THROWAWAYS
Work Culture and Consumer Education

THROWAWAYS

Work Culture and Consumer Education

EVAN WATKINS

STANFORD UNIVERSITY PRESS

STANFORD, CALIFORNIA

Stanford University Press
Stanford, California
© 1993 by the Board of Trustees of the
Leland Stanford Junior University
Printed in the United States of America

CIP data appear at the end of the book

Stanford University Press publications
are distributed exclusively by Stanford
University Press within the United
States, Canada, and Mexico; they are
distributed exclusively by Cambridge
University Press throughout the rest of
the world.

FOR DIANE

Acknowledgments

As always, a great many people contributed a great deal. I want especially to thank Helen Tartar, Ann Klefstad, and Karen Brown Davison at Stanford Press for their careful work with the manuscript, and Hazard Adams, Charles Altieri, Carolyn Allen, and Roger Meiners for reading drafts of several chapters and giving me invaluable suggestions. Pamela Fox, Susan Jeffords, and Lisa Schubert put up with the manuscript from the beginning, supplied most of the good ideas, listened patiently to the rest, and made it seem worthwhile by the example of their own work no less than by what they taught me about mine. Diane taught me what was important to think about.

A much earlier and different version of chapter 4, under the title "Television Programming and Household Flow: Critical Analysis of Mass Culture in a Politics of Change," appeared in *The Centennial Review*, and an earlier and different version of chapter 3, under the same title, in *boundary 2*.

Contents

	Introduction	I
ONE	Stranded at the Crossroads: Technology, Obsolescence, and the Production of the Past	15
TWO	Class-as-Lifestyle: Social Organization in a Service Economy	41
THREE	"For the Time Being, Forever": Social Position and the Art of Automobile Maintenance	83
FOUR	Politics of Change in Mass Culture Education: Television Programming and Household Flow	106
FIVE	When I Win the Lottery: Educating Taste in a Consumer Culture	134
SIX	"What Are You Doing Here?"	164
	Works Cited	219
	Index	225

THROWAWAYS
Work Culture and Consumer Education

Introduction

The ruling ideas of a culture, Marx's familiar aphorism claims, are the ideas of its ruling group. Narratives of social change would then seem to be unlikely carriers of ruling ideas. Social change is a touchy topic for ruling groups. Yet as the *Manifesto* anticipates, and as *Capital* explains at great length, capitalism is an economy of change. Thus ruling ideas in a capitalist economy must nevertheless in some way make sense of changing conditions, however uncomfortable or potentially treacherous the task might be. Antonio Gramsci's concept of "hegemony" complicates considerably any understanding of what exactly creates and maintains the "rule" of ruling groups. But whatever else is involved, Gramsci argued, relations of hegemony are always educational relationships. In the conditions of a capitalist economy, narratives of change might then be best understood as a contested pedagogy: who tells the story of change, what narrative teleology is plotted, how roles are assigned, and, most crucially, which lessons are taught. Narratives of change, in other words, are about the determination of social position.

Social Darwinism affords a convenient example of how such narratives function. It involved attempts to "adapt" often disturbing stories of natural change into explanations that taught people how to think about social mobilities. That is, its ideology linked stories of change in biology to stories of change in the social field, for educative ends. The encoded teleology of reward for the socially "fittest" helped domesticate the available picture of natural change. On the other side, nature obligingly remained in place, to supply hermeneutical corroboration for narratives of social change. Social

Darwinism's master narrative was also a field guide for plotting the symmetries of structural *ex*change, an educational paradigm of change that permitted the continuing naturalization of ruling social position.

Like social Darwinism, what I will call "technoideological coding" in the following chapters also works educationally concerning configurations of social position. As the name suggests, however, the field of reference here is not nature but technology; social disaster is not the equivalent of biological extinction but of obsolescence; and survival is no longer the name designating "the fittest" but what identifies the obsolete as relics from the past, those left behind by the innovations of the present. By linking "technology" and "ideology" in this way, as technoideological coding, I mean to suggest as well how such coding can register change directly. Unlike nature, technology as a field of reference already implies continual and often unpredictable changes. In these circumstances, and so far from a necessary precondition, some Darwinianlike reinterpretation of nature can become just an afterthought. Technoideological coding permits the internalization of changing conditions as within the range of ideological signification from the beginning, with the result that dominant ideologies need not be expected to appear coherent and stable by means of freezing a temporarily existing configuration of social position under the sign of some universalized normative model. Rather than such adaptation to new conditions made visible across a map of structural exchange between nature and the social field, positional dominance as technoideologically coded requires a continual production of new terms defining the social field.

In the next chapter, I want to sketch very quickly the emergence of technoideological coding and, by way of Donna Haraway's brilliant exploratory analysis in "A Manifesto for Cyborgs," the correlative disappearance of what she calls "natural coding."* The immediately

---

*Any number of books—Jules Henry's *Culture Against Man* is a particularly good good example—have discussed at length the social effects of an economy of so-called planned obsolescence. And Jürgen Habermas, perhaps to an even greater extent than other currently influential theorists, has emphasized the intrusive power of technocratic systems and "systems analysis" in people's everyday experiences. My general line of argument in what follows will nevertheless remain on the whole closer to Gramsci than to these directions of more recent work, for it is Gramsci's understanding of hegemony as involving specifically *pedagogical* relations that seems to me most directly useful in recognizing just how that intrusive power functions in the inter-

crucial point, however, is that in contrast to the kind of stories that appear in ideologies such as social Darwinism, the master narrative of a technoideological coding of social position is a myth of survivals as the unfit, no longer integrally productive components of the present, those who failed to capitalize on the profit-bearing power of change. Survivals are relics, throwaways, isolated groups of the population who haven't moved with the times, and who now litter the social landscape and require the moral attention of cleanup crews, the containing apparatus of police and prisons, the financial drain of "safety nets," the immense maintenance bureaucracies of the state.*

There are a number of reasons for identifying this master narrative as mythic, but its power lies first of all in how it mystifies its own temporal scene, its own legitimizing powers of social definition within the terms of present configurations of position. Like Marx's fetishized commodity, the obsolescence of survivals then appears to supply independent and variable laws of motion, as if no *present* process produced the positional configurations of obsolescence, and time was merely a passive-voice language for the story to be told. In the familiar images supplied by both the Reagan and Bush administrations (recently in response to the events following the Rodney King verdict), throwaways, as the populations of "urban ghettos" for example, are simply now useless survivals from the past. This disguises how present social organization in its Reaganite configurations produces groups of throwaways by defining the "pastness" of the past to which "they" belong.

While helpful, however, the analogy to commodity is also potentially treacherous: Marx's point was that fetishism makes commodi-

---

stices of mass culture. In this context, theorists such as Haraway and Chela Sandoval and others have a special value for me. If necessarily in terms of contemporary circumstances, very different altogether than what Gramsci saw in Fascist Italy, their arguments as well are organized around what resources are available among nondominant groups to be mobilized for a countereducation. In contrast to Jürgen Habermas, that is, and in common with Gramsci's political project, their analysis of dominant social formations is then always engaged first with an eye to where exactly those potentially countereducational resources might best be put to use.

*Or alternatively, survivals are simply "disposed of" as waste, as Simon Watney describes the effects of a public discourse about AIDS: "The 'homosexual body' is 'disposed of,' like so much rubbish, like the trash it was in life" (80).

ties seem, precisely, "natural" objects, their "metaphysical subtleties and theological niceties" then open to interminable investigation. But throwaway populations aren't at all natural in this master narrative of survivals, any more than breaker point ignition systems in the cars now beginning to fill junkyards or vacuum tubes in the televisions still occasionally to be found in Salvation Army stores. Oppositional "demystification" must correspondingly involve rather different operations than the process of exposing the natural as in fact ideological. Technoideological coding requires no natural frame of explanation to legitimize its powers to educate concerning configurations of social position. So far from preserving constants of positionality and resisting social change, its master narrative *capitalizes* change, projects as its narrative "hero" a performative agency everywhere engaged in the innovative capitalization of new possibilities rather than hoarding position like a miser. Thus oppositional politics, like oppositional demystification, faces a very different set of mobile, shifting conditions of hegemony, what Chela Sandoval recognizes in her strategic praise of "survival skills" in "U.S. Third World Feminism: The Theory and Method of Oppositional Consciousness in the Postmodern World": "The differential mode of oppositional consciousness depends upon an ability to read the current situation of power and of self-consciously choosing and adopting the ideological form best suited to push against its configurations, a survival skill well-known to oppressed peoples" (15). Their survival often depends upon pushing against a dominant social designation of them as surviving relics, throwaways.

It's no secret that, historically, institutional public education in the United States has played crucial roles in establishing the visible architecture of expectations, qualities of work, and measures of assessment that surround the determination of social positionalities. At the same time, however, ideologies of public education made each of these indices seem naturally determined. I argued in *Work Time* that assessment by "merit" presupposes at least the possibility of identifying inherent intelligence and ability across the entire student population, however much in practice these qualities proved rather difficult to isolate in any consistent way. Thus student work could never quite be assessed solely in relation to utility, progress, or whatever, but is judged as revelatory of inherent qualities, signs of some ultimate student "merit." The realization of expectations valorized the acquisition of educationally certified skills and knowledges but always within the parameters of what that individual "merit" might permit. In my concluding chapter, I want to turn specifically to questions of how the political culture of Reaganism (a term I will parallel to Stuart Hall's term "Thatcherism") has made use of the narratives of technoideological coding and found ways to direct them toward the "reform" of public education, and the redefinitions of expectations for work and assessment procedures that reform implies.

In these terms, Reaganism is far from over with Clinton's election. As I will argue later, Reaganism as a political culture has become very much a part of what Gramsci would identify as an everyday "common sense," the often unacknowledged assumptions that "make sense" of the current political situation. For Gramsci, "common sense" is not a unified political philosophy or a consistent interpretation of existing conditions. Clinton's specific educational policy initiatives may well then differ in emphasis from the directions visible during the Bush administration. Common sense, however, functions to establish boundary conditions in effect, within which a certain range of policies will seem plausible and realistic, while those falling outside that range will seem in contrast naive, dated, or simply out of touch with contemporary "reality." Educational reform under the Clinton administration, for all it may differ in emphasis, nevertheless will likely continue to observe the boundary conditions of Reaganism's political common sense. Clinton's campaign insistence that "choice" not be extended beyond the public school system to private schools, for example, certainly differs from Republican proposals, but the key concept of "choice" echoes everywhere Reaganite assumptions about the larger context of how educational possibilities are determined. Thus before reaching the point in the argument where we would consider how this common sense might affect the reform of educational institutions, it seems a good idea to explore in some detail Reaganism's more primary fields of technoideologically coded investments in education: a so-called service economy and a consumer culture.

I mean then to understand these fields—service economy and consumer culture—as indeed *educative*, which means more than identifying ideological agendas or manipulation. Public education is "mass" education, as consumer culture is "mass" culture. But consumer culture is not about "massing" any more than public education is. Like public education, its payoffs always involve the differentiations and distinctions of social position; like public education, it speaks to and with the languages of rising social expectations; like public education, it promises the positional rewards of mastering crucial lessons across an elaborately structured "curriculum" of subject areas; and thus, like public education, it involves continually contested zones and intricately negotiated individual itineraries. Unlike public education, however, consumer culture, insofar as it deploys the resources of technoideological coding, needs no comprehensive frame of legitimation in the natural, no bottom-lining "merit" to rationalize and explain the determinations that emerge. Thus, perhaps not surprisingly, both elitist "high" culture dismissals as well as any version of a Baudrillardian "hyperlogic" of consumption walk right by its educative powers on roughly the same track, albeit signposting that track with completely different values. Reaganism as a now arguably hegemonic political culture became so in part by learning to be more observant than these two orientations, and by following up that observation by occupying the territories of consumer culture imaged as a manifestation of the "free market order."* At this point, even the knowledge that things are a bit more complicated than that image implies does little without a contesting of this politics of occupation.

Reaganism had the incentives of a necessity for corporate restructuring, technological modernization, and an emergent service economy in the United States. Such economic interests are real enough, however they have been obscured by the bad philosophizing of economic determinism and the mystifications of "the last instance," which have little to do with economics. A service economy requires a different work force and very different perceptions of work than the linked programs of training and assessment in public education

*To recognize as much is not immediately equivalent to endorsing the formation of some U.S. equivalent to the "New Times" agenda Stuart Hall and others have proposed in Britain. It is, however, to understand what Frank Mort has claimed about Thatcherism in Britain in "The Politics of Consumption" as no less true of Reaganism, as I will argue at length in my concluding chapter: "Thatcherism's orchestration of consumption has been adept at channelling perceptions of growing personal prosperity into its own political discourse equating the ring of tinkling cash registers with political and cultural freedoms" (163).

were organized to supply. Consumer culture—or, as I would prefer to identify it, consumer education—afforded a better field of possibility, if also a whole new set of problems emerging within the diverse spectrum of constituencies Reaganism engaged. For there's no reason to think a service economy "serves," as it were, only one set of interests, or that it exists in some elaborately preplanned monadal harmony with the processes of consumer education. Most important for my purposes, a service economy involves often very complicated redefinitions of what exactly constitutes "economic interests," in ways that I think make it possible to intervene in economic sectors of the social field, in opposition to Reaganism, without at the same time relying on the metaphysics of economic determinism. It's true enough that privileging "the economic instance" has effectively negated a great many directions of oppositional politics, without a dominant order having to do anything. But it would be a disaster to leave economics in the hands of Reaganism—while Reaganism may yet succeed in making poverty culturally obsolete, being poor remains a devastating economic condition.

In what follows, chapter 1 is about obsolescence and obsolescence stories—how technoideological coding produces educational narratives of social position. My general point is a very simple one: positionally, obsolescence involves conditions of both cultural and economic production *in the present*, not what has survived, uselessly, from the past, as obsolescence stories would have it. Throwaway populations are not the survival of the unfit, the waste of change. They are produced by and indispensable to present social organization. Chapter 2 is about the intersections of a service economy, public education, and the consumer education acquired through consumer culture, which I will focus through the general concept of class-as-lifestyle. "Class" in this sense of mobile, shifting lifestyle identities has become the privileged social category of technoideological coding, supplying the available indices of social position by producing the obsolescence of now "older" categories of race and gender, as if the latter were no longer an effectively determining force of positionality. Technoideologically coded narratives of social change are class-as-lifestyle narratives, which locate race and gender as still-surviving relics of a rapidly disappearing past.

My account involves a certain range of detail, yet the argument nevertheless proceeds as if these intersections of service economy, public education, and consumer culture functioned like some massively totalized reflection of a dominant power where everything fitted neatly into place. That is, it's an argument that seems to fly in the face of all those familiar poststructuralist claims that there is no closed, self-defining totality of "the social." Things don't really fit; totalities leak. In my account, however, the internalization of change in dominant politics made possible by technoideological coding is about exploiting continually new possibilities of "fit." And while it's nice to know such totalizing aims may never ultimately succeed, there's no reason to expect throwaway populations to be happy with what—however "inevitably"—leaks through with each new shift in dominant configurations. Not only is that patronizing, it conveniently ignores how it's the unfit, the relic, the throwaway who are forced to pay for your knowledge of slippages and incongruities.

Chapters 3, 4, and 5 are about pedagogical operations across certain fields of consumer education, to register—especially in chapters 4 and 5—oppositions and resistances to totalizing "fit," as well as the attractions of what consumer education promises, which are considerable. My discussions will then brush close to a great deal of recent critical attention to "mass culture" and various means for extracting "popular culture" from it. But I'm not particularly interested in supplying readings of mass culture constructions, or in collapsing distinctions between "high" and "mass" culture. Education educates, and I'm interested in what people learn and how they use it and where they can and can't go with their learning. Consumer education concerns the work of a service economy no less than consumption, the organization of social space every bit as much as cultural "taste," and its curricula no more obey familiar academic identifications of cultural fields than its assessment measures conform to standards of merit.

My concluding chapter necessarily involves a more direct consideration of the political culture of Reaganism; it is about Reaganism's interventional presence within the fields of consumer education and its reform directions for public institutional education. Yet the force of that "necessarily" can't really be dictated solely by the logic of my argument, much as I would like it to be. The range of political analysis projected by Reaganism has already begun to produce an increasingly visible discourse about "us"—that is, about people like myself trained as textual scholars and teaching in humanities

departments in U.S. universities and colleges. While such recognition may perhaps gratify some desire to be a designated political
threat to a dominant power, nevertheless the effects on "us" aren't
really the crucial issue. What those discourses involve—beyond all
the gratifying woo-woo noises about how "tenured radicals" have
subverted educational institutions and are in the process of destroy-
ing the very fabric of Western culture*—are educational reform
agendas, the implementation of structures of isolation, and increasingly complex and far-reaching policy decisions that are not likely
to cause much more than psychological damage to tenured radicals
in the near future. But these agendas will have devastating effects
on those throwaway populations whose interests and expectations
tenured radicals often claim to be positioned to work for within
educational institutions.

I do realize that a great many of "us" as humanities teachers
are covertly or openly pleased with how recent developments of
Reaganism would ease "our" return to the proper tasks of literary
and historical scholarship, and to reading the great philosophers instead of mucking around endlessly with economics and ideologies
and "mass culture" and all that, where "we" don't really belong
anyway. But at some point it must surely occur to anyone that obsolescence is a dangerous game for everybody who doesn't know
the rules, can't recognize the playing fields, and continues to depend on the resources of what worked in the past. After all, those
"proper tasks" of scholarship have only been around in roughly this
form for at most eighty years or so, despite the wistful intimations
of immortality with which they're surrounded, and no Lloyds in its
right mind would step in with insurance cover given the actuarial
tables of cultural highway carnage. While you may feel threatened by
how your department seems "swamped"—in Margaret Thatcher's
famous phrase—by women and minority "ideologues" and MTV-
eyed postmodernists, the far greater danger to your brilliant reconstruction of the chronology of Plato's dialogues or Conrad's short
stories lies in assuming such things will have an important or prolonged role in the school culture reform inherent in Clinton's education for choice no less than in Bush's *America 2000* agenda. And I'm

---

*The reference is to Roger Kimball's book *Tenured Radicals: How Politics Has Cor-
rupted Our Higher Education*.

convinced this ought to be obvious with even a little more mucking around elsewhere.

Like Stuart Hall with Thatcherism, I think there's much for left politics to learn from Reaganism in the United States. Good learning isn't really imitative, and I'm not suggesting at all that left politics should construct parallel versions of Reaganite individualism, market order, the entrepreneurial state, or educational marketability, and should certainly not parallel its technologies of social motion. The general point, again, is a very simple one. Where Reaganism is, left politics has to be also, with genuinely alternative possibilities. This isn't easy to accept because it means acknowledging that Reaganism has largely controlled and directed cultural and political innovations, that it has made the "new" new and "change" change, for all the imagery of avant- and vanguardism as left properties. Then this means figuring out as well where Reaganism is, how it got there, and how to make "there" *here*, before obsolescence becomes for many a permanently terminal condition.

Thus my emphasis on repair—on making use of the socially designated obsolete, both technologically and ideologically—is hardly intended as a dismissal of new, creative political possibilities. And certainly I do not counsel any return to the pieties of traditional socialisms or Marxisms, whatever those might be. Obsolescence in my argument involves the conditions of the present, rather than what is left over from the past. I have two reasons for my emphasis on repair. First, "newness" is not only a relative term, but a term, like so many others, that marks out a contested field of cultural value. The stakes in "newness" then have everything to do with who has authority to define what counts as new. It is, of course, conceivable that a political left in some form could learn to beat Reaganism's political culture at its own game of definition (although I find little evidence such a form has emerged in the United States to date). But "repair," as I will use the term, refers to a mode of understanding and a multiple set of practices whose aim is to construct conditions of possibility for a different politics altogether, where there are no winners and losers at the game of newness dictated by techno-ideological coding. Thus, while the survival skills of repair do not enable repossession of the cultural and economic riches that come with the command of the new, this doesn't imply that repair can't be inventive. Any politics that would set out to abolish the endlessly intricated social distinctions of winners and losers has to be endlessly inventive. Raymond Williams realized well enough (if for somewhat different reasons) that this revolution would be a long one indeed. The shifting survival skills of obsolete groups continue to create conditions of revolutionary possibility, precisely by their inventiveness in repair.

Second, to the extent the political culture of Reaganism has recognized perhaps more profoundly than any previous regime the social capital available from the command of the new, it is also relentlessly condemning whole groups of the population to having available *nothing but* what is correlatively designated as the obsolete—ideologically again, as well as technologically. In September of 1991, in a speech entitled "Post-Modern Politics: The Search for a New Paradigm," given at the Washington Rotary Club, James Pinkerton, then deputy assistant to President Bush for policy planning, offered the following defining examples of the postmodern new:*

> Every human institution goes through a life cycle of youthful enthusiasm, maturity, and finally obsolescence, incompetence, and death. So it is with modernism . . . What do I mean by post-modern?
>
> Going to business school is modern. *The One Minute Manager* is postmodern.
>
> "Coke is It"—modern. It focuses on the product—suggesting that Coca-Cola is a unitary totality that will solve your problems. Pepsi's "You got the right one baby—uh huh" is post-modern, because it shifts the focus from the product to the person, acknowledging that the sovereign consumer, not the giant company, is the ultimate arbiter of what is and what is not "it."
>
> PC—political correctness—is modern dogmatism. The PC—the personal computer—is post-modern because it expands choice and freedom.
>
> The effort of the left to defeat Clarence Thomas for the Supreme Court is a modern effort to impose monolithic conformity; the left is terrified that Thomas' post-modern thinking on empowerment and individual achievement will threaten their monopoly on the Black agenda.
>
> Communism is modernism on steroids.

It may seem a bit surprising to academics to hear an official of the Bush administration claiming the term "postmodernism" as his own, in a speech before the Rotary Club of all things, and as applicable to something like Clarence Thomas's views about empower-

---

*I want to thank Diana Paulin for getting me a text of Pinkerton's speech and pointing out its appropriateness to my argument.

ment. But if you take account of what I've been suggesting about Reaganism's occupation of consumer culture, it shouldn't really be surprising, and in any case, Pinkerton already anticipates that surprise:

> Some professors might claim that post-modernism is associated, like them, with the Old Paradigm left. But this has more to do with the left's ability to assign labels than the essence of post-modernism. Indeed, since the contemporary post-modern era has seen the death of collectivism and the renaissance of free market economies, one could certainly draw the opposite conclusion!

Thus I think it would be a mistake to read that speech—which contains a great many defining examples of the postmodern from consumer culture—as a co-optation of the term postmodern, as if all the radical cultural innovations for which "once upon a time" postmodernism could stand as a sign have now been taken over and assimilated for the purposes of a dominant political culture. The telling move, rather, is how "political correctness," to take one example, is consigned by Pinkerton to the obsolescence of the modern. This demonstrates everywhere a power of defining the new, and like it or not would identify those of us invested in "pc," in whatever multiple ways and for whatever reasons, as henceforth obsolete. In such circumstances, the test of oppositional political inventiveness is not to keep ahead of the game by scrapping political correctness in favor of a still newer set of terms and practices that might enjoy at least a diminishing half-life of excitement before Bush & Co. get hold of them as well. Reaganism has capitalized newness, and hence nothing will more surely perpetuate "politics as usual" than continuing in this way to play winners and losers.

Despite all the things about contemporary political organization in Western democracies that Gramsci so brilliantly anticipated, the *political* importance of consumption escaped him entirely—not entirely without reason, for Gramsci's circumstances were very different from ours. The toys he played with as a child growing up in Sardinia, for example, were pretty much the same toys his grandparents and great-grandparents and great-great-grandparents had played with. Some time ago, I spent an afternoon with one of my Italian friends who grew up in the brutal poverty of Calabria at a museum in Reggio Calabria, with him delightedly pointing out displays of toys from 1,000, even 1,500 years ago, that were the same toys he had played with. As a Communist party worker for 20 years, he, like Gramsci, had had very little to say in his countless speeches throughout Calabria about consumption. A consumer world with huge mass marketers of children's toys such as Toys "Я" Us had little immediate political relevance to the groups he addressed.

That situation has changed dramatically, however, and in the United States the politics of Reaganism has created powerful connections between how people become consumers and how they become citizens. Marxists have not always thought very carefully about those changes, have too often accepted uncritically the gender values coded into the division of production as active, public, social, and masculine, and consumption in contrast as passive, private, psychological, and feminine. Even what advertisers recognized a long time ago—that economics itself dictated a crucial role for advertising in the public, social world of women's activities and power as consumers—was misrecognized as simply a matter of duping and manipulating a passive population. And what Reaganism understood all too clearly as the social promise of rising expectations articulated across consumer fields was misrecognized as just a matter of co-optation and embourgeoisement.

Gramsci himself had almost nothing to say about consumption, but the political education of citizens was perhaps the most pervasive theme throughout his writings. "Every relation of 'hegemony,' " he reminds us again, "is necessarily an educational relationship" (SPN, 350; QC, 1331). He also had a great deal to say about public education in Italy, for under the Fascist government, public education underwent a massive reform known as the *riforma Gentile*, named after Mussolini's first minister of public education, the Hegelian scholar and intellectual Giovanni Gentile. The reform promised a far more democratic system of education—it's still the basis for the organization of public education in Italy—and a much greater access to educational opportunities. Gramsci wrote at length about the *riforma Gentile* in the *Notebooks*, but for my purposes the most immediately salient summary passage is the following: "[Under the proposed reform] the labourer can become a skilled worker, for instance, the peasant a surveyor or petty agronomist. But democracy, by definition, cannot mean merely that an unskilled worker can become skilled. It must mean that every 'citizen' can 'govern' and that society places him, even if only abstractly, in a general condition to achieve this. . . . Thus [with the reform] we are really going back to a division into juridically fixed and crystallized estates rather than moving towards the transcendence of class divisions" (SPN, 40–41; QC, 1547–48).

What Gramsci saw in the *riforma Gentile* was a promise of rising social expectations and greater powers of citizen governance being simultaneously negated by new political limitations imposed on the positions promised: "We are really going back to a division into juridically fixed and crystallized estates." And it doesn't seem to me farfetched to recognize a very similar form of promise and negation at work in images of the freedom of a "market order," as they appear throughout the field of consumer education inherited from the *riforma Reagan*. "Modern politics," Pinkerton claims, "is a reflected artifact of modern art." Bush's postmodern politics, he suggests by inference, has its source in the postmodernism of consumer culture, with its promises of freedom from constraints.

Like Gramsci facing the long-term, far-reaching political implications of the *riforma Gentile*, we too face a remarkable political period of promised change—but with its educative powers located in the intricacies of consumer culture. And like Gramsci, I believe those promises arrive with a new set of political limitations for whole groups of the population who are being identified by Pinkerton and others as obsolete, as throwaways: "We are really going back to a division into juridically fixed and crystallized estates." There is, in other words, a rapidly closing territory in which it's necessary to find ways to intervene, to carve a space for educational alternatives.

In his capitalizing of newness, however, Pinkerton has left political correctness (along with Coke, business school, and a whole host of intriguing stuff) on an always growing ideological junkyard of the obsolete. Like "yesterday's" technologically primitive boombox, pc then becomes available as one more thing to repair and use, a device on which to play for all it's worth a political music that won't rest with the social divisions of winners and losers, and by which it's possible to challenge effectively all such constructions as Pinkerton's postmodern, which would perpetuate the politics of his still-white, still-determined-to-win, still-supremacist club. As the junkyard grows, it will become more and more difficult even to find the clubhouse in the midst of all the debris flying from its windows.

Stranded at the Crossroads: Technology, Obsolescence, and the Production of the Past

NBC will not be able to predict a winner at 8:32 . . .
—Gil Scott-Heron, "The Revolution Will Not be Televised"

Charles Babbage's *On the Economy of Machinery and Manufacturers*, published in 1832, was one of the first sustained arguments to realize the importance of new industrial technologies to the temporal organization of work and to the principles of a division of labor in capitalist production. But what is often overlooked in Babbage is his anticipation of how technological developments affected not only individual but also national positions and importance within the field of industrial production. In some simple and direct sense, Babbage took the values implied by a notion of "progress" for granted. What interested him was that an industrial economy put progress up for grabs and introduced an intense competition among nations to be in the forefront of progress. Thus a great deal would be lost unless a nation's social priorities recognized a linked chain of determinations that at bottom rested on continual technological innovation. Babbage himself had a lifelong fascination with developing new machinery, including a very early version of the computer. He understood technological innovation, however, as less a matter of "nature" in any sense, even of natural resources, than of the allocation of specifically social and cultural resources toward the end of developing new technologies of production. British cloth was cheaper than cloth made in India, obviously not because England possessed greater resources of raw materials, but because "British looms" were far superior to Indian technology, yielding comparable production at one-seventh the cost of labor (17n).

Babbage's argument thus depends on a different field of reference than, for example, the familiar social designations of women as emotional, tribespeople as savage, and the working class as physically gross. Rather than implying closeness to a "state of nature" like these designations, a reliance on out-of-date technologies for manufacturing cotton cloth or a failure to adopt the new office machinery that made double-entry accounting so much easier would signify in Babbage's calculations the potentially nightmare results of technological obsolescence.* And neither an abundance of raw material nor a demon work load nor permanently depressed wages could compensate for the liabilities of obsolescence. That is, the opposition that drives Babbage's argument is not a version of nature/culture, but is located within the organization of the field of social relations, a function of the effective positionalities that derive from technological innovation or obsolescence. Beyond the necessity of developing new technologies, Babbage was not particularly interested in exploring the question of *why* certain groups of the population, and certain nations, seemed more or less capable of throwing resources into such development. But obviously it interested others, and to some great extent the growing visibility and utility of arguments like Babbage's altered significantly the terms of inquiry.

Prior to Babbage's work, and in the conditions of a still nascent capitalism, constructions of the natural capabilities of individuals and of whole social groups supplied virtually the entire field of reference for determining the "appropriateness" of specific configurations of social position, if often in divergent ways. Wordsworth's familiar praise of "rustic and humble life," for example, was dismissed as naive even by contemporaries such as Coleridge, but clearly Wordsworth had glimpsed a potentially double signification of being closer to a "state of nature." What you lose in terms of "refinement" and "progress" may be more than amply compensated for by what you gain in "real" permanent resources of imagination and imaginative energy. Far more acutely than Wordsworth, however, Mary Woll-

---

*Such "backwardness" might be made to seem closer to nature, however, by the process Raymond Williams identified in *The Country and the City* as ideological myths of some unbroken, organic continuity of the past, of course shattered forever at about whatever time one happened to reach puberty. That is, for Williams one of the effects of a continually changing social world is to encourage the illusion of some dramatic break from the heretofore natural, organic unfolding of society, where, as he points out, that "break" then always obligingly conforms to the patterns of one's own individual history, and hence will appear at very different times depending on who is making the argument.

stonecraft was led to question the very indices of the "natural" as, precisely, constructions that functioned to rationalize the determination of social position. Given, for example, Rousseau's insistent litany of constraints he deemed it necessary to impose on women, Wollstonecraft was able systematically to expose the process of *cultural* education that produces both women's sexual behavior and the appearance of a "natural" law governing it: "This cruel association of ideas, which every thing conspires to twist into all their habits of thinking, or, to speak with more precision, of feeling, receives new force when they begin to act a little for themselves; for they then perceive that it is only through their addresses to excite emotions in men, that pleasure and power are to be obtained" (117). And in case you still don't get the point, she adds in a footnote to "cruel": " 'Cruel' because ideas, once irreversibly set, determine a girl's future mode of thinking and acting." Once assimilated, ideas of sexuality operate as if by natural law. For Wollstonecraft, that is, what the claim for the workings of "nature" supplies in the circumstances is the surest indicator of a culturally constructed system of domination.

Wollstonecraft may have had her own dream of the natural, as Wordsworth did. Nevertheless, and in the tradition of earlier writers such as Lady Wortley Montagu, Anne Finch, and Elizabeth Tollet, constructions of natural law and appeals to "permanent" characteristics of female nature were for Wollstonecraft necessarily open to interrogation as, again, signaling powerful cultural motivations at work. From a much later vantage point than Wollstonecraft's, however, Marx and Engels were able to recognize how the insistence of the natural might in fact pose an obstacle not only to socially subordinated populations, but to capitalist expansion itself: "The bourgeoisie cannot exist without constantly revolutionizing the instruments of production, and thereby the relations of production, and with them the whole relations of society" (87). What had intervened in the long interval between Wollstonecraft and the *Manifesto* was a general and pervasive recognition of the relation between "progress" and dominant social position on the one hand, and on the other the importance of technological innovation that had so obsessed Babbage—what Marx and Engels imply in their phrase "revolutionizing the instruments of production." In circumstances of continual technological modernization of production, ideological constructions then seem required to make sense of the changes by an after-the-fact process of *re*naturalizing the determinations of social position within the shifting networks of "the whole relations of society."

Race, to take an obvious example, could continue to be recognized as a natural division of human populations only to the extent that the ideological meanings of race likewise shifted to accommodate the changing positionalities of racially marked agents—that is, in the situation of African-Americans in the United States, from rural, agricultural slave labor to urban, low-level industrial workers. It's little wonder specifically ideological production became under capitalism a diverse, multiple, pervasive, and necessary operation. Renaturalizing must be an ongoing, even "avant-garde" process, usefully buttressed by myths of a scientific and scholarly "progress" of knowledge as well as of technologies. Such progress, that is, could account for why older images of "the natural" were simply not as yet very "accurate." In my context, however, the immediate point has to do with how the separation between Babbage's opposition of technological innovation / obsolescence and ideals of progress with their constructions of "the natural" began to collapse. While obsolescence may not be a state of nature, there seemed an obvious social utility in being able to explain why some groups rather than others seem perennially positioned on the downside of innovation/ obsolescence.

In relation to arguments like Babbage's, and to the recognized importance generally of new technological developments, ideological renaturalizing began to assume the status of a kind of metarationale. That is, rather than functioning as an immediate field of reference for explanations of stratified relations of social position, constructions of the natural could occupy the higher ground of "disinterested" inquiry into what the social process of stratification had made visible. Later still, the visibility and prestige of social Darwinism, for example, might be grasped most easily as the result of its specific and often very elaborate linkages between constructions adjudicated on the one hand across the boundary lines of nature and culture, and on the other by indices of technological change and development. For if "nature herself" made certain life forms obsolete in a process of natural selection, then surely technological change, like biological adaptation, dictated a corporate and social survival of the fittest. And conversely, a language of "natural" population groupings could be made available to describe technological development. Like some astonished "native" tribesperson blinking in amazement at the sophisticated equipment of "the white man," day-before-yesterday's technology is then designated "primitive" in comparison to the latest apparatus. Fetishized constructions of "nature" and of "technology" have been so often and so regularly opposed to each other in political argument, in whatever multiple combinations, that it seems to me worth remembering clearly how in ideological explanations of configurations of social position they have as frequently cohabited quite happily (as in social Darwinism).

Recent political critique, however, has to some great extent altered the contours of familiar debate by refusing from the outset any appeal to nature, even as grounds for oppositional practices. Thus in "A Manifesto for Cyborgs," to take a particularly dramatic example, Donna Haraway generates a list of "dichotomies" that inform what she calls the transformation "from an organic, industrial society to a polymorphous, information system" (592).* The con-

*Haraway's list of dichotomies is as follows (592–93):

Representation	Simulation
Bourgeois novel, realism	Science fiction, postmodernism
Organism	Biotic component
Depth, integrity	Surface, boundary
Heat	Noise
Biology as clinical practice	Biology as inscription
Physiology	Communications engineering
Small group	Subsystem
Perfection	Optimization
Eugenics	Population control
Decadence, *Magic Mountain*	Obsolescence, *Future Shock*
Hygiene	Stress management
Microbiology, tuberculosis	Immunology, AIDS
Organic division of labor	Ergonomics/cybernetics of labor
Functional specialization	Modular construction
Reproduction	Replication
Organic sex role specialization	Optimal genetic strategies
Biological determinism	Evolutionary inertia, constraints
Community ecology	Ecosystem
Racial chain of being	Neo-imperialism, United Nations humanism
Scientific management in home/factory	Global factory / electronic cottage
Family/market/factory	Women in the integrated circuit

junction of "organic" and "industrial" in that formulation recognizes
how what Haraway will refer to as "natural coding" has been linked
in complementary ways with the technological terms of industrial
development and progress, and as a result hers is a formulation that
clearly cuts across "older" political strategies of opposing nature
and technology, radical as well as conservative. More important for
Haraway, however, "the objects on the right-hand side" of her list
of dichotomies, characteristic of the newly emergent information
society, "cannot be coded as 'natural,' a realization that subverts
naturalistic coding for the left-hand side as well. We cannot go back
ideologically or materially" (593).

    The warning about the impossibility of "going back" is directed
at radical political criticism, the way in which critique has itself often
resorted to natural coding as a lever to challenge existing configurations of social position. For Haraway, "Feminisms and Marxisms
have run aground on Western epistemological imperatives to construct a revolutionary subject from the perspective of a hierarchy of
oppressions and/or a latent position of moral superiority, innocence,
and greater closeness to nature" (606). In her context Wordsworth,
for example, might well appear as an early and "naive" avatar of later
and much more complicated appeals to the radical political virtue
of closeness to a state of nature. And for Haraway, any would-be
revolutionary project grounded in a reproduction of the natural is at
once self-defeating, and a disingenuous nostalgizing of what after all
was hardly a congenial social world for nondominant populations.
Haraway is under no illusion that a recognizably postmodern world
of "fields of difference" obliterates all distinctions of positionality.
The point is that while some "differences" are indeed "playful; some

Family wage	Comparable worth
Public/private	Cyborg citizenship
Nature/culture	Fields of difference
Cooperation	Communications enhancement
Freud	Lacan
Sex	Genetic engineering
Labor	Robotics
Mind	Artificial intelligence
World War II	Star Wars
White capitalist patriarchy	Informatics of domination

are poles of world historical systems of domination. 'Epistemology' is about knowing the difference" (592).

But while it may be true enough, as Haraway argues, that left politics has often hung itself on a dream of the natural, it's also true, as I've suggested, that the ideological effects of natural coding have supplied a reliable epistemological barometer of "world historical systems of domination." Anne Finch's remarkable poem "The Spleen," with its challenge to an emergent scientific medical discourse of women's bodies, like Wollstonecraft's critique of Rousseau later, and like Marx's attack on the assumed "natural laws" of bourgeois economics, all in one way or another afforded radical traditions of analytic resource for subsequent attempts at constructing sensitive weather instruments to register new forms of "the natural" as in fact the approaching squall lines of oppressive intensities. There were continually new forms, as the ideological process of renaturalizing continually projected always more "accurate" versions of the natural. It's possible to grant, provisionally at least, Haraway's argument that even such refined versions of natural coding have ceased to characterize the contemporary information society composed of the features on the right-hand side of her list. But at that point, the "epistemological" problem for oppositional criticism lies not only in the difficulty of resisting the temptation to rehabilitate the natural but also in the attractions of that ensemble of critical practices that took their epistemological bearings from recognizing the ideological function of constructed "natures." In these new circumstances, "knowing the difference" becomes a newly formidable task.

Whatever the current status of natural coding, however, it seems to me unquestionably true that what I will call in parallel terms the technoideological coding of obsolescence/innovation has accelerated dramatically in importance. Obsolescence occupies only one slot (opposite "decadence" on the left-hand side) in Haraway's list, but arguably it informs each of the other features she lists as well. "Robotics," for example, not only replaces "older" categories of labor in the organization of industrial production, but among other things stands as a compacted narrative of the threat of Japanese car manufacture that drove GM to its highly touted Saturn plant as an escape from the increasingly pervasive perception consigning GM to obsolescence in today's market. "Microelectronics"—which for

Haraway functions as almost a metatechnology, as "what mediates the translation of *labor* into robotics and word processing; *sex* into genetic engineering and reproductive technologies; and *mind* into artificial intelligence and decision procedures" (596; Haraway's italics)—nevertheless betrays in its prefix the coding of innovation/ obsolescence. For micro is relative; yesterday's micro is micro no longer, not because, like "labor," it's now part of a "natural" past, but because, like Babbage's Indian cloth manufacture was in 1832, it is now obsolete.

As I suggested, Babbage's argument had already clearly realized the positional effects of technological innovation, but throughout the nineteenth and well into the twentieth century, it was preeminently some version or another of natural coding that continued to supply the explanatory rationale for those effects. To some extent the importance of new technologies of industrial production displaced natural coding as the immediate reference of positionality in the social field. Despite Marx and Engel's sweeping assertion in the *Manifesto* that "the whole relations of society" underwent continual change with the "revolutionizing" of the "instruments of production," however, what I've described as the renaturalizing of configurations of social position did more than keep pace. Renaturalizing also elaborated new technologies of knowledge that (as Foucault has argued) produced whole new fields of relevance for determining social relations of position. Things changed, but so did the powers of natural coding. At times in "A Manifesto for Cyborgs" Haraway seems dismissive of Foucault's analysis, as if his focus of attention was only a problematic of historical reconstruction. But I think it possible to make sense of that apparent dismissal by recognizing that for Haraway what's finally at stake in the emergent information society of the present is less some complete disappearance of natural coding than its loss of general explanatory authority. It may or may not have disappeared completely (indeed, arguments for its disappearance seem to me difficult, given the prominence of such fields as sociobiology), but it's no longer needed to explain the social changes made possible through technological innovation.

The latter perception, however, accounts in part for the relative optimism of her essay in comparison to Foucault's own work and to Foucauldian analysis generally. Insofar as women have almost invariably been positioned as the victims in any version of natural coding, the displacement of its explanatory authority can appear a hopeful sign. "The cyborg," Haraway argues, "is not subject to Foucault's biopolitics; the cyborg simulates politics, a much more potent field of operations" (594). Thus, in her list of dichotomies, "fields of difference" on the right-hand side of the list replaces "nature/culture" on the left. I read this as an indication of her sense that within the social organization of fields of difference, natural coding no longer supplies an authoritative explanatory rationale. Likewise, however, fields of difference then no longer yield a natural sign system for a left politics by means of which, as in Wollstonecraft and Marx, oppositional critique could get its epistemological bearings. What still seem to be obvious positional inequalities in configurations of social relations can't be understood through demystifying the rationales of the natural.

One sign of the difficulties of relying on such demystification is that even relatively sophisticated Marxist analyses, for example, have been led to suggest that gender and race—in the past familiar vehicles of natural coding—no longer function as primary systems of domination, as if when they are no longer naturally coded, they no longer enforce the social determinations that nevertheless continue to assign women and people of color to nondominant positions. William J. Wilson's *The Declining Significance of Race* is perhaps the most visible example, since it has been used so often by conservative ideologues to underwrite their own opposition to liberal affirmative action and antidiscrimination laws. In fairness to Wilson, what he actually had in mind was more, not less, government intervention, which he saw as necessary to hasten a declining significance that wasn't declining nearly rapidly enough, and his analysis of labor market segmentation remains an enormously useful account of existing discriminatory policies in the marketplace. The point is simply that by not recognizing race as a primary determining factor in those policies, Wilson's demystifying argument doesn't get very far in understanding, and challenging, the roles of newly produced racial meanings in contemporary culture. That is, the problem is not only the habitual Marxist tendency to think of class as always a more fundamental socioeconomic reality. It's a failure of epistemology to "know the difference," as Haraway might put it. Natural coding of social position was never anything but an ideology of explanation.

Thus while it is now rare outside of a virulent neoconservatism

to find racist arguments overtly cast in terms of the biological in-
feriority of "blacks," nevertheless there is no lack of visible "explanations" for why a "black urban underclass" remains black and
underclass. Like yesterday's technology, "such people" are, quite
simply, obsolete. That is, the meaning of race in this form of explanation is not referred to some metarationale of natural coding, but
is instead coded directly across obsolescence/innovation as black-
stagnant/black-rising: on the one hand, a residual survival from a
rapidly vanishing past, still clinging to the broken shards and fragments of a no longer viable culture, and on the other a rising black
middle class which, "cyborg-like" if you will, learned to modernize
itself, and which thus evidences a profound "unfaithfulness" to any
putative origin in a myth of "natural" races.

Nicholas Lemann's two-part *Atlantic* article, since expanded into
book form, affords a convenient illustration. His argument would
locate the "actual" origins of a northern urban black underclass in
the cultural heritage of a now disappearing rural South, a culture
that, however enabling in its original surroundings, becomes profoundly dysfunctional when preserved in the radically new and different conditions of northern industrial cities. Thus it's not at all
an argument about how "blacks" are naturally "that way." Urban
ghetto populations for Lemann are no more natural than an outdated technology. Like 8-tracks and vinyl records in a CD world,
they're just rummage-sale cheap, endlessly grinding out "Songs of
the South"—while microelectronics in its latest digitally processed
form mediates the translations of rap into MTV. Nevertheless, there
should be no doubt either that this is still very much an argument
about the meaning of race. The social itineraries available to "blacks"
are plotted everywhere in relation to "white" positionalities as a
norm. Technoideological coding doesn't diminish the significance
of race, even if it does alter profoundly how racial meanings are
produced.

The optimistic gamble of Haraway's essay lies in the premise that
while cyborgs are, as she says, "the illegitimate offspring of mili-
tarism and patriarchal capitalism, not to mention state socialism,"
nevertheless "illegitimate offspring are often exceedingly unfaithful
to their origins" (582); there's no teleology guaranteeing the reproduction of origin. But what that premise ignores is the potential usefulness for dominant positions of the *unfaithfulness* of the unfaithful.

As I suggested, in the continually changing relations of a capitalist economy, natural coding could retain its authority of explanation only by becoming an ongoing process of ideological renaturalizing. Yet there are still limits to what natural coding can accomplish even as mobilized in this ongoing process. It's more difficult for the two-hundredth new explanation of the natural characteristics of a race to be quite as convincing as the third or fourth; explanations of race that remain faithful to their origin in the natural eventually become a liability rather than an asset, a simulation of racism suitable only for mockery by the "enlightened" programming of recent network television, for example. Arguments such as Lemann's, in contrast, are themselves cyborglike in their unfaithfulness to any origin in a biologically assumed nature of race. But that very unfaithfulness means the trick can be worked over and over again with no loss of efficacy. Because it makes no natural claims about race, Lemann's own argument can become obligingly obsolete should someone generate a "better" explanation than rural Southern heritage for the persistence of a black urban underclass. Like 8-tracks, carburetors, and rotary phones, it will simply join the frozen, garish relics strewn across the itineraries of technological change.

What Haraway identifies as the collapse of boundaries distinguishing ideological constructions of "the natural" from ideological constructions of "technology" may well make a myth of cyborgs possible. But technological innovation must always produce technological obsolescence, and that collapse of boundaries then makes people available to the operations of technology's informing thematics of obsolescence. Technologies, like people, travel; they have a certain social mobility that is neither random nor uniform. The technoideological coding of dominant politics structures "fields of difference" so that nondominant populations travel the same routes to the same places as obsolete technologies. That is, technoideological coding can "do without" the authority of natural coding to explain configurations of social position, because in this master narrative of residual, obsolete survivals from the past, it generates its own rationale for the stratifications of the social field. Thus oppositional politics in contrast must then involve a recognition that such itineraries of the obsolete mark not survivals from the past, but the conditions of ideological production of a dominant politics in the present.

"We cannot go back ideologically or materially"; attempts to pit "the natural" against "the technological" are as futile a hope as any other construction of nostalgia. In later chapters, I will have a great deal to say about nostalgia as a function of dominant politics, a way of preserving its master narrative of survivals from the past. But rather than playing, as an alternative to nostalgia, new ways to link avant-garde art and vanguard politics across the newly emergent sectors of technology, I want to pursue instead the *production* of obsolescence as a condition of technoideological change. That is, I will be less interested in the implications of recent technological developments than in what happens to "yesterday's" innovation: where it goes, to whom, and what alternative uses can be made of it. As so-called third world countries, as well as part-time workers, a great many racial and ethnic "minorities," and poor people generally in the United States know all too well, obsolete technologies don't disappear as they become obsolete. Obsolescence means the possibility of *appearance*; it is a precondition for the availability of technologies to these groups.* And avant-garde assumptions aside, what's true of technologies in some sense may also be true of ideologies.

Before anticipating too quickly the argument of later chapters, however, I will look briefly at the changing conditions of technological innovation. Even in the more strictly economic terms of industrial production, there remains a sense in which obsolete technologies not only don't disappear, but in fact often continue to be integral to the success of new technologies. I'll begin then at some distance from media studies and the postmodern, from obviously cultural fields—not because ideological constructions are unimportant, but because technologies, even micro ones, do involve material apparatuses, and it's good to get some sense of their movements and

*The *use* of technologies socially designated as obsolete, however, is rather different in any case than the use of designated innovative, "cutting-edge" technologies, precisely because the value of such obsolete technologies can indeed be figured first in terms of use rather than in terms of their relative newness or innovation. Lisa Schubert pointed out to me in conversation that my argument about the use of the obsolete in this sense thus has a certain relevance to Susan Willis's argument in *A Primer for Daily Life* about restoring the importance of use value in a social context where everything is measured by exchange: "Where I think Willis's argument is similar to your book is that, when you think about it, when a commodity is rendered obsolete, it loses much of its exchange value and manifests to a greater degree its use value."

uses in production. It is here that technoideological coding's master narrative of survivals locates its own field of reference.

I

A focus on the material apparatuses of technologies, however, can't imply an arrival at some unambiguous level of brute facticity. The "same" phenomenon will neither look nor function as "same" across the social field. In the late fifties and early sixties, for example, television appeared to a number of theorists within literary culture as a massive new development in communications technology that would eventually absorb and rearticulate in completely new forms the entire field of communications. That is not quite how it looked to anyone at work on the development of circuit board technologies, for whom there seemed to be, instead of simply "television," an immensely complicated bundle of multiple, intersecting fields of technological research, where no one could say for sure what exactly would happen next and what the effects might be. Neither perspective was necessarily right or wrong, more or less "global" or more or less "local." No vast schema coordinated all these developments, assigning roles and levels of specificity in advance.

Clearly, technological obsolescence is not a natural phenomenon, but beyond that, even in terms of a material apparatus, obsolescence must be produced in specific ways. "Television" doesn't automatically make "radio" obsolete, nor for that matter did transistors make vacuum tubes obsolete automatically. Not only are different and shifting levels of material apparatus involved—the comparison of television to radio is not the same kind of comparison as transistor to vacuum tube—but the determination of obsolescence is itself a function of use that requires the interventional establishment of some field of equivalency. An assertion such as "television made radio obsolete" both obscures this process of intervention and ignores how in certain fields—say, weather information and emergency communication aboard pleasure boats—technological developments that may have begun somewhere within television research functioned to revolutionize radio reception and transmission.

The movement of material apparatuses, and likewise the production of obsolescence, is bound up everywhere with the significations of equivalent use, and consequently with ideological production understood less as the kind of metarationale supplied by themes of "progress" than as a process of transcoding. Prior to any signs of "progress," transcoding involves the more immediately necessary process of rewriting any one systematic ensemble of relations into the terms of another in a way that permits a migration of the useful through now unimpeded flow channels across the field. The obsolescence of breaker-point ignition systems in automobile engines, for example, might be represented in advertising constructions as the result of technological "progress." However, ideological production functioned first in that determination of obsolescence through a process of transcoding that rewrote the relation of the automobile's electric system to its fuel system from the model of temporally linked cause and effect, within which breaker points functioned, into the synchronic spatiality afforded by systems models of computers. Within the general equivalences made available by this reassembled relationality, it then became possible to see how an electronic ignition specifically might serve a use equivalent to breaker points, and hence mark the latter from that point on as obsolete.

Technologies thus move across the multiple sectors of the social field in doubly complicated ways. While it is true enough, as any number of critics have pointed out, that high-level research and development is typically high level indeed, involving the interlocking upper reaches of corporate, financial, military, and academic institutions, new technologies nevertheless don't uniformly move from the top down, spreading more and more widely in the process. The establishment of equivalent use that produces specific indices of innovation and obsolescence is (to put it mildly) an uncertain, uneven process, as the legal tangle of patent laws and applications ought to suggest. And here, perhaps better than anywhere, is the place to observe often striking contradictions between (crudely) the material and the cultural resources required for the development and use of new technologies.

The financial cost of facilities involved in the actual research for and production of any given material apparatus of technology may or may not in some grand final accounting be recovered through its use and sale. But far greater profits are likely to emerge elsewhere as a result less of throwing greater financial resources into the process "from the top" than by establishing different equivalencies of use that permit the spread of the technology elsewhere. The remarkable proliferation of electronics firms —in the Silicon Valley; in San Diego, Los Angeles, and Orange counties of Southern California; and by now in more northern cities such as Seattle and Portland— is hardly a direct result of a sudden access of cash flow through these geographical sectors to fund R & D work. It results primarily from marketing by entrepreneurial firms that opened new territories of equivalent uses requiring only relatively slight and rapid alterations of already existing technological apparatuses. The dizzying rises, collapses, expansions, and buyouts of such firms suggest something very different from uniformly measured flow from "top" to "bottom." Obsolescence and innovation at any given moment seem perpetually up for grabs.

But this is not quite a picture of some capitalist heaven where "free competition" has at last been restored to its rightful role as final arbiter of the newest and best, and where "the little guy" with brains, hard work, and initiative can compete equally with long-established firms. "Stress," Haraway remarks, is the "privileged pathology affecting all kinds of components in this universe" (594), from the material apparatus itself to individual firms and people. Stress in this form, however—as "communications breakdown," failures of transcoded equivalencies, and so on—is also a pathology *of* privilege, of what occurs within the privileged positionalities of being immediately at stake in the movements of technologies, in producing their indices of obsolescence and innovation. For beneath these layers of turbulence lies what in contrast will then seem a kind of terminal condition of obsolescence, where, so far from a pathology, such stress as always would be a luxury, the somatic *frisson* of anticipation that might signal escape.

In the fashionable image of what Haraway labels the "global economy/electronic cottage" (replacing "scientific management in home/factory" in the left-hand column), the garment industry appears a relic. Historically a site of many major, embattled confrontations in the political economy—from the institution of the "family wage" to the unionization of women—it now seems, as Baudrillard might say, that "the stakes are no longer there" (133, n. 2). Thus it may well come as a surprise to find that in the great corporate restructuring of the last three decades the organization of management, the increasingly complex chain of subcontracting work, the development and use of new technologies, and the hiring patterns of

the garment industry resemble nothing so much as the most sophisticated electronics production, the very emblem of the new. At the
same time, however, the comparison is doubly revealing. The similarity, that is, tells you where to look in electronics production for
what becomes clear enough in the garment industry, namely, the
"paradox" that while perhaps it is linked to the rapid-paced information system of a global economy, the "cottage" is not, or not
only, a wired-up electronic marvel but more immediately something resembling a negative afterimage of the worst sweatshops of
the industrial "past."*

Fernández Kelly and García's research, on which I've been relying for the comparison, turned up any number of "instances where
women with experience as operatives in the garment industry literally had to become managers or owners of small operations in
order to maintain the living standards of their families" (62). As
now owner-operators out of their homes, however, these workers
do not of course spend their days (and often nights) at the controls
of sophisticated machinery. In one case reported by Fernández Kelly
and García, "an older woman had used a sizeable disability pension
received by her husband to make the initial investment in five used
sewing machines and in the hiring of seven workers" (62). Her firm,
like others in similar circumstances, then becomes one of the sub-
contractors for large corporations, paid by the local job, and often
hired in the first place not by the corporation itself, but through the
efforts of a broker whose function is, precisely, to line up available
small operations for subcontracting work at the cheapest rates and
the quickest work, and with an inevitable cut of her or his own.

Studies like Fernández Kelly and García's document how electronics production, no less than the garment industry, depends on
workers, working conditions, and technologies that bear little resemblance to the image of a relentlessly globalized high-tech world.†

*The "post-Fordism" hypothesis that has occasioned so much attention in Britain
(see, for example, Robin Murray's "Fordism and Post-Fordism") as a sign of "new
times" registers quite accurately an emergent restructuring of corporations and the
labor force, but perhaps without fully recognizing this "after-image" effect.

†Evelyn Nakano Glenn and Charles Tolbert's study of stratification yields corroborating data by focusing on the composition of the work force and relative wage
levels in computer-related occupations across a number of different fields. What
Fernández Kelly and García's research explains about employment practices within
electronics manufacture itself, Glenn and Tolbert's explains about the effects of the

A home/shop where work is carried out on used sewing machines or, in electronics production, with a kind of miniature assembly line of detailed handwork spread out on an old drafting table, may—eventually or already—be linked by computer to a corporate office hundreds of miles away. But even the spatially immediate juxtaposition of these different technological apparatuses in the home can signal nothing so much as the newly created and immense social distances of positionality separating the home worker from the layers of corporate management. A current term such as "economic destabilization" is then not quite enough to describe these changing conditions of production.

It's true that the technological modernization of the garment industry, like the emergence of electronics production and other new operations, does destabilize the divisions of the social field that had itself organized industrial production. It affects everything, from the location, size, and distribution of the work place, the gender and racial ethnic composition of the work force, the distribution of that work force—no longer "massed" in factories—even the very geography of industry, and of the corporation itself. Destabilization, that is, is relative everywhere to the divisions and categories of the past, and to the potential for equally dramatic effects of new technologies and new uses for them in the future. But it is *not* necessarily relative to the always present immediacies of positional distances at any given moment in the process of technoideological change. In the next chapter, I will look in more detail at what exactly has been de-

---

electronic machines produced, such as computers, as they are used in production elsewhere. Dividing occupations into five categories of both "skill" and "wage"—computer scientist, programmer, equipment repairer, equipment operator, and data entry keyer—they report that "60 percent of white males in computer occupations are located in the top two occupations (computer scientist and programmer). In sharp contrast, only 23 percent of the women of color are employed in these top occupations; instead, they are overwhelmingly concentrated (77 percent) in the lower-level computer operator and data entry occupations. White women do not fare much better than their racial ethnic counterparts, but white men have a considerable advantage over racial ethnic men, among whom only 42 percent are in the computer scientist and computer programmer occupations" (323). Their data are especially important to counter a widespread perception that new computers in different occupational fields open up new employment possibilities. As I'll suggest, what that perception ignores are the new layers of occupational stratification that ensure positional distances.

stabilized in the emergence of a postindustrial "service" economy in the United States. The restructuring of industrial production in garment manufacture and elsewhere is clearly only one part of a much larger recent economic history. Ideologically, however, the concept of destabilization ignores how the very process of change itself may be as positionally structured (by relative degrees of cultural and economic capital) as the categorical divisions it breaks down.

In the technoideological coding of obsolescence/innovation, innovation can only be innovation for the time being; today's technological apparatus is as important for what it makes possible in future developments as for what it might be used for today. In such circumstances, however, those who occupy dominant social positions can't assume the permanence of such a position, nor rely only on the power of producing innovations before anyone else to ensure dominance. If, as Pierre Bourdieu has argued in *Distinction*, dominant positions are always marked by the social distance of distinction from others, then in an unstable field of continually shifting positionalities, dominance requires what can be called the capitalization of change. That is, the *positional* "profit potential" of innovation and change is a matter of extorting the maximum of distance and distinction from each shift that occurs in the social field. Thus rather than simply producing the conditions of change, whether new technologies or whatever, dominant social positions must depend on an emergent distance between what henceforth can be temporally marked as "old" and "new" in the reconfigurations of positionality. That distance functions like a kind of "surplus value," over and above the "fact" of change and the labors of innovation, and is available to be realized as the social capital of distinction from "the others" condemned to a now rapidly disappearing configuration of what used to be.

Hence it's not the case that conditions for a Hispanic garment worker in Southern California don't potentially "improve" in some sense by means of the change from factory laborer to home subcontracting "entrepreneur." They might, or they might not, or the change might be necessary, as Fernández Kelly and García point out, simply to maintain a living wage. But the positional significance of "entrepreneurial owner" will not remain the same either. Relative to the position of a corporate manager, there may exist an even greater distance between the one and the other than between the position of factory worker and manager. Money is not the same as capital, and likewise the power of movement—from factory worker to owner in this case—afforded by a newly destabilized, changing field of positionality is not the same as the capitalization of change, the realization of positional "value." It is the latter that at once yields "new" freedoms and benefits, and yet also consigns whole groups of the population to the residual status of survivals from a rapidly disappearing past, rather than being integral to and produced by changing requirements of the present. The capitalization of change, that is, depends on narratively locating such presently produced positionalities as survivals from the past. These social divisions of "fields of difference" have everything to do with how the relations of temporality to obsolescence are determined.

II
_____

The various natural codings of "progress" often borrowed a temporal language of past, present, and future to configure ideologically assigned indices of position. In much of the rhetoric of colonialism, for example, "native" could mean not only non-European populations existing closer to a "state of nature"— with all its often contradictory valences—but also being stuck in the past, at some always more remote point in the eschatologically marked temporality of Christianity, or alternatively in the development of industrial civilization. For the language of temporality itself observed an organic unfolding of past into present into future, and in so doing facilitated the multiple alignments of a natural coding of progress with the technoideological coding of obsolescence/innovation. The "native" is stuck in the past; the "obsolete" is simply the slippage into the past of what had once been the leading edge of change.

With the displacement of the natural as a foundational code of temporality, however, such determinations become considerably more complicated. In a postcolonial field of "developing" nations, of "first," "second," and "third" worlds, and of multinational capitalism's designation of "core" and "periphery," technologically very similar operations might seem in one context—say, Oldsmobile's Lansing plant—in danger of becoming an obsolete holdover from the past, and yet in another identify the developing industrialization of an export processing zone in specifically marked regions

of the "periphery," like Volkswagen's Brazil plant. Similarly confusing temporal effects—confusing, that is, from the perspective of
an organically unfolding temporality—can be seen in a completely
different kind of example, in the variously charted itineraries of
modernism into postmodernism. Here is where the obsolescence of
"the modern," so far from slipping into a quietly marginal death in
the past, might seem instead a movement into a centrally consoli-
dated orthodoxy still imaged through the persistent avant-gardism
of the postmodern, like the nightmare of the living dead, a putative
Hegelian owl of Minerva become Count Dracula. Or alternatively,
it might seem necessary to cherish "the modern" as the last, best,
still surviving hope of genuinely oppositional practices before the
relentless co-optation of the postmodern into the culturally dominant—less like a vampire feeding off the living than a promise of
rebirth gestating in the very belly of the prison-house. Or finally, as
Lyotard sometimes seems to suggest, perhaps the modern is merely
a curious blip in the otherwise steady development of a postmodern
consciousness. Both materially and culturally, any temporal determination of obsolescence seems obligingly mobile.

This temporal mobility nevertheless evidences certain positional
regularities. Like the natural, technoideological coding is constitutive of the distances and distinctions of stratified social position.
Without foundational grounding in the natural—the organically unfolding—time itself can function as a readily available index of capitalization in any given circumstances, making visible the positionally profit-bearing power of change. Electronics production supplies
a conveniently prototypical image of internationalization in these
terms. Since the mid-sixties, when Fairchild opened its semicon-
ductor assembly plant in Hong Kong, and General Instruments its
microelectronics assembly in Taiwan, it has seemed imperative for
domestic electronics production to change in order to "survive."
And change it did, in fact continuing to grow well into the eighties.
But a successful capitalization of change required more than geographical movement within the United States and the decentralization of production through the proliferation of small firms and
subcontracting. It also required a drastic restructuring of the work
force, increasingly split between upper-level, high-skill technicians
and management and finance professionals, on the one hand, and
an always larger available pool of unskilled and semiskilled labor

on the other. Using the Labor Department's own projections, Fernández Kelly and García point out that electronics manufacture in the United States "will have required fifty times more janitors than engineers by the end of the century" (56).

Beyond U.S. borders, in assembly plants in Hong Kong, Taiwan, and before long in Singapore, Malaysia, the Philippines, and elsewhere, the emergent social positionalities of a work force could be rationalized as if a necessary cost of "development," of the industrialization of new export-processing zones in these countries. But within the United States, even when the actual work force might include large numbers of recent immigrants from many of the same countries where assembly plants were now running; when women greatly outnumbered men both in the United States and in other countries; and when similar natural language might still retain local ideological uses—"Asian women are good with their hands," and so on—an explanatory rationale nevertheless had to be fundamentally different. For within the United States, a new work force composed primarily of racial ethnic minorities replaced white men to some extent, and white women to an even greater extent. And a language of linear, organic temporal development can function neither to mask nor to rationalize such reassigned positionalities occasioned by the domestic effects of internationalization and corporate restructuring. Nor can the more brutally simple natural coding of "good with their hands" and the like, without some rather curious epicycles to explain why white women were to be perceived as not quite so good with their hands as they used to be.

In these circumstances, the mobility of temporal determinations of obsolescence became functionally crucial as a form of explanation. Indigenous white populations who recognized the necessity of profiting from change could "earn" the positional distinction that located them in high-skill occupations (conveniently forgetting, of course, the fifty-to-one odds of engineer to janitor), and likewise the distance from which to oversee the work of populations newly arrived in the work force. Indigenous white populations unwilling to recognize this necessity became obsolete—their occupational, wage, and lifestyle expectations sadly out of key with the present.* The

*Lee Iacocca made this clear in his often-repeated "explanation" of how in the midst of Chrysler's crisis of change, he had a lot of jobs available at $17 an hour, none at $20 an hour.

newly arrived people of color in the work force teetered precariously
between the alternative itineraries marked out by such white innovation and obsolescence, and meanwhile supplied cheaply available
labor by "teetering" always in the same way, forever stranded at an
always mobile crossroads. In a landscape of constant social change,
this crossroads promises decisive changes in direction, but nothing
ever emerges but this promise.

There is, then, a certain coherence here, but not one that would
uniformly link innovation/obsolescence to an organically unfolding
temporality, which in fact could "work" only in the absence of such
linkages. Stripped of its naturally coded metarationale, technoideological coding becomes capable of projecting its own explanations
of positionality in the capitalization of change by means of its own
variable indices of the "now," the "not yet," and the "no longer"
as temporally visible measures of such capitalization. The "not yet"
need not at all obey any inherent teleology to become the "now," and
the "no longer" can strike at any point in the configuration of the
"now" without necessarily jeopardizing the rest of it: an inestimable
advantage over a natural coding of time. It's not a "coherence" only
of the random; this isn't a long way of saying that obsolescence is
temporally relative. There is relation, to be sure, but in specifically
structured ways, which mark out the utility for dominant positions
of making obsolescence what *determines* time, and not the other way
around, for with that reversal of priority, no necessity exists to discover any other and "deeper" reasons why certain populations don't
"move with the times." A displaced white working class is a survival
from the past *because* it is obsolete; a culturally "stagnant" urban
black underclass can be distinguished from a rising black middle
class as likewise a survival, because likewise obsolete, and so on.
Obsolescence splits and divides up the social field by producing its
temporalities as structurally coexistent layers.

Thus theories of the postmodern that locate their coordinates in
the synchronicity of information systems, simulations, and the collapse of familiar binaries (surface/depth, public/private, and so on)
can rarely speak relevantly about the conditions of obsolescence,
insofar as such coordinates reproduce the very narratives of temporal survivals supplied by the discourse of obsolescence. Baudrillard
writes, in that curious footnote to "The Ecstasy of Communication": "All this does not mean that the domestic universe—the home,

its objects, etc.—is not still lived largely in a traditional way—social, psychological, differential, etc. It means rather that the stakes are no longer there, that another arrangement or lifestyle is virtually in place, even if it is indicated only through a technological discourse which is often simply a political gadget" (133, n. 2). Determining where exactly the stakes are at any given time is what positional dominance is all about; the assumption of a "virtual" coexistence of "lifestyles" establishes the necessary field of equivalences that obsolescence can temporally configure into a still surviving "traditional" way and an emergent "new" way. Thus it can be made to seem as though Hispanic garment workers are where they are socially because they are clinging to an obsolete interior psychology or to a now dysfunctional domestic culture, rather than because they must work in conditions produced by a "technological discourse" that appears to be a mere "political gadget" only if you're positioned somewhere else altogether.

Ernst Bloch's well-known formula of "nonsynchronous fragments" is here a useful reminder that materially and culturally, change is an uneven process; whatever may be "virtually in place" is never in place all at once virtually, let alone actually. Nevertheless, in terms of the configurations of social position, it would be a mistake to let that formula account for all temporally marked displacements. It doesn't just happen that the social field evidences nonsynchronous, fragmentary movements, and as my examples in the last section were intended to suggest, even the synchronically immediate doesn't imply some as yet temporally unmarked conjunction. It is of course necessary to keep in mind the similarities that do exist between the conditions of factory workers in the garment industry in the late nineteenth and early twentieth centuries, and the conditions of garment workers in Southern California today; as it is to remark the similarities between purportedly old-line industries such as garment manufacture and emergent industries such as electronics. But the nonsynchronous appearance of what then seem like working conditions surviving from the past is itself produced from within the organization of production in the present. What the similarities tell you is not simply that change is uneven, and that some things still persist. As I will argue in the next chapter, they tell you that the process of change has been structured in ways that generate new configurations of the social field that are no less marked by

the distances and distinctions of positionality than configurations in
the past.

III
_____

It is in the context of such a recognition that the optimism of
Haraway's argument can help forestall drawing the immediate implication that oppositional politics are impossible, or at least that
oppositionally organized politics in the past made no headway. Both
assumptions involve reproducing the technoideological coding of
obsolescence/innovation, as if past political practices are merely an
obsolete ground that must be cleared before anything more promising can begin, because obviously they didn't succeed. But if Haraway is right, and natural coding no longer possesses the authoritative status of metarationale of explanation, if it has been displaced
as the ultimate field of reference for the determinations of social
position, surely part of the reason lies in the success of oppositional
politics. Industries such as garment manufacture must now look
to create the political conditions that can yield a large population
of nonunionized immigrant labor, for example, because unionized
labor forced a certain redistribution of profit and a reconfiguration
of the social relations of management and labor. In doing so it made
it increasingly difficult to locate *any* potential pool of labor as just
"naturally" available. There is good reason not to overestimate the
effects of that success; however, that's a rather different matter than
dismissing "older" oppositional practices out of hand or succumbing to the nostalgic left politics of the "authentically native," which
demands that nondominant groups look the part, as it were.

Nevertheless, to expect Hispanic garment workers to evidence
the signs of some set of cultural practices now socially designated as
new is no less illusory than the politics of the "native." At best, it's
merely a relocation of the avant-gardism of the postmodern, which
lets academics continue to get the latest cultural news, every hour
on the hour. At worst, it ignores what it's like to have to live within
that grinding logic of necessity. What the capitalization of change—
as made possible across the indices of technoideological coding of
obsolescence/innovation—means in terms of social position is the
forced congruence of the nondominant and the obsolete, in all their
multiple forms. This means in turn that it's not the socially desig-

nated newest and latest—materially or culturally—but the obsolete
that nondominant groups find most immediately available to work
with. The crucial recognition in this context is that obsolescence
is not at all a survival from the past. It is produced by and integral to the conditions of dominance in the present. And because it
is integral to these conditions, it is potentially dangerous to them.
There's every reason dominant ideological productions work very
hard to endlessly construct itineraries of the obsolete as survival narratives, to flood so-called mass culture with nostalgic reproductions
of a fading past—because obsolescence when reproduced as nostalgic object is no longer dangerous. It's then just a hopelessly outdated
survival, perhaps even one to be cherished affectionately against the
"deteriorations" of the present, as, for example, in the last two decades of Hollywood films celebrating the "lost" macho values of
the working class. All of which on the one hand then functionally
obscures how an obsolete working class is continually being produced now—out of whole new populations in the work force—to
sustain "corporate restructuring," and on the other recontains the
threat posed to positional dominance by the necessity of presently
produced obsolescence.

For left politics the crucial point, again, is that the threat to positional dominance can inhere neither in the dream of the authentically native that Haraway criticizes nor in the avant-gardism of
commanding the new. Groups consigned to obsolescence by a dominant politics don't have access to the cultural freedoms to generate
brilliantly new simulations and excesses of this postmodernism, any
more than they can possess the material benefits of the latest technologies. That is, culturally the issue isn't whether any specific form
of the postmodern is "oppositional" or "co-opted"—presumably it
might be either—or whether postmodernism generally is now culturally dominant. The more immediate issue is where avant-garde–
identified innovations of the postmodern can come from in the first
place—which suggests that it's not a good idea to pin a lot of political
hopes to the possibilities of such postmodern oppositionality. This
is the case not because the postmodern can't be "genuinely" oppositional, or because it's already "virtually in place" everywhere as in
fact the cultural logic of multinational capitalism, but because until
its forms—like "yesterday's" technologies—become obsolete, not a
whole lot of people can make use of whatever oppositional directions

those forms might make possible. Indeed, specifically cultural innovation, in whatever versions of avant-garde ideology, has always
lent itself to the survival narratives of technoideological coding by
obligingly dispensing with "yesterday's" new form, new assembly,
new configuration, and so on, as if "co-optation" and the like signaled an end to their oppositional usefulness rather than a conflict
just underway. The disdain directed at the use of yesterday's new is
just the flip side of "Gee, you don't seem like an Indian from the
reservation."

The recognition of obsolescence as presently produced, however,
is a way to break the links of survival narratives that equate the obsolete with the fading past, the residual, the nostalgic, the politically
ineffective. What may seem co-optation by the dominant from the
angle of entry into cultural fields imposed by innovation imperatives is from another angle simply a high-level turbulence. Its fallout
yields lots of previously unavailable stuff, which may indeed be con-
scripted as necessary to keep the conflict going. Nevertheless, as I
will argue in subsequent chapters, the "stuff" of both material and
cultural junk can also often be patched, repaired, reshaped, rapidly
distributed, and deployed toward other kinds of ends altogether.
That revolution, Gil Scott-Heron's title reminds us, in present circumstances will not be televised. But it might usefully be, were
television itself to join the "survivals" of obsolete technologies.

Class-as-Lifestyle:
Social Organization in
a Service Economy

There does seem to be massive statistical evidence for a shift in employment patterns in the United States. Since Victor Fuchs's 1968 study, *The Service Economy*, done for the National Bureau of Economic Research, growth trends in the service sector Fuchs documented have continued to accelerate. Very recent statistics indicating a potential slowdown of growth don't really alter the general picture since World War II; the slowdown occurs relative to the pace of the eighties, when growth was even more spectacular than previously. Nevertheless, it remains difficult to generalize about what exactly has changed that would make the term "service economy" seem appropriate, and what might conceivably justify the increasingly widespread perception of some fundamental change in the very organization of the economy. Undoubtedly in the United States the labor force classified under food service, for example, has increased dramatically in comparison to auto workers, but it's a long jump from statistical comparisons between specific occupations to generalizations about a service economy. As George Stigler had pointed out over 40 years ago, the very way in which census categories define service occupations is by no means stable. And if, like Harry Braverman in *Labor and Monopoly Capital*, you maintain that, strictly, "service" means labor "offered directly to the consumer," where "production and consumption are simultaneous" (360) since no vendible product is involved, then many of the occupations that fall under census categories of service (and which then lend the support of statistical data to perceptions of change) are nothing of the sort. Indeed, for all his seems a common-sense definition, Braverman has some considerable difficulty in isolating occupations that might fit it exactly.

While Braverman's challenge to perceptions of fundamental economic change thus begins in questions about the definition of service in census categories and the like, in "Is There a Service Economy?" Richard Walker proceeds instead by linking the growth of so-called service occupations to the corporate restructuring of major industries. He argues that as corporations became more and more expansively multinational, with great distances separating production sites, and with the home office in still another location, the relative proportion of "indirect" and "hands-on" labor within the corporation changed accordingly. The former now occupies a complex zone of service personnel interposed between the actual production of a commodity and the consumer. The result, however, is then less a transformation from one kind of economy to another, "industrial" to "service," than a series of linked developments in the process of how an industrial economy functions. That is, the emergence of new sectors of service occupations is largely a creation of and is sustained by the restructuring of industry. Bennett Harrison and Barry Bluestone have made Walker's thesis crucial to their own account of corporate restructuring in *The Great U-Turn*, and Stephen Cohen and John Zyman propose a similar kind of description in *Manufacturing Matters*. And indeed, if you suspend for the moment Braverman's questions about the definition of service, even census and Labor Department statistics permit a slightly different means of support for Walker's thesis, by way of a series of generalizations from the data.

First, occupations that by whatever rationale of definition are classified as "service" do represent generally growing fields, in sharp contrast to those classified under industry, which have been uniformly stagnant or declining. Second, average salaries in the service sector will be appreciably lower than in manufacturing and industry generally, despite the relatively recent inclusion of categories of "financial service" workers and others who may hold high-paying jobs. Third, the labor force of the service sector will include a much larger percentage of women, young people, and people of color. Fourth, that labor force will be much less likely to be unionized. And finally, occupations classified under service are very often extensions, modifications, or divisions of labor that in the past did not function directly in the calculation of wage labor for profit. That

is, they would have belonged within what an older Marxian terminology labeled "unproductive" labor within a capitalist economic
organization—but they now are clearly very much a part of that
organization.

These generalizations do seem to me faithful to the statistical data,
but if you look to them for help in actually defining what the shift
to a service economy is all about, what exactly has changed in and
through this shift, the answer must be simultaneously "a great deal"
and "not much, really." Clearly there has been a massive movement
within the total labor force from some occupations to others, and if
it is difficult to isolate an essential distinction between the poles of
movement, certain correlations are possible, as my generalizations
suggest. Yet just as clearly, there has rarely been a time in the history of a capitalist economy when a similar movement couldn't be
observed from older and more heavily capitalized to newer, emergent, and less capitalized production; from relatively high-wage to
relatively low-wage labor; and from a relatively homogeneous to
a relatively more heterogeneous labor force, involving the infusion
of whole new categories of workers. That is, from this perspective at least, the shift seems merely the same again, and more of
it. Housing starts may be down, but the employment in "entrepreneurial" housekeeping services is up; so businesses are selling more
clean houses than new houses, with—surprise—a labor force composed primarily of women being paid much less than the primarily
male labor force in housing construction. That hardly seems a basis
from which to claim some dramatic shift in the whole structure of
the economy. Walker's thesis that what we now see is simply an extension rather than a transformation of an industrial economy looks
considerably more plausible.

My generalizations, however, like the statistical data and arguments like Walker's, are written from the point of view of production. Even syntax conspires to suggest that "industrial" and "service"
are adjectival modifiers of "economy," and it's very easy here to
slip from syntax to significance, as if because "industrial" identifies
a particular kind of economic production "service" must as well,
whether the same kind or a different kind. If you think first in terms
of consumption, however, the terms are not parallel by any means.
You can buy a service, but not an industrial. In part, that is, the definitional slipperiness of "service" lies in how, unlike "industrial," it

points simultaneously to consumption as well as to production and labor. And definitions that ignore the conditions of consumption, as I've suggested, make little headway. But if, again, you begin in terms of consumption, it seems to me possible to recognize some clearly etched differences.

Occupations classified by the census data under manufacturing and industrial production involve almost no interaction between worker and consumer, while those classified under service very often involve extended periods of such contact. The auto worker at a GM transmission assembly plant (classified as an industrial worker) may in fact use diagnostic computers and other equipment similar to the auto-repair worker who rebuilds transmissions for Aamco (classified under service); may even possess at least roughly similar labor skills; and arguably there is a vendible product in both cases. That is, you don't just buy the Aamco worker's services, you also buy a rebuilt transmission. As a consumer, however, you'll never see the GM worker—even if she or he's located in the United States—while you're likely to have some direct contact with the Aamco worker. With other service-classified occupations, the contact may be much greater. In other words, what from the perspective of production appears to be "indirect labor," as Walker describes it, from the perspective of consumption appears to be directly *visible* labor. To modify Braverman's definition slightly, what's at issue is less a matter of some simultaneity of production and consumption than the relation of *service workers to consumers*, the emergence of multiple, variegated structures of contact between a work force and a "consumer force."

Workers are also consumers, and vice versa, as was the case throughout the development of an industrial economy as well. But the emergent structures of contact between the roles of worker and consumer affect the identity of work and consumption, where it's no longer then quite so clear what exactly is "role" and what "identity," or (as I'll suggest later), what it means to work and what it means to consume. It's become almost a truism that the emergence of a service economy involves many such destabilizations of familiar categories and oppositions. Destabilization is not only a matter of the collapse of familiar categories, however, but of what happens to social space. Contact between service worker and consumer affects the labor process by permitting the invasion of consumers into the very space where the work occurs, and it alters consumer behavior, which likewise happens in the same space as the labor of service work. The consumption of services often involves bringing workers into your home, which for the duration becomes openly available space, and conversely service work may be carried out from your home, which then makes it available space for consumers. Leisure time is not necessarily time spent by yourself or with family and friends, but is often spent in situations where the space is crowded by any number of service workers performing any number of tasks. Further, consumers are often forced to compete with each other for attention from service workers, who likewise will often compete among themselves—in department stores where sales personnel work on commission, for example—for consumers who look like big-ticket purchasers or big tippers. And finally, anxieties can easily arise, for consumers especially, if you feel yourself in the "wrong" space, a more upscale department store or whatever than you are used to. All of which leads to endlessly refined indices of perception of others' behavior, for clues about what potential comfort zones might be available.

In this sense destabilization brings together, in the same social spaces, people who occupy those spaces across multiple and often conflicting interests, values, and behaviors. And it thereby creates conditions that can lead to intense antagonisms, which are only heightened by the breakdown of categories that no longer supply the norms of behavior in the situation. Even the simplest, most routine everyday behavior can become a "problem" requiring negotiation. If you're working in a union warehouse, standard ten-minute break times every two hours afford the obvious opportunity to head for the bathroom. If you're cleaning someone's gutters, in contrast, having to go to the bathroom involves "problems" for everyone: permissions asked and granted; anxieties about whether the bathroom is clean or not and what exactly might be on view in it, about getting to and from the bathroom covered with gutter muck; if you're getting paid by the hour, how to account for the time all this takes, and even if by the job, the necessary prolonging of the time the home is available space for both worker and consumer, and so on. All of these problems are likely to be complicated by gender difference—who is to be home for what gender of worker—and often "racial anxieties," and the fear of exposing any of the above to view. These sorts of things may seem utterly trivial, and the example a silly one, but this is itself a perception that irritates, as you know that nevertheless you have to go through them, behave in some way when you do, and feel majorly stupid if you try to take still further time to consult with others to anticipate every possible contingency in advance. In a service economy, social space is anxious space, and for reasons I'll describe in more detail, it generates social antagonisms and conflicts.

It shouldn't then seem farfetched to recognize that a service economy will appear ideologically in terms that function to manage and defuse the potential for antagonisms. That is, the issue isn't which comes first, economic change (however defined) or ideological change. One of the conveniences of the notion of a service economy is that it forestalls such likely interminable debate, insofar as by pointing simultaneously at production, labor, and consumption, it implies that economic transactions are in any case always ideological as well, and vice versa. Likewise the potential for antagonisms can be recognized in either economic or ideological terms. The resources of technoideological coding, however, obviously speak to both, and as I will argue, work less to obscure the specifically social character of relations than to reconfigure potential antagonisms in ways that plot the obsolescence of what in the context will then appear as "the merely social," categories such as gender and race that within the field of natural coding were assumed to be relatively fixed and stable.

The importance of consumption in a service economy can be registered across any number of different forms, from the increasingly powerful role (with respect to production) of marketing and market research analysis within corporate organization to the ways in which indices of social position become visible first in consumer terms. But consumption, as Tania Modleski, among others, has argued, is not only an economic category, but itself has identified a gender-specific social space. To the extent that in an industrial economy "work" meant primarily industrial labor, at factory or warehouse, it was assumed to be done by men, while consumption on the other hand was centered in the home, involving primarily women (a division advertisers were quick to take advantage of early in the century). Obviously both men and women did work outside the home, and just as obviously for women at least, the home couldn't really

be the site of the leisure time activities it was so often imaged to
be. Yet the dominant concept of an industry-driven economy permitted this range of familiar dualisms—production/consumption,
workplace/home, labor/leisure, masculine/feminine—to maintain
a certain equilibrium of distribution, to seem normative in its symmetry.

It might then be anticipated that one effect of the structural importance of consumption in both the economic and the cultural organization of a service economy will be the masculinization of consumer
practices, and correspondingly the feminization of service labor. This
is not simply a matter of more men being more directly involved in
consumer purchases, of both goods and services, or of the high percentage, statistically, of women in service occupations. It involves
how the roles of worker and consumer are no longer categorically
identified through a stable gender division, and how work processes
and the practices of consumption are likewise marked ambiguously.
Indeed, one indication of the masculinization of consumer roles is
that it "suddenly" seems "important" in contemporary culture to
understand that consumption no less than "real work" presupposes a
particular effort, even the exercise of often remarkably sophisticated
skills and knowledges. There no longer seems anything particularly
"natural" about men actively working and women passively con-
suming. As Susan Willis suggests in *A Primer for Daily Life*:

> It may well be that capitalism, having exploited the women's market,
> is now reaching out to make men equal to women as consumers. It is
> true that many more men now participate in shopping as a leisure-time
> activity (particularly in shopping malls) than would ever have dreamed
> of doing so in the past. Gender roles are changing, but so too are the
> economics of commodity capitalism. (100)

In the next section of my argument, I will first trace something
of the detail of this destabilization of gender identifications, and
then connect it to my discussion of the technoideological coding of
racial meanings in the first chapter. While not strictly parallel, both
do involve a certain refusal of natural coding, and, more important
for my immediate purposes, together they suggest how it is that
class emerges as the preferred social category of technoideological
coding. That is, gender and racial divisions as obvious sources of
social antagonisms become through these destabilizing operations

indicators of obsolescence, of the persistence of "older" categories in the midst of a social world whose positionalities are to be assigned instead primarily in class terms. Thus perhaps the most immediate ideological sign of how the potentially violent antagonisms of those crowded social spaces of a service economy are reconfigured will be the destabilizations that produce the obsolescence of gender and race, rewriting them into class terms. This then implies that "class" in this sense is produced precisely by producing the obsolescence of gender and race, as the latter become primary vehicles of techno-ideological coding's master narrative of survivals. The term "white supremacy" is seen by bell hooks as more useful than "racism" to identify how people of color are being exploited in the United States ("Overcoming," 24), and I would suggest that "class" as it functions in technoideological coding carries much of the authority of that white supremacy, by plotting white norms as "merely" class indicators. Nicholas Lemann's argument (discussed in chapter 1) is once again a convenient example: it's not a "racist" argument dedicated to excluding blacks; it's a white supremacist argument in hooks's sense, subsuming white norms into a narrative of class mobilities ostensibly applicable to anyone.

Class, however, is no less obviously than gender or race a social category, and class division is likewise a potential source of social antagonisms. In the third section of this chapter, I will argue that a shift of class-assigned positionalities from production to consumption allows class itself to be transformed from a stable social category into what I will call class-as-lifestyle, which features instead a mobile, performative individual agency as its central term of identification. Antagonisms in this new social configuration can then be narratively resolved into the encounter structures of performance, organized (not surprisingly) around the worker/consumer contact so pervasive in a service economy. Antagonisms, that is, aren't assumed to disappear.

Indeed, in the literature of consumer self-help through which I'll focus the argument, the contact zones of a service economy are explicitly plotted as zones of combat. But what this narrative emplotment attempts is a certain redistribution of performative roles, such that at different times everyone is assumed to have different stakes in the combats, with the result that no one would have any particular reason to want to change the *scene* of combat. That is, everyone will want to perform "better" in whatever given circumstances at whatever time, but without ever altering the ground rules in which everyone is to have an equal investment. Rather than leading to potentially prolonged and intense conflicts across fixed positions, crowded social spaces simply become occasions for the performative mastery of anxieties.

"Class" then seems perhaps a dubious way to designate what are after all foregrounded as performative lifestyle "options" of individual agency, but that it remains appropriate I would argue for several reasons. First, and however individuated in performance, lifestyles are nevertheless available to generalization by focusing on both the expectations and the anxieties of performative agency—the double horizon of class within which lifestyle options are realized. Hence the science of class in a service economy is no longer really sociology, but psychology, as it functions in market research analysis, for instance, as the means for charting generalizable horizons of expectations and anxieties. Indeed, "lifestyle" as I will use it is a term borrowed from market research into consumer behavior, where it names a certain configuration of attitudes, values, and expectations that enables the prediction of future buying patterns. In "The Politics of Consumption," for example, Frank Mort emphasizes the importance of market research analysis in *political* determinations of "lifestyle" patterns, and in linking the term with "class," I mean to expand that definition considerably—but it is important to preserve the emphasis on consumption implied by the market analysis that is my point of departure.

Next, to the extent class is produced upon the obsolescence of race and gender as social categories, the persistence of the latter must be accounted for in class terms in some way. Otherwise, any narrative assertion of their survival will be suspect. Within an "older" terminology of class division, as it was figured by dominant class interests, it was of course the working class that played the invidious role of prolonging and exacerbating the antagonisms of class division, motivated by "resentment," "laziness," "lack of respect" for their "betters," and so on. Here, in contrast, as I'll argue in the second section of this chapter, the notion of a working class itself survives as the designated repository of all those now obsolete ideas about race and gender, as the sector where people are perceived as still stubbornly clinging to such outdated variables of conflict by refusing to adapt to the radically changing lifestyles of the present.

Finally, class-as-lifestyle also plots a certain kind of class division, one having less to do with the criteria of successful individual performance in any given circumstance than with class-marked powers of performance itself. Performance is not the same as the possession or acquisition of positional resources, in any form those resources might take, from simply time and money to very specific and socially certified skills and knowledges. Performance implies the power to deploy whatever resources you might possess in whatever specific circumstances exist. Thus, analogous to Marx's initial model of class division in *Capital*—between those who have only their own labor power to sell, and those who can deploy capital in the purchase of labor power, machinery, and raw material—it is possible within the field of consumption to recognize a class-as-lifestyle division between those who have only their own resources to engage in consumer practices, and those who can capitalize their resources in and through the individuation of performative agency. What counts, in other words, is less the positionally acquired money to buy a high-tech stereo system, for example, or for that matter the system itself, than a position that only *emerges* in and through the performance of getting the system in the first place and the subsequent performances in which it continues to be deployed. Increasingly, then, advertising constructions sell products as part of a larger process of educating consumers in strategies of performance.

I've described these ideological operations that plot social antagonisms as narrative structures, the complementary teleologies of technoideological coding's master narrative of survivals. But no narrative can yield possibilities of hermeneutical corroboration without the detailed organization of material practices. Narratives don't produce obsolescence; they tell you how to read that material organization as they emplot its ends. In the growth of an industrial economy in the United States, the development of an institutional public educational system became increasingly important to material organization in all kinds of ways, from the stratification of individual qualifications for jobs to the skills of literacy that permitted the use of new and more pervasive forms of advertising to reach potential consumers. In the last section of this chapter, the importance of education to the material organization of a service economy as well as an industrial economy will be shown, against two major structural shifts.

First, ideologies of rising social expectations have been largely relocated from the connected circuits of educational certification and occupational availability to the field of consumption and consumer practices. As a result, so-called mass culture assumes a primary pedagogical role, mass culture is also mass education. That is, insofar as ideologies of rising expectations supplied the foundational rationale for "selling" the development of public education to the public, once relocated they function to transform mass culture into a pedagogical field as well. And to that extent, mass culture is not only a matter of ideological "manipulation" or "resistances" to ideology, but like educational institutions is part of the process of determining configurations of social position. Second, as a system of public education thus loses its putative ground of public appeal, not only does the familiar rhetoric of crisis that has always surrounded public education intensify, but the functions of the schools will change considerably. If, as I will argue, mass culture is also a mass education in the "universalizing" performative powers of class-as-lifestyle, public education is then increasingly positioned to maintain and enforce class-as-lifestyle division. Schools become what a great many students perceive them to be: obsolescence factories. But in them obsolescence, again, must be understood not as a rapidly disappearing survival from the past, but as what is produced in the present as functionally necessary to social organization.

Briefly and generally then, technoideologically coded indices of social position project the organization of a service economy in and through pedagogical narratives of consumer lifestyle practices, relationally articulated across class-variable powers of individual performative agency. Class in this sense is itself a mobile category, keyed everywhere to performance rather than to the acquisition and possession of cultural and economic resources. As performative, class is identified through the obsolescence of gender- and race-marked categories of social division and conflict, where the latter appear as so many surviving relics from a rapidly disappearing past. In contrast to race and gender divisions, class division is then acknowledged to exist throughout the crowded, anxious spaces of a service economy. But class conflicts in these destabilized "combat zones" involve the criteria for successful or unsuccessful performance rather than struggles over the possession of resources or over fundamental shifts in the social territories where conflicts are fought out. Relations of hegemony, Gramsci reminds us, are always pedagogical, and the growing importance of mass culture education and the corresponding talk of "crisis" and "decline" of institutional education function materially to reorganize the field of social practices around the narratively plotted structures of technoideologically coded positionality.

What my argument will offer, in other words, is a "clean" (if admittedly complicated) picture of social change, linking economic, cultural, and educational factors through the multiple narratives of positional identifications supplied by technoideological coding. In reality, of course, the picture is not quite so clean. I will then focus subsequent chapters more directly on those interstitial zones of confusion and disruption that smudge the picture's clean outlines, as well as on oppositional challenges to the emergent politics of a service economy from groups technoideologically coded as obsolete in specific circumstances. Yet if there is no necessary, inherent teleology that would guarantee the eventual realization of some totally integrated circuit of the social in technoideologically coded terms, likewise there are no guarantees that oppositional politics or anything else will prevent such ultimate clarity. All that can be said with some degree of certainty is that "it hasn't happened yet"; the best chance that it won't depends on understanding how it might and doing what's possible to change the process.

I
———

The perception of service work as feminized is now quite common, but the issue is complicated by the ambiguities of the term of reference—the work force? the labor process itself?—and by the further ambiguity of what exactly counts as a service occupation. The latter are in any case remarkably diverse, by whatever definition. The assumption I've outlined, however, that service work will in some way involve contact with consumers, does suggest one place to begin thinking about what diverse service occupations nevertheless have in common in terms of a labor process. That contact makes service work in whatever form available to be exploited as a marketing tool; to the extent that it is visible to consumers, service labor can also advertise. The service worker not only does the job but also advertises the service firm or herself/himself as a supplier of services. Service work thus helps "solve" what advertising theory has recognized for some time as the most immediately necessary task of marketing: establishing contact that can attract consumers' attention to what is being sold. This doesn't mean that services are never advertised in any other way, it does mean that once engaged, the labor process of service work can be seen as one of the most effective marketing tools for future sales. Whatever else it may involve, the organization of service work at some level will then be determined by the requirements of advertising. Susan Willis's argument in *A Primer for Daily Life*, for example, can tellingly link the apparent exoticism of the workers' costumes and the like at Disneyland to the more familiar service work of McDonald's employees ("At Disneyland, workers are referred to as actors, made to wear costumes and transform their labor into roles. At McDonald's work is trivialized. Rather than being regarded as producers, the employees are seen as burger assemblers" [60]), in part because in both cases workers are required above all to advertise the firm in the process of their work.

In contrast to service labor, industrial labor typically conjures up images of men working on machines, but in fact service workers also typically operate machinery of some kind, from air wrenches and vacuum cleaners to computers, fax machines, and pizza ovens. The variations here are potentially as great as in industrial labor, and as a result, the use of machinery is hardly a means of distinguishing a service labor process from the labor process of industrial work. But again (if often in variable ratios), advertising will in some sense be part of the job of service work. That is, flight attendants may have relatively less responsibility than auto repair workers for machine operation, and work on different machines; they will have relatively more responsibility for marketing, as the most visible emblem of the airline's "public image." But to whatever variable extent, both will be expected to advertise. Advertising thus makes visible within the terms of the labor process itself the functional role of structures of contact between worker and consumer in distinguishing service work in all its diversity from other occupations.

As service occupations change, the demands of the work within any given occupation will often become more diverse as well. In contrast to industrial labor, which over the course of time in any given production operation will tend to become more specialized and uniform, service work in contrast tends toward greater diversity. A convenient illustration can be found in a recent *U.S. News & World Report* story, rather gleefully pointing to an "innovative" experiment by the Primus Companies hotel chain, in which "a breakfast hostess at one of the firm's Homewood Suites can be shifted to the front desk at checkout time, then make up beds in the afternoon" (49), tasks that alter appreciably the ratios among different kinds of job demands, as well as involving different specific skills. Employees are "trained" and rewarded "accordingly" for the new responsibilities, the article notes, but it's not likely the rewards are by any means commensurate with what the company would have to pay for hiring workers for each separate task. While the labor-cost differential may supply the motive for such reorganization of work, however, what makes the "experiment" possible at all lies in the conceptualization of these different tasks as linked in one way or another to the function of service personnel as marketing for Homewood Suites. Because a breakfast "hostess" both hostesses and advertises, a checkout person both checks out guests and advertises, and so on, it then seems at least plausible that the same person might perform a great many more of the tasks involved. Advertising not only structures any given task—across a great many different fields of service work—in relation to worker/consumer contact, but also permits the coordination of diverse tasks within the same location of work in relation to that contact.

There's nothing, however, that marks advertising work in itself as specifically feminized labor. Indeed, despite how what is actually done in an advertising agency, for example, may exist at a great distance from either the "heavy labor" of men in factory or warehouse, or the corporate decisions about production, financing, and so on, of management personnel, it remains possible nevertheless to preserve a certain masculine ethos about the process of work. The work in question involves highly elaborated skills and knowledges assumed to be the more successful the less "outsiders" know about or see them. That is, it constitutes an exclusive territory of privileged knowledge that, so long as it gets results, leaves controlling details of organization and decision making relatively "in house," and thus lends itself easily enough to a sense of masculine autonomy in the labor process. Service work is also advertising, but in contrast to this exclusivity of territory, it can function as advertising only to the extent the labor process is open to view. The worker must then not only perform the job in accordance with whatever requirements she or he has been trained to meet, but also perform it to the visible satisfaction of the consumer if the advertising is to be successful. Thus the advertising component of service work affects the positions of worker and consumer as surely as it affects the organization of the job. The consumer's position will more closely resemble "boss" or "overseer," the continuously "intrusive" presence of outside judgment, than a role to be consigned by ideological principle to the "passively feminine." Men may of course be working service jobs, and women be consumers of services, but the specific forms advertising takes in service labor mean that the *role* of worker must involve pleasing whoever occupies the *role* of consumer, submitting his or her work to the judgment of the consumer. Service work then appears relatively feminized in relation to the masculinization of consumer positionality.

Obviously everyone can't consume the same amount of services. For reasons I'll discuss later, the notion of a "consumer society," of everyone's activities as increasingly oriented around consumption, supplies an ideologically dangerous rationale of social antagonisms. But just minimally, it should be clear enough that both class and race positions affect not only who will be engaged in what kind of service occupation at what level, but also who will be primary consumers of services. The immediately crucial point here is that the perception of service work as feminized in turn then functions to assign masculine characteristics to class- and race-marked potential for high consumption of services. That is, it may in some sense be your class position, for example, that permits both the financial resources and the cultural values that encourage greater consumption of services, but the exercise of that consumption is realized not only in class-marked but also in gender-marked terms. Thus the destabilization of gendered roles of worker and consumer makes gender available as a constitutive factor of class position.

Yet at the same time, gender doesn't function uniformly or indiscriminately in these terms. While even upper-level service occupations may involve a labor process that seems feminized in some sense, they also yield much greater resources for the consumption of services than lower-level occupations. Anyone located in such an

upper-level job is then permitted a rather remarkable gender mobility. In a paper entitled "Abject, Technician, Metonym: The Acquiring Editor and the Scholarly Community," Stanford University
Press humanities editor Helen Tartar supplies an example uncom-
fortably close to home:

> J. G. Bell, formerly head of the Stanford Press editorial department, was
> to his staff a revered figure of heroic dimensions and was held in awe
> by scholars and press personnel across the country. . . . One day during
> my first year at the press, he noticed, looking over the draft of a letter I
> was about to send to an author, that I had not sufficiently qualified my
> suggestions (this is not, I assure you, an ironic characterization of what
> I had written). He came to my office and tactfully suggested excellent
> revisions, saying that I should write such letters like a "little girl." "I'm
> a little girl," he said, "all editors are little girls." (10–11)

What in the context may seem an incongruous admission on Bell's
part nevertheless observes nicely the mobility I'm describing. The
recognition that there's a sense in which the services he performs
can be perceived as feminized work—"all editors are little girls"—
in no way compromises the masculine identifications of the power
of his position, as derived not only from an internal hierarchy but
also from the resources made available by the position. And conversely, the power of the position doesn't at all prevent a recognition
on his part of the work as feminized. Gender, that is, becomes a
constitutive factor of class position not as a categorical social division identified in natural, universalized terms, but as a differential
marker of relative mobility, a class freedom of movement across
gender roles.

I suggested in the last chapter that a technoideological coding of
obsolescence/innovation alters how racial meanings are produced,
as in Lemann's argument, which no longer relies on assumed natural
characteristics of race. And the gender mobility available to upper-
level service occupations functions in something of the same way.
Given that mobility, the assumption of gender as a natural category
can seem obsolete, something whose negative polarities need not
really trouble anymore someone in a position such as Bell's, who is
quite willing to admit to being in certain situations "a little girl."
Likewise, however, by a relatively easy leap of ideological logic,
those for whom gender roles *are* troubling, for whom they come
fraught with all the conflicts and antagonisms of a divided social

field, can themselves be perceived as survivals from the past, precariously left over to stand blinking in amazement at the rapidly changing features of dynamic social spaces no longer organized in fixed gender terms. Like Lemann's black underclass, they simply haven't "moved with the times." Although the instances are not strictly parallel, I do think it possible to recognize in both cases how this "logic" is expressed in class terms. That is, escape from the obsolete racial culture of the urban ghetto is imaged in terms of a rising black middle class, just as escape from the "prison-house" of fixed gender roles appears in the mobilities available to those in upper-level service occupations.

Historically, the ascendancy of a bourgeoisie made class, unlike gender and race, an avenue of universalization as well as a means of distinction. For all the ways in which "the natural" supplied rationales for the positionalities of a working-class population, it wasn't (in principle, at least) impossible for certain individuals of the working class to become good bourgeoisie. If they had the "right stuff"—and in the bitterly contested victories of more liberal arguments, the right conditions of opportunity as well—they could not only "pass," but be transformed. This was unlike African-Americans, say, who might eventually become middle class, but not be white; or women, who might achieve a certain middle-class equality, but not be men. Class, that is, continued to function as a measure of distinction, and hence a vehicle for natural coding, but in principle it also represented a universalizing potential unavailable to categories of race and gender.

Technoidcological coding, in contrast, undercuts the foundationally natural grounding of race and gender categories as well as of class categories. Nevertheless, because it doesn't do away with the positionalities of race- and gender-marked agents, those positionalities must be rewritten into the terms of class as simultaneously universalizing and distinctive: *anybody* must be able to change with the times, but not everybody does. As a result, gender and race will then be "preserved" in their very obsolescence as available ways to mark the difference. Thus the ultimate implication of arguments like Lemann's at this level of ideological construction is nothing less than an assumption that while "we" may be able to determine the "real" origins of a black urban underclass in an obsolete culture, "they" in fact remain where they are because they continue to act, precisely, *as if* naturally coded "blacks." Just as women who, for example, "accept" the conditions of part-time, low-wage service employment do so because they continue to act as if they were naturally coded women, necessarily responsible for child rearing, home stability, and so on. These are "in reality," however, simply *lifestyles* such people choose, or can have forced upon them. Technoideological coding, that is, realizes the universalizing potential of class insofar as it works toward the elimination of a natural ground for gender and race as well as class; no ultimate barriers can exist to that universalizing potential. At the same time, however, it maintains class as also a mark of distinction by rewriting race and gender into "choices" preserved within certain class-specific lifestyles.

It is crucially important to register alternative possibilities in this determination of lifestyle—"choose" or "have forced upon"—for unlike natural coding, technoideological coding cannot afford any *automatically* assumed ideologies of "blaming the victim." Such ideologies must themselves be rewritten into new forms. Obsolescence/innovation can exhaustively code the social field only at the expense of recognizing that no one is "naturally" obsolete. If it's possible to "choose" obsolescence for yourself, the possibility must also be acknowledged that such obsolescence can be forced on some people through the "choices" made by others. That is, to the extent fixed categories of race and gender "stubbornly" continue to survive into the present, there's always the chance they will also continue to be used to victimize specific individuals.

Thus within the terms of technoideological coding, no charge of gender or racial discrimination can be summarily dismissed, simply assumed to be the "victim's" own fault. But what *can* be dismissed is a claim for structurally systematic discriminatory practices as anything more than an effect of now obsolete choices made by specific individuals in specific circumstances and imposed on others. (As Senator Hatch repeated over and over at the Clarence Thomas confirmation hearings, "sexual harassment," so far from being "normal" male behavior, is an aberration; it is engaged in only by certain individuals whose attitudes make them "monsters." In other words, sexual harassment is never a matter of systematic, socially sanctioned violence to women, but only of the attitudes of monstrously "outdated" individuals.) The result of such a dismissal of systematic discrimination is that any argument for the rights of victims of discriminatory practices based on the "merely social" categories of gender and race will be assumed to accord victims (in current vocabulary) "special rights," that is, privileges that are no less obsolete than the now "illusory" systematic discriminatory practices they claim to redress, because they are claims based in the "merely social."

Further, in circumstances where obsolete "choices" seem not only to persist, but to persist in producing discriminatory practices, the class coding of obsolescence must also be available to suggest their likely source. This source will be those who occupy lower-level, "working-class" jobs. In contrast to those in upper-level occupations, for whom gender mobility, even racial mobility, need pose no problem, "working-class" people will see such mobility in others as a threat, having not yet learned themselves to take advantage of it. In everything from Hollywood films and TV sitcoms to the routines of comedians such as Andrew Dice Clay, a "working class" becomes a focus of fascinated attention. On the one hand, it must be kept at a distance, as the repository of now obsolete and often discriminatory values and behaviors. But on the other, it can also be cherished nostalgically as a reminder—if a bit "extreme," perhaps—of what to do when "minorities" and women get too "pushy" about claiming "special rights." At least good old "working-class" values permit no such nonsense—never mind that an actual working class in a service economy is now largely composed of women and "minorities."

The initial Bush administration response to the jury verdict in the case of Rodney King's beating is a good indication of how deeply embedded in a common-sense vocabulary this purported working-class source of racial discrimination has become. In sharply distinguishing between the violence of King's beating (for Bush, something that could only be addressed by a "continuation" of due process of law) and the violence of the "riots" in Los Angeles (which must be addressed instead by the extraordinary steps of mobilizing National Guard and Army units), Bush's televised speech attempted not only to avoid but to put out of play the inconvenient fact that the jury in the case was predominantly white and upper middle class, as was the jury selection pool and trial venue. In the class imaginary I'm describing, that "fact" simply doesn't signify. It's impossible to imagine discriminatory practices perpetuated by a non–working-class group. If indeed justice "miscarried," the explanation has to lie elsewhere, and will be revealed in the "continuation" of due process

at the federal level. The "riots," "looting," and "mob violence" in
Los Angeles streets in contrast are then readily available to be coded
as just that, "mindless" mob behavior having nothing at all to do
with social conditions or with the beating of King, a point Bush
stressed over and over. To acknowledge any connection would bring
that inconvenient fact swinging directly back into view.

Class typically (not just in Marxist arguments) has retained some
direct reference to occupational stratification, as I have used it to
designate upper-level and lower-level service occupations. Class-as-
lifestyle, however, not only implies a relatively greater importance of
cultural variables in the determination of class-specific positionalities, but a shift generally away from work, production, and occupation to consumption as its primary location. (Andrew Dice Clay,
for example, dresses like he's going to a masked ball rather than to a
job at Minit Lube. He can be made to look "working class," that is,
only in consumer-identified rather than in occupationally identified
terms.) Rather than trying to play "cultural" and "economic" definitions of class against each other, I want the notion of class-as-lifestyle
to register a shift of cultural as well as economic variables from
production to the field of consumption. Just as, within corporate
organization, it is marketing that now largely determines the process
of production, class-as-lifestyle ideologies imply that it is the expectations to be realized in a particular lifestyle option that drive occupational choices. From the perspective of class-as-lifestyle, while it
may be accurate enough to argue (as I have) that specific occupational levels yield greater resources for consumption, that only tells
half the story. The very "choice" of occupation in the first place is
assumed in this logic to derive from consumer expectations.

What must be asked in these circumstances is then less a matter of how class-as-lifestyle ideologies function to obscure "underlying" economic realities than how they plot the antagonisms and
conflicts that occur at the intersections of class-specific lifestyles involving both cultural and economic factors. As my examples are
intended to suggest, in rewriting "natural" versions of blame-the-
victim assumptions, in producing conditions for the simultaneous
maintenance and obsolescence of constructions of race and gender,
and in the linkages of "choice" with changing social positionalities,
technoideological coding's master narrative of survivals is also and
everywhere a story of class conflict, if not exactly a Marxian one.

It is played out on a screen filled with the competing performative strategies of individual agents; and what exactly "performance" involves is perhaps easiest to understand in the context of that by-now-massively available literature of consumer self-help in mass culture. Such self-help literature offers perhaps the clearest paradigm of mass culture as educational: as a series of lessons in how to perform.

II

Consumer Reports (and Consumers Union, its parent organization) made its national reputation as an independent advocate for consumer interests, as a way for individual consumers to gain access to information that might give them a fighting chance in a marketplace battlefield. On the one hand, it was unlikely any individual would possess the necessary knowledges to comparatively evaluate always more technologically sophisticated competing products, let alone the resources of time and money to put into the process of evaluation with each product that might be considered for purchase. And the development of market research analysis on which advertising increasingly depended made it unlikely that individual consumers would have any other way to see through the glittering promises of advertising. In these circumstances, *Consumer Reports* could supply at least a partially effective answer to both dilemmas.

Subscriptions, contributions, and the like paid for growing research facilities and trained technicians who could in fact then evaluate competing products on behalf of the consumer. Against the resources available to advertising through market research analysis, *Consumer Reports* could offer to consumers data collected from increasingly elaborate surveys of its readership about their actual experiences with the products, which could then be put to use as a check on what advertising constructions promised. All of this was presented in a smart, no-nonsense style, complete with readable graphics and careful translations of high-tech jargon into more familiar terminology. Corporations—GM being the classic example—did not typically look with favor on the magazine, and there was a great deal of flak directed at how in the course of its development *Consumer Reports* took on more obviously "politicized" issues such as health care, government regulatory agencies and laws, environmental effects, and so on. Yet in a sense, everything about the magazine was political from the beginning, since it presented itself as intervening in an *already* adversarial relation (hence GM's anger) that pitted consumers against large corporations and their allies. Indeed, this way of drawing battle lines was enormously important to *Consumer Reports'* success, enabling it to build a large and relatively diverse readership despite corporate, legal, and occasionally government attack. A no-advertising policy was scrupulously maintained, and the magazine was ready to file suit at a moment's notice against any use of its claims in marketing; this policy was at once the effect of this drawing of battle lines and a constitutive factor in identifying them clearly in the first place.

With the emergence of a service economy, however, even *Consumer Reports'* own articles have begun to register a significant shift in adversarial alignments. If you're a frequent reader, as I am, think how often over the last five years or so especially you've encountered recommendations such as the following from a report on brake and muffler shops in August, 1989:

> But judging by our readers' experiences, independent garages [as opposed to chains such as Midas, etc.] have the best chance of leaving you a satisfied customer. Of course, that judgment is an average of thousands of experiences ranging from the best to the worst, so it's no guarantee that just any garage will provide good service. If you have a local shop whose service you like, stick with it. (530)

The corollary is that if you *don't* like the service, then statistical data and informed expertise aside, go somewhere else.

That seems common-sense advice, and familiar enough, but because it acknowledges what increasingly appears a fact of consumer life in a service economy: the importance of the individual service worker in any transaction. Presumably the advice would then apply not only to independent garages, but to corporate chains such as Midas or Meineke if in the particular shop you dealt with, you liked the personnel and were generally satisfied with the work. The crucial point is that the recommendation also acknowledges that marketplace battle lines that involve services can't be drawn clearly between individual consumers on the one hand and large corporations, professional associations, and government agencies on the other. Potential conflicts instead seem more frequently to lie within the contact zones of consumer and service worker. And in that situation, the kind of information *Consumer Reports* can arm consumers with may be of relatively little immediate use, as the recommendation scrupulously recognizes.

Such scrupulousness, however, is not a prominent feature of that rather different and growing body of literature (and now videos) aimed, like *Consumer Reports*, at individual consumers, but which, unlike *Consumer Reports*, locates itself directly in the contact zones avoided by the recommendation above. If the question *Consumer Reports* sets out to answer can be understood in terms of what information an organized consumer union might usefully make available to individual consumers that they couldn't generate on their own, this literature in contrast is one form of individual self-help literature, dedicated to instructing individuals in how to mobilize performative strategies in their encounters with service personnel. *Consumer Reports* in its article will try to acquaint you with at least something of what is involved in brake and muffler work, with the corporate history and structure of chains such as Midas, and with typical advertising practices. Consumer self-help literature instead may supply a quick inventory of ways service technicians will try to persuade you to authorize more work than you actually need done, delay completion of work, insist on price "uppers" and so on, but the primary emphasis will fall on elaborating the reasons why service workers might feel they can get away with this stuff in any individual situation. The assumption is that that's in fact what you most need to know, in order to develop successfully your own counterstrategies. In other words, what this self-help literature has to offer is not the resources of a kind of consumer equivalent of a labor union, an organization to counter the power of the institutionally organized interests you face in the marketplace. Rather, it offers the testimony of psychological warfare in the contact zones of worker and consumer.

There should be little surprise that antagonisms exist in these zones. Structures of contact not only make it possible for consumers to see the work being done and question its quality if they wish; workers *also* see consumers, are afforded often astonishingly intimate glimpses into their lives, their surroundings, their habits, their possessions. Service work makes visible, often in minute detail, the sometimes immense social distances separating those positioned to afford high levels of consumption of services, and those (the "lower class," women, young people, people of color—overlapping categories that encompass very different groups of the population) who compose the majority of the service work force. Here, distance is not a matter of some TV or film representation, but appears in the midst of daily work, right in front of you, a reminder around every corner you turn as a service worker. A service economy creates conditions that might well lead to particularly intense, widespread, violent, and prolonged conflicts. Unlike in an industrially driven economic organization, the very social spaces of labor, of leisure, of home life, of consumption, are everywhere potentially open to view from other and dramatically different positions.

Consumer self-help literature affords a particularly good clue to the management of that potential for social conflict, first of all because in its variety it addresses in specific detail an immense range of circumstances of consumption, from diet and fitness (where you must then deal with the "professional" services of health "experts") to auto repair, insurance, salespeople of all kinds, child care, and so on. More important, it doesn't try to disguise the existence of antagonisms across that consumer field. Its intensities of imagery derive from the recognition that in the conditions of a service economy, service workers may have reasons to be "out to get you." Consumer self-help literature explicitly understands zones of contact as also zones of combat, and advises you to proceed accordingly. As it is a literature selling itself to consumers, one would hardly expect to find in it any unflattering assertion that service workers have "good" reasons to be out to get you individually. Hence that long-familiar litany describing resentful, lazy, disrespectful service workers is a staple. Functionally, however, instruction in consumer self-help doesn't rely on how to spot such qualities of service worker character, but rather depends on elaborating "winning" strategies in the encounter. Thus its narrative perceptions of what constitutes performance encounters explain a great deal about the larger ideological configurations in which antagonisms are plotted.

In the next chapter, I will look in more detail at the self-help literature of car repair and purchase, since the importance of the automobile in the United States represents a remarkable conjunction of technological and ideological change and their effects. In the immediate context, however, it's worth emphasizing again that unlike *Consumer Reports*, consumer self-help literature on the whole doesn't attempt to supply you with the benefits of informed expertise for product evaluation, but rather with performative strategies. From the perspective of the kind of recommendation *Consumer Reports* typically presents, such advice will then appear substantively empty, devoid of either informational content or expert opinion. The notion of performance, however, is intended to register how for self-help literature, what's at stake in the encounter is not who knows what, but the relative positions of the agents involved in the transaction. Information and expert opinion are then not only themselves merely instrumental, but for consumers potentially very risky instruments to deploy. They yield territorial advantage, condemn you to playing on someone else's ground.

No matter what data you come armed with, for example, it's inevitably a finite quantum. Thanks to *Consumer Reports*, perhaps, you may come in for a brake job with, let's say, some recently acquired knowledge of calipers and brake pads, but if you're then told your rotor runout exceeds manufacturer specs, you have no recourse. From that moment on, the terms of the encounter will be scripted by the auto repair worker and your performance dictated by the worker's direction. Thus consumer self-help literature seems relatively unconcerned with such "substantive" issues as knowledge of vertical runout or lack of parallelism, and more concerned with how to maintain for yourself the power to script the encounter. Self-help literature, in other words, offers strategies for individual empowerment through performance rather than, like *Consumer Reports*, the service of experts who for the price of the magazine deliver technical information.

It's at this level that the self-help literature I'm describing rejoins a larger ideological configuration of how social antagonisms and conflicts are plotted in a service economy. The implications of thinking first of performance in this sense have to do with a certain redefinition of the very field of consumption. *Consumer Reports* assumes that finally you're "there" temporarily, in transit, because for whatever reasons you need something done in order to get on with a life that has made available to you the resources to get it done. The point is simply that the "there" of consumption, however temporary in your eyes, is nevertheless affected by the pressures of all kinds of interests, and hence you're wise not to walk into it blindly if you want to walk out quickly with what you came for, at a price you feel is a fair one.

The emphasis on performance in consumer self-help literature suggests in contrast that what consumption is all about is, precisely, the conflicts of relative positionality. It's not where you go to real- ize the benefits of a position acquired somewhere else, but where position itself is realized in the first place. Service workers may then indeed have reasons to be out to get you, as consumer self-help lit- erature emphasizes over and over. But those reasons don't derive from the fact that they are service workers. For what's assumed as "temporary" in the circumstances is not your role as consumer in the encounter, but the service worker's role as worker. That is, in "larger" terms, and just like you, that worker is always and every- where engaged in the performative realization of position in the field of consumption, and only temporarily, toward the end of that realization, involved in the instance in the labor of a service occu- pation. Ultimately, then, the service workers' reasons to be out to get you are the same reasons you're out to get them. In a so-called consumer society, people perform for the same stakes, in the same universalizing field of consumption, and perform "successfully" not by assuming any positional resources as givens but by capitalizing on whatever resources they possess through adopting the best available strategies in any performance relations.

It would then be a mistake, I think, to see this ideology of an all- pervasive "consumer society" narratively structuring antagonisms and conflicts toward some vast operation of recontainment, obscur- ing the specifically social with a foregrounding of individual en- counters. While it's true enough that the agency of performance is endlessly individuated in the instances of consumption, to the ex- tent that position is always relative, this is no less a vision of the social. That is, it would be more accurate to recognize how the "consumer society" is a narrative structure that relocates social an- tagonisms and conflicts from the scene of occupational stratification, the organization of work and the market segmentation of labor, to the scene of consumption, where performances are enacted. Thus class-as-lifestyle ideologies register not only the prominence of an individual agency of performance—"lifestyle"—but also the rela- tionality of positionally realized performances as social, as finally a matter of class and class division. Such division is unrecognizable as such only if your field of reference continues to be labor and occu- pational stratification rather than consumption. The perceptions in consumer self-help literature are useful here also; what constitutes "winning" and "losing" strategies of performance helps identify the organizing class terms of class-as-lifestyle division.

Briefly and generally, performances are "lost" when you make the mistake of relying on already acquired positional resources, and worse, blaming yourself for not having more of them. Performance is not a matter of what you know or what you have, but of your capitalization of resources in the circumstances. If you head for a doctor's office in awe of a professional expertise you'll never possess; if you take your car for repair with fear and trembling that as a woman you're walking into masculine territory; if you worry whether the maid at an upscale hotel will count the bathtub rings you've left; if you're intimidated by how the clothing salespeople always seem dressed better than you—you're doomed from the start. The alternative is not that you must then learn to distinguish yourself "as an individual" from the attitudes implied by these social categories, or acquire permanent characteristics of aggressiveness and intimidation (in certain circumstances, the latter may be a real disadvantage). It's rather to learn to think of all such things as performative rather than defining, as so many roles for the occasion to be invested should they seem appropriate in the event. The point of the endless triumph stories consumer self-help literature tells is not that you, too, can acquire a wealth of socially certified resources. Obviously everybody can't, and self-help literature isn't likely to sell itself to consumers by promising the tedious labor of acquiring more resources. The point is that whatever you have can be performed to advantage in any situation. The field of consumption as imaged in consumer self-help literature is universalizing to the extent that it both encourages and promises the realization of endlessly rising social expectations in the performative capital of consumer practices.

Marx emphasized long ago that you can think of work in terms of what he called "concrete labor," that is, the physical-intellectual effort of transforming a particular material into something else; or in terms of "abstract labor," the social organization of work, having to do with the relations among those engaged in a particular labor process. His focus on the use value and exchange value of commodities, however, while obviously important as a way of restoring an understanding of the connections between commodities and the labor of their production, nevertheless led him to ignore what consumer self-help literature implies about performance: consumption is not only a matter of commodities and commodity exchange, but is itself a process that, like labor in production, might also be thought of in terms of a specific physical-intellectual effort and in terms of organized social relations. There is after all a certain effort involved in shopping, in the selection and utilization of goods and services, no less than in the labor of their production, and it doesn't seem farfetched to recognize as well that that effort occurs in and through specific organizations of social relations. Theories of conspicuous consumption point quite clearly to the social relations in the process of consumption, and assert the priority of those relations over the effort of selection and utilization. The latter, that is, is understood to be determined by the former, just as in Marx's discussion of concrete and abstract labor in capitalist production, abstract labor dominates.

Such theories also emphasize the differential signification of consumer social relations; consumption is to be conspicuous in order to supply a visible index of differentiation, and is organized so that differences can be arranged in stratified hierarchies. However, these social relations are more often than not understood by an extension of a basically Marxian concept of the exchange value of commodities consumed. (Thorstein Veblen is the obvious example of such understanding, but Guy Debord and Jean Baudrillard, as later and more sophisticated versions, would serve as well.) It's then easy to slip from a recognition of differentiation and stratification into an assumption that such markers nevertheless are ultimately empty. Like commodity exchange value, social differentiation has no real ground of meaning in anything beyond the visible indices of exchange in any given situation. Like commodity organization, which tends toward an always purer condition of exchange equivalents, the consumption of commodities tends toward pure "spectacle," a system of purely relational status. There's no point at all to eating your food off enormously expensive designer plates, beyond the status they yield in circumstances that may well change overnight to favor some other visible marker; this procession of change, in Baudrillard's logic, then leads finally to a sort of frantic glut of consumption beyond even the temporarily stable meanings of visible markers.

But if consumption, like labor, involves a specific process, then for all the ways in which these social relations may determine, like abstract labor, the concrete effort of selection and utilization, they don't get rid of that effort, even in a Baudrillardian universe. You still must actually do the work of buying these plates rather than others, and actually eat your food off them or display them at "conspicuous" occasions. How you go about this may indeed be determined by hierarchically organized status relations—or some sheer excess of proliferation "beyond" hierarchy—but you still have to do it. Thus while these markers of status may be epistemologically empty, having no foundational ground of meaning whatsoever, nevertheless they continue to involve specific efforts of "concrete consumption." And as consumer self-help literature recognizes, such "concrete consumption" may then take up a great deal of time, no matter whether, from some lofty stratosphere of philosophical insight, the work process is perceived as just meaningless, empty, wasteful, "hyperreal," or whatever. Consumer status is never just a game of empty signifiers, not only because of the often destructive effects of organized status relations, but because it at once depends on and organizes the terms of considerable investments of time, effort, skills, and knowledges, every bit as much as the organization of labor in production Indeed, as I suggested in the last section, one effect of the destabilization of gender-identified roles of work and consumption is to make the work of consumption more visible and obvious.

Practically the first lesson Marx supplies about labor transactions in volume one of *Capital* is that, however historically it came to be the case, people arrive at the scene of such transactions with very different resources: workers have only their own labor power to sell; owners have capital that can be invested in the purchase of labor power, among other things. Consumer practices are likewise marked by differential resources among consumers, but in this context, even for the purposes of a deliberately ahistorical, structural model such as Marx's, it would seem impossible to understand either resources or groups of people as quite so neatly divided, or even to indicate in any convenient simplification how exactly "resources" might be calculated. Being able to spend large amounts of money in comparison to other people in a consumer field obviously helps, but as everyone knows by now it's no infallible guarantee of the acquisition of status. Having a lot of time to take up with purchases may help also, but if that time must be invested in deciding between, say, a Honda Civic or a Toyota Tercel, it won't likely overbalance the ten minutes in which someone else may "intuitively" arrive at just the right BMW 835i. Examples here are potentially endless.

The idea of class-as-lifestyle, however, suggests a rather different way to think about the situation than trying to devise some exhaustive calculus for assessing consumer resources, even one as sophisticated as what Pierre Bourdieu supplies in *Distinction*. As consumer self-help literature implies, the performative indices of lifestyle don't depend directly on expending resources—whether of time, effort, money, skills, or whatever—in the process of "concrete consumption," but instead on the capitalization of always changing conditions of resource. It might be possible, in this context of consumer practices, to preserve something of the explanatory simplicity of Marx's initial model of labor transactions in capitalist production by thinking in terms of those who have *only* resources to bring to the process, and those in contrast who can capitalize changing conditions of resource. This is as deliberately simplistic and ahistorical as Marx's initial account, but it is so for a similar purpose: to make structurally visible across the field of a "consumer society" the kind of class division Marx was intent on describing in the field of capitalist production.

Consumer self-help literature then suggests in rather more concrete detail the difference between having consumer resources and deploying consumer capital. The latter is performative, a matter of what you do with resources on the occasion rather than an acquisition or a permanent possession of resources sufficient to any occasion. Performance, that is, has something of the same relation to consumer resources as capital to money. You don't become "rich" by hoarding either resources or money. Advertisements and commercials for both products and services suggest a similar kind of concrete detail. While magazines like *Consumer Reports* will advise you to view advertising skeptically that seems to promise qualities having little to do with the product or service itself, the notion of performance in self-help literature can be easily enough extended to recognize that such promises are what the advertising construction is all about. Possession of the product or the benefit of the service is merely a kind of resource to be put into play in performative capitalization. Advertising, like consumer self-help literature, educates you about strategies of performance, and you're likely to buy the product as well because it functions as a "model resource" through which you learned the strategies.

Class-as-lifestyle is then both a universalizing category, insofar as its field of realization is consumption as the endless horizon of rising social expectations, and an identification of class division across the mere possession of consumer resources on the one hand and the performance of consumer resources on the other. Rather than disguising or recontaining "the social" within the terms of individual agency, it reconstructs social positionalities through, first, a shift from the social field of production, occupation, and labor to the no less social field of consumer practices; second, a shift in importance from the relative stability of possession or acquisition to the mobilities of performance; and finally (and this remains to be discussed) a relocation of those long-familiar ideologies of rising social expectations from an institutional educational system to the multiple opportunities and promises of the field of consumption. This relocation is especially important to understand, for in explaining class-as-lifestyle division, my account—like Marx's initial model of class in *Capital*—has avoided anything much about how it is division appears in the first place, how it is that some consumers have only their own resources and others command the capital of performance. The promises of consumer self-help literature aside, it isn't really just because the latter read self-help literature and the former didn't. But it is, I think, very much a matter of education, just as the class divisions of an industrial economy were reproduced, maintained, and extended by a public educational system. What I'm describing as a relocation of rising expectations suggests that education will function rather differently in any class-as-lifestyle division, but no less importantly. And perceptions of the current crisis of public education will then be useful indicators of that changing function.

Nevertheless, while class-as-lifestyle involves more complicated operations than simply the ideological decomposition of "the social," the organization of social relations it offers across the field of consumption both obscures a great deal and at the same time evidences often intense contradictions that must be accounted for ideologically in some way. What it obscures, through technoideological coding's master narrative of survivals, is the *present* dependence of that field of consumption on the relations of production, occupation, and labor as replotted in a service economy. These forms of labor are not then survivals from some rapidly disappearing industrial past, or merely "temporary" locations to be subsumed under the universal category of "consumer" in ideologies of a consumer society. The obsolescence of work—and workers—in this sense must be continually produced in the present. And the production of obsolescence has now been assigned largely to the institutional formation of public education. Schools have become functional instruments of class-as-lifestyle division. It might then be anticipated that the specific contradictions of "still surviving" gender- and race-marked positionalities will be fought out in the schools, because, more generally, public education will be expected to contribute in every way possible to the material organization that permits the hermeneutical readability of the narratives of class-as-lifestyle I've been describing.

III

It's no secret that a public educational system in the United States developed together with the growth of an industrial economy, and that the great expansion of public education after World War I coincided with the new political priorities of industrial change. As the large-scale specialization of production operations and the capitalization of new industries increased dramatically, workers could assume a relatively greater job mobility, and likewise then a greater sense of worker autonomy in relation to any given manufacturing concern. The investment of time and money in training workers for often rapidly changing production tasks, no less than the higher wages necessary to attract skilled workers and to enlarge the consumer base of sales to absorb increased capacities for production, threatened future expansion. Educational reform and expansion offered solutions to all these dilemmas. The development of vocational training programs shifted the cost burden of training to the public sector. The antagonisms of workplace struggles for control could be defused by increasingly complicated programs of educational certification for occupational slots; the schools could take from the workplace the task of assigning people to their places. The growth of literacy through universal education generated a public whose patterns of consumption could be influenced through media advertising constructions that could be disseminated widely throughout the country.

The exponential growth of public education (between 1905 and 1930, the percentage of an age group who completed high school jumped from roughly 9 percent to nearly 45 percent [Conant, 3]) necessary for such "advantages" to be realized could hardly be sold to the public in quite these functional terms. Universal education was instead sold largely on the basis of its authority to create and realize rising expectations democratically. A system of universal education would purportedly maximize the efficiency of political, economic, and social institutions—by selecting the best available people for specific positions and training them accordingly—and at the same time equalize opportunities for everyone to rise as high as their individual talents, motivation, and work would allow. For at least a couple of reasons, such educational promise could not operate as merely a disguise, a massive obfuscation of the real purposes public education served for an expanding industrial economy.

The potential advantages to an industrial economy were contingent on the consent of the great majority of the population to a comprehensive public educational system, and elitist dismissals of the "mass" aside, such consent is never secured for long without at least some visible payoffs. Equally important, a greatly expanded educational system not only required a greatly expanded work force but a cheap one, if the advantages the system offered were not to be offset by its sheer cost. Hence the first target audience for the promised values and benefits of education had to be the potential work force of educational institutions, people who would believe in and be committed to work for educational ideals to the extent of also being willing to work for considerably less money and social prestige than the responsibilities of the positions might seem to imply. Women were then one obvious group to recruit. At the elementary level especially, schooling could be made to seem merely an extension of "women's work" at home, and in the immediate circumstances of early twentieth-century reform women were cheaply available. Women could also be assumed to have a real stake in and see the values of educational promises of equalized opportunity *for everyone*, in ways that would keep them cheaply available. The price, of course, was that women could then also use whatever resources the positions might permit to ensure that promised educational ideals were actually realized. This was another reason, perhaps, that those who recruited teachers chose women; they may have been seen as less likely to use these resources in formidable ways.

It is politically crucial to recognize how this educational system has functioned to stabilize, maintain, and enforce the oppressions of an industrial economy and of a given political organization. At the same time, however, to dismiss educational ideals as simply ideals— as "false promises," or just "wrong"—is also to dismiss the working lives and sacrifices of countless people, primarily women, who in often extraordinarily difficult circumstances fought successfully to supply some real content to those promises in any number of instances, and whose lives then attest to the value of the ideals. Many of us now in position to recognize and understand the larger-scale social functions an educational system has carried out historically nevertheless owe that positioning, absolutely and without qualification, to their struggles. We then owe them a little work of our own that continues their struggle, and continues it in ways that don't forget who was there first and what it cost them on our behalf.

Public education as a universal means for the realization of rising social expectations was nevertheless a dubious proposition, even if, through the struggles of any number of teachers and students, in certain instances it could and did work. For many people much of the time, however, education was necessarily a protracted period of "cooling off," of being reconciled to the inescapable conclusion that their abilities would take them no further. I argued in *Work Time* that such determinations of "merit" had as a ground, beyond all the complicated variables of cultural background, opportunity, motivation, and so on, what in the context of this argument might be understood as a kind of natural coding of "intelligence" (Watkins, 117–20). That is, while ideally at least education could eventually equalize cultural variables, intelligence in contrast was understood as a "natural" given, the limit beyond which the educational process couldn't be expected to compensate. Ultimately, expectations had to be bounded by what innate intelligence permitted. The immediate difficulty, not surprisingly, was that intelligence as the ground of merit proved remarkably difficult to isolate from all the variables. Thus evaluative intelligence testing became fairly rapidly one of the most politically contested educational operations.

The long-range "problem," however (as ultimately with any natural coding of social position, but especially in a situation such as educational institutions that encouraged and rewarded rising social expectations even as they were busy cooling them off), was that a whole lot more people wanted to be intelligent, thought they were intelligent, and could find reasons to support a conviction of their own intelligence than a deeply stratified social organization could allow to possess the social rewards of intelligence. Too many educationally certified intelligent people for too few prestigious and rewarding social positions meant lots of crisis alarms in "public" discussions of an educational system, from the why-do-we-assume-college-education-is-for-everyone morality play, to the tragedy of lower standards, the melodrama of grade-inflation menace, the mystery of the lost competitive edge, and so on. All of which would be wonderfully entertaining cabaret, since nobody ever fingered themselves or their own children for the preferred choral response ("What's the matter with you, you stupid or something?" "Well, yeah. Yeah, I am"), except for the fact that they wreaked havoc on countless lives without in the least "resolving" the "problem" even in its own terms.

Despite the violence of one crisis after another, the work of dedicated teachers, among other things, meant the educational system continued to produce more educationally certified people who thought they deserved more social rewards for the certification than they received. An economic, political, and social system that is organized to preserve dominant positions for a few without the expense and hazards of dictatorially suppressing the rest doesn't have a lot of options beyond convincing as many people as possible that generally, rising social expectations are all to the good and can be realized, while at the same time finding the most efficient means of convincing that same population that individually, they don't quite have what it takes, but after all where they are isn't really all that bad. Public education worked fairly effectively toward that double end until eventually it began to glut out on the sheer numbers of people who took the "rising expectations" part seriously enough and refused to submit to the "cooling off" strictures of the second half.

From the other side, the "problem" was exacerbated by the changes in the organization of labor as it moved from an industrial to a service economy. Because the divisions of labor in industrial production tended to generate more and more specialized unit tasks for workers at every level, industrial production also permitted more and more complicated, intricate stratifications of work. As Harry Braverman argues in *Labor and Monopoly Capital*, such stratification doesn't really reflect the skill levels of the jobs in relation to the capabilities of individual workers; there's little reason to think most workers in any given industrial operation couldn't perform most of the jobs. Stratification, however, does take advantage of the division of labor to make available a certain field of realization for ideologies of rising social expectations: potentially, there seems always somewhere higher to go in the organization of industrial production, in finely differentiated levels. And increasingly, educational certification became the gatekeeper of those higher levels. While Braverman is undoubtedly right that skills are not really the issue, nevertheless higher levels did carry at least some relative privileges of pay, prestige, and control over the work.

Most lower-level service occupations permit much less stratification than industrial production. Differentiated tasks are more likely to be combined than to be sorted out in stratified sequences to different workers. Most lower-level service occupations, that is, are also "terminal." Possibilities for advancement must then lie in moving to another service job, but this is more often than not simply a lateral move. A solution lies in the lure of "entrepreneurship," but statistics overwhelmingly demonstrate that this is inviting disaster. There's little need to point out the substantial cost benefits to major corporations hiring service personnel, franchising services, subcontracting piece work, and so on. But whatever the benefits to corporations individually, the process also creates the potential social liability— as more and more individual corporations pursue those benefits—of decomposing the connections that linked occupational stratification, educational certification, and rising expectations in the first place.

The "solution" that has emerged in a service economy / consumer society involves first the destabilization of natural coding, to which the educational system linked by means of its determinations of "merit"; and second, the relocation of ideologies of rising social expectations into the class-as-lifestyle–structured fields of consumption. Current perceptions of public education's crisis, then, in their often bewildering multiplicity of terms, are perhaps rightly understood as responses to the development of a qualitatively different set of circumstances for public education. The two elements of the "solution" imply that it's a crisis having to do with the foundational rationales of public education, the very grounds on which it was sold to the public, rather than with how best it might carry out specific functions or mediate locally contradictory social imperatives.

In the last chapter of this book, I'll look specifically at the emerging "school culture" reforms of Reaganism under the Bush administration as a politically directed response to this crisis. Here, though, it's easy enough to recognize how conservative critics of educational crisis have much less compunction than their liberal counterparts about directly indicting the lack of knowledges and skills of "today's students" as a sign of crisis. Liberal critics will be understandably hesitant, for example, to assign reasons for low SAT scores and the like to unqualified teachers, poor educational practices, and un-caring, stupid students. The litany of information conservative critics are more than willing to generate about what students don't know is treated by liberals as something to be explained by a whole host of more complicated intersecting factors. Despite the violence of these now familiar debates, there does exist a kind of common ground in the assumption that whatever exactly it is, and for whatever reasons, there's a lot of "essential" stuff that students don't know. And if you suspend for a moment your own notions of what's "essential," it might be surprising to discover what multiple storehouses of data different students do possess.

MTV, to take an obvious example, may look to some edu-cators like an occasion for often remarkably complex analyses of the "excesses" of postmodern simulation and so on, and to others like simply a monotonous blur of lights and sounds. But what at least some middle- and high-school students might know is where you can actually get suspenders most closely resembling the ones worn by the lead singer of Guns N' Roses in the concert video of "Knockin' on Heaven's Door." Other students know entirely different things about different phenomena, none of which is likely to qualify as "essential" to anyone up on the textual variants of *Piers Plowman B*, the proliferation of self-reflexive ironies initiated by Dire Straits having won best video of 1986 for "Money for Nothing," or the approximate geographical location of Florida. But it would be a real mistake to assume that students don't really know anything, and it doesn't do a lot of good to be appalled at what they know without having at least explored the possibility that they know what they know because there seems to them good reason to know it.

My assumption is that more often than not students know best the intricacies of consumer practices in whatever sectors of consumption seem most available to them; and further, that they know such things not as the "hyperreal" of some frantic "mass" imperatives beyond meaning, but in at least something of the same ways their great-great-great-great-grandparents (or their parents, as the case may be) might have known the best-shaped blade for hoeing or the best working rhythm of a sewing machine treadle: because these details count, because they are immediately significant influences on daily behavior in relation to others, contributing to exactly how those relations are constituted and helping to determine what possibilities might be open in the future. That is, students may not be "smart" consumers in a *Consumer Reports* sense, and as recent surveys delight in pointing out, things such as APR disclosure and extended warranty contracts may leave them utterly baffled. But it's then equally plausible to assume that such surveys have identified the wrong stakes in the wrong fields to assess student epistemologies of what counts as knowledges. In my hypothesis, it does little good in any case to bemoan the "deterioration" of a social world that's gone from the good, solid skills of hoeing and sewing to the choice of suspenders, or like Baudrillard to celebrate its apocalyptic ecstasies of "refusing" meanings. Both just get in the way of recognizing such knowledges as significant, as after all registering quite accurately a relocation of ideologies of rising social expectations from institutional education to the fields of consumption.

To imagine, as educational critics often do, that students are somehow "tricked" into thinking that the availability of look-alike Axl Rose suspenders is a more important piece of information than the location of Florida is to misunderstand completely the contexts in which these bits of information are located. It's to assume that students somehow evaluate their relative importance in a vacuum and, perversely, opt for the former bit over the latter all too often. It's not just that buying suspenders only assumes its importance within the complex terms of consumption and its ideologies of rising expectations. Knowledges such as geography also arrive to students within a context, in the terms of an educationally organized curricular structure, and whatever screaming attempts might be made to get "them" to recognize the potentially vital importance of *any* such bit of information can't obviate the force of that awareness. This occurs for perfectly good reasons. If intensities of knowledge about consumer practices suggest the importance of educational *fields* of consumption, relative lack of interest in "school" knowledges might well then suggest less a perception of the unimportance of such knowledges than a perception of the obsolescence of the educational field in which they're located. That is, in whatever confused and confusing ways, such perception suggests at least some awareness that one primary institutional victim of technoideological coding's master narrative of survivals is the system of public education. Because schools are perceived as a survival, a carryover from some now rapidly disappearing past, the knowledges that arrive in the context of education come surrounded by reasons to doubt their importance.

Obviously that perception is not shared by all students or felt by all in the same way. But it does suggest some cause for concern about how teachers will track "good" students, that is, students who respond with interest and attention to things like geographical location and the rhyme patterns of sonnets. "Good" students will very often be those who have nothing to fear from the designated obsolescence of an educational system, who already have access to what seems immediately important and can then afford to value knowledges learned in school as part of the resources of their own performative agencies. These students have the luxury of detaching knowledges from their institutional context to be evaluated in their own terms, where indeed all kinds of things can become important and enabling. What schools in a service economy must produce in overwhelming numbers are not "good" students in this sense, but "bad" students, who will then become available to fill the enormous and growing number of terminal occupations and carry out the interminable labor of a service economy on which a consumer society depends. And "bad" students will appear in increasing numbers, since—again— they're usually not so bad as to be unable to recognize that there seems little to gain from school-acquired resources. That is, the most effective way to ensure that schools produce lots of bad students is not really by "raising standards" and the like, but by taking away reasons to acquire educationally certified resources, by making schools a primary institutional producer of obsolescence.

To the extent, however, that ideologies of rising social expectations have been relocated to the field of consumption and consumer
performances, that field also becomes educative, a matter of organized pedagogical practices. Rather than a curious anomaly, consumer self-help literature might then be better understood as paradigmatically typical, as perhaps an extreme form, yet revealing of
what occurs across an enormous range of so-called mass culture constructions. A Guns N' Roses concert video is after all first a performance, foregrounding everywhere the performative agency of Rose,
Slash, and the others. And if as a consumer you're being educated
how to perform, and how to aspire to such privileged positionalities
in your own everyday performances, knowledge of at least where
to get the appropriately similar suspenders with which to practice
performance doesn't seem a response that is any more "irrational,"
stupid, or beyond meaning than looking up a footnote reference in
The Wasteland. It's a bit literal, maybe, but most incipient knowledges
are. To study contemporary education in the United States means to
study contemporary mass culture, and the kind of critical analysis
often enough directed at educational institutions must also be directed at mass culture. That is, it's necessary to ask more than how
mass culture semiotic systems are structured, whether or to what
extent they "manipulate" their audiences or "induce" consumption,
or in what ways audiences "resist" manipulation. No critical analysis of educational institutions would limit itself to such questions,
because it's no mystery that an educational system has had a major
role in determining configurations of social position. And I think
it necessary to assume that similar functionalities exist for mass culture constructions. Much of the detail of argument in subsequent
chapters will involve an analysis of these functions.

Yet analysis will likely take place, and may lever potential political
effects within the organization of educational institutions—that is,
within structures now designated as obsolescent. Obsolescence here
doesn't mean that something will soon and automatically disappear;
it means rather that this thing will remain functionally crucial—in
this case to class-as-lifestyle divisions. In the next chapter, I will turn
directly to mass culture as itself a pedagogical field of social positionalities. But that discussion must be framed by the reminder that
such critical study of mass culture pedagogy can be put to political
use, precisely, within the obsolete institutional structure of public

education. Thus it's a good idea to get some preliminary sense of what that obsolescence implies in current circumstances.

I argued earlier that the universalizing emergence of class-as-lifestyle is constituted across the obsolescence of race and gender as relatively stable social categories, which as categories have also been the source of longtime social antagonisms and conflicts. Thus it might be anticipated that so far from being assigned, as in the past, the task of resolving social conflicts—such as "racial tensions"—schools will now be seen as places where *such conflicts themselves survive as obsolete*, where indeed "class" itself survives, not as lifestyle, but, like gender and race, a source of antagonisms. It is in these terms that Reaganism's critiques of education make their most powerful ideological contribution. Such conservative critique imagines malign visions of, for example, curricular reform for multicultural literacy, attention to different "identities," encouragement of "superficial" and "unscholarly" pursuits such as cultural studies, and so on, as what "ideologically" dominates an educational process, and what then works to perpetuate the "illusion" that older categories of gender, race, and class still exist in the social world. In this imaginary it is as if, were it only possible to get rid of how schools promote them, the social antagonisms and conflicts generated across these categories would simply disappear as well into a process of educating students for the "real world" of endlessly realizable expectations. "School culture" reform, in other words, proceeds by first of all isolating the schools as responsible for perpetuating social antagonisms.

Correlatively, the current crisis of education has also produced a whole series of creative alternatives, from the proliferation of (often) church-sponsored private education to that now perennial Republican proposal of tax credits and other incentives for private education, the diversification of "options" and "tracks" within public education itself, the exploration of means of funding other than property taxes, and so. These reforms are premised on "choice"—that is, on making education relatively more "up-to-date," more congruent with other sectors of the field of consumption. You "choose" your children's education just as you choose your washing machine, stereo system, or what suspenders to wear. But reform in these terms is doomed in advance to affect very little in the general structures and process of public education for most people. With the relocation of ideologies of rising social expectations away from a public educational system and into consumer fields, schools become more available to police and enforce class-as-lifestyle division. Rather than being in any real sense a gatekeeper of access to "better" social positions, schools become merely a way of preserving access—and "choice"—for those who don't need it anyway, while producing the rest as terminal. Public education itself (as anyone anxiously contemplating a first elementary- or secondary-school post knows all too well) is increasingly a divided structure, because increasingly, schools must produce the social divisions of class-as-lifestyle.

All kinds of pressures will intensify to make the public schools available to produce these divisions. For all the ideologically powerful promises of class-as-lifestyle in universalizing the field of consumption, and all the attractions of performatively enlarging the figure of individual agency, and all of consumer culture's educative instruction in mastering the anxieties and antagonisms of performance, nevertheless, the production of the obsolescence of so many hands and minds, so many eyes staring across the social distances of a service economy, remains a precarious operation, which will pressure institutions of education to contribute everything possible to the task. Political criticism will find the task of challenging those pressures complicated everywhere, not because students are "ignorant" and just haven't yet been made to see what's really going on, but by the fact that they're not ignorant, and they do see enough to know that most challenges are infinitely easier from the relative security of university positions. This must always be remembered in mobilizing any possibilities of analysis to produce a countereducation. What must also then be remembered is the struggles of teachers in the past, primarily women who were underpaid and socially devalued in the cruelest ways, but who took it on themselves to organize collectively and work individually for the benefit of all of us who were their students.

THREE

"For the Time Being, Forever": Social Position and the Art of Automobile Maintenance

One of the most obvious features of so-called mass culture is the dynamics of cultural change, with its often dizzying parade of new technologies as well as new forms and fashions. Thus theorists of contemporary culture are continually pressed to construct models of change that can register the flickering rapidity of each new development while at the same time establishing some conceptual coordinates to help make sense of the fact of change itself. The prefix in "postmodern," to take an obvious example, suggests in retrospect that the term might have begun life as a simple (if perhaps already exasperated) period designation, an attempt to combine the maximum of saturation potential—it can absorb almost any newly emergent cultural phenomena—with at least a minimal gesture toward a familiar conceptual segmentation of regularized change. But as anyone familiar with the term's complex itineraries knows well enough, "postmodern" very soon seemed to become a reflex symptom of the conditions it was designed to explain, more useful finally to assist in the identifications of the modernism that came before than for a description of the present.

One result of this inadequacy has been the refashioning of other kinds of terms to address more directly the conditions of cultural meaning in the present that permit the velocities of change. Thus in contrast to his use of "postmodern," for example, which has

---

The phrase "for the time being, forever" comes from Dick Darman, George Bush's budget director, in response to congressional questioning in April 1990 about how long Bush's "no new taxes" pledge would last. "Forever" ended June 25, 1990.

ballooned almost to the point of theological immensity, Fredric
Jameson's elaboration of pastiche remains more specifically useful
to his analysis. It is capable of specifying something about a wide
range of cultural forms at the same time that it projects a theoretical
means to focus the combinatory structures of self-referentiality and
emotional evacuation that characterize for Jameson the current epistemological field of cultural change. Likewise, in contrast to a term
such as "consumer society," Baudrillard's concept of simulation also
functions, if in a rather different way than pastiche, as a focusing
of the dissolution of reference in the contemporary epistemological field. Nevertheless, the invitation to reconstruct in detail some
preceding moment of cultural history implied by the periodizing
implications of postmodern and consumer society cannot be abandoned completely in the deployment of terms such as "pastiche"
or "simulation." Much of what they have to address as change will
involve what Raymond Williams, in an interview shortly before
his death, called "the endless nostalgic reconstitution" (Heath and
Skirrow, 10) of the past so visible in everything from films to rock-
and-roll revivals and "oldies" stations, to fashion, and to television
programs and commercials.

The advantage for Jameson in his use of "pastiche" is how, unlike
"postmodern," it can direct attention specifically to the details of an
apparent paradox: how it is that a certain "sheen" or "look" of the
past is achieved in ways that yet appear in a contemporary context
as something unexpected, new, and obviously different altogether
than anything available in the past. For Jameson, the concept of pastiche makes sense of the paradox by suggesting that, unlike parody
or satire, this form of contemporary cultural production works by
emptying objects of their densities and depths of significance, with
the result that the construction is neither "really old" nor "really
new," but inhabits a kind of structural timelessness by preserving
adjacent to each other the signifiers of both. Thus, not surprisingly, although Jameson doesn't emphasize the point, the most immediately available pastiche object is typically some visually foregrounded apparatus of a now obsolete or outdated technology—the
omnipresent cars endlessly prowling the streets of *American Graffiti*,
for example. Or think of how often in *Chinatown* Jack Nicholson's
bandaged nose is framed against that distinctively shaped thirties
telephone receiver; or, for a nonfilm example, how against the back-

ground of stacked Marshall amps, electronic circuitry, and all the familiar paraphernalia of current rock performances, Neil Young—himself a figure first familiar from late sixties and early seventies rock—emerged center stage at the most recent Farm Aid concert with a much-battered acoustic guitar.

Given this often detailed presence of obsolete technologies, however, there seems to me good reason to consider the marketing of nostalgia in rather different ways than through the primarily epistemological coordinates established by pastiche or simulation. That technology looms so large in nostalgia products is a curiously skewed indication of their masculine identifications—masculine, because the use and control of technology has been traditionally associated in U S. culture with men and men's work; skewed, because the emphasis here seems as much on the reconstituted details of day before-yesterday's technology as on the sheer destructive power of masculine force invested in it. It is this destructive power that Gillian Skirrow finds played out again and again in video games, for example, in what she calls "hellivision":

> All aspects of life, particularly sexuality, being so closely scrutinized, death remains the only secret. However, as it is only in the fantasy of the video games that a single suicidal enemy is a real threat to strong power, there seems little potential for a discourse from the position of death becoming an oppositional force to be reckoned with. On the evidence of the games the preferred male solution seems to be to bury themselves in the mother's body with their fantasy weapons and forget about the very real dangers of the world outside until these dangers manifest themselves as disputes about boundaries, as in the Falklands "crisis," in which case they can be understood and dealt with by playing the war game, again. (Skirrow, 140–41)

In contrast to this "preferred male solution"—which obviously worked for the United States as well, in the Gulf War—nostalgia's foregrounding of obsolete technologies can perhaps be understood initially as linking a technological extension of traditional masculine power with the restitutive, restorative values of low-tech skills that are more typically associated with women and women's work. It's a linkage that in masculine terms then becomes less a battle within and against the mother's body than a need to adopt the "female" skills of restorative labor in order to create in an alien present some dimly remembered sense of masculine power that is appearing to slip irretrievably into the past. Whether any "oppositional force" can emerge through these operations is doubtful, just as with the "preferred male solution" Skirrow describes in video games. However, to understand nostalgia critically in terms of shifting social positions of gender (and of race and class, in ways I'll suggest in a moment) rather than through the epistemological conditions of cultural meaning does at least imply the means of constructing different models of cultural change. For if indeed mass culture is also an educational process, then the kind of change in mass culture constructions registered by a term such as pastiche will nevertheless involve both an instructional message and, as Skirrow argues, a certain interventional force affecting the configurations of social position. What pastiche tells us in this context is that the message has to do with the irrelevance of representational powers of signification; that is, you've got the initial point of such retro constructions when you've ceased to anticipate corroborating echoes from either the depths of your own immediate surroundings or from any forgotten recesses and interiors of the past that could be revealed by archival research. Epistemologically, as Jameson's use of pastiche suggests, this might appear simply as a kind of emptiness of reference, but instructionally it accomplishes a powerful refocusing of attention, shapes and foregrounds a scene in which some as yet unplotted performative possibilities will emerge across surface textures.

At the same time, the instructional refocusing functions interventionally to destabilize the source material of social identifications. Signifiers of positionality, that is, will in this newly constructed scene appear randomly distributed across a depthless surface, and for that reason will seem uniformly available, unmoored from their locational source to be deployed in whatever multiple performative scripting you might "choose." Like any educational process, what nostalgias promise is that the more completely you've absorbed the instructional message, the more you've enabled your own powers of social mobility. Nostalgia offers itself as a relatively more sophisticated educational achievement than, for example, video games, not because you've got to wait until you're an adult to have something to be nostalgic about, but because by comparison the often single-minded teleology of performance in video games here gives way to multiple potentials that video games can only approximate through the itinerary of change that emerges as you move from one level of the game to another.

Nostalgia in any case is not about the past, as Jameson's argument itself makes clear enough, but about possibilities in the conditions of the present. What it produces as "past" might then be more accurately understood as still another aspect of its instructional message, having to do with the subject that exercises cultural theorists such as Jameson and Baudrillard—namely, models of cultural change. In this rather different context, technological artifacts continue to function prominently, but no longer as simply visible markers of temporal differentiation. To the extent that what's at stake instructionally is a conceptual modeling of the process of change, the temporal differentiations of technological apparatuses—"telephone receivers used to look like this"—must be made to yield an explanation for the perceptual field itself that identifies the "used to look." And if you've absorbed the first lesson, you know better than to seek corroboration by dusting off magazines or whatever from the thirties, which could in any case only confirm (or deny) representability, without addressing the mechanisms of change. Nostalgia is about present conditions of possibility, however, and thus one very good clue to the instructional messages constituted through the appearance of "older" technologies can be seen in the ways in which new, high-tech apparatuses are marketed.

Patricia Mellencamp locates the gender divisions that frequently emerge in such marketing, where "unlike machines marketed for women, machines addressed to men often have excess power, e.g. 160 mph sports cars, rifles, machine guns and hand-held missiles, and the unearthly decibels of stereos. Washing machines or vacuum cleaners with excess power become either sitcom jokes, as in *Mr. Mom* or *Lucy*, or a horror film nightmare. For women's machines, excess power is rarely a desirable, salable component" (219). Further, within this gender division, excess power is figured very differently along class lines for men. Thus Mellencamp's list might be extended to distinguish, for example, between the ultrasophisticated, expensive, and expandable apparatus of top-end rifles and, in contrast, the "crude" explosive force of .357 magnum handguns widely sold in secondhand stores. Similar distinctions can be made between the sophisticated, expandable power of a new Porsche 911 and the sheer quantum of engine displacement power available in an old Chevy V-8. You might then think of roughly parallel kinds of class distinctions for women in the marketing of Jenn-Aire ranges, say, in contrast to Sears's Kenmore basic electrics. Marketing of new technologies, that is, clearly observes both gender and class lines of division, but it might be anticipated that these intersections will be at once complicated and replotted in relation to what after all this marketing of the new is intended to displace, what will now appear in the context as yesterday's technologies: the field of nostalgia constructions. And conversely, the instructional messages of the latter's modeling of cultural change will then assume the importance of such constructions in relation to the marketing of the new.

I've picked my examples from Mellencamp's list to neatly align the marketing of new, "sophisticated" technologies with upwardly mobile middle-class men, thereby leaving older, "cruder" technologies to working-class whites and men of color. The alignment is by no means completely accurate in marketing, but it is common enough to follow up on one particular area where the selling of nostalgia intersects directly with technological change: in the field of automobile care and maintenance. The literature of car care affords a conveniently localized example of the cultural plotting of technological change, at the same time that it makes more easily visible the social positioning of groups of the population than other, more widely discussed constructs of film, television programming, music, and so on. Further, it is not only obviously gender- and class-marked, but it can also suggest a great deal about the double cultural projection of racial categories: inside the United States, where they are intricated in increasingly complex ways with gender and class, and outside U.S. borders, in the already huge and growing marketing of obsolete technologies to so-called developing nations.

Finally, the literature of car care belongs within the larger category of consumer self-help literature, which supplies perhaps the most paradigmatically typical field of mass culture constructions as educational. Given the importance of the automobile in U.S. culture, it's as appropriate as anything to focus both the instructional messages and the interventional force of mass culture education. In pursuing the argument in these terms, I'm suggesting that mass culture is not merely material to be theorized about, but is in the same business as cultural theory. Part of the instructional message will involve models of cultural change that articulate in some considerable detail technoideological coding's master narrative of survivals. With that detail available, it then becomes rather easier to recognize how for all the differences in political values that might inform epistemological readings of mass culture through terms such as "pastiche" or "simulation," the models of cultural change that emerge in such readings are nevertheless strikingly congruent with that technoideologically coded narrative of survivals and its models of change as they appear in mass culture constructions.

I

Out of context, such terms as "care" and "maintenance" don't typically suggest masculine activities, and as a result when deployed concerning car work they have been linked with more immediately recognizable masculine ideologies of automotive performance and individualistic, even "frontiersman"-style, appeals to do-it-yourself stuff. But what interests me here particularly is how the effects of changing automotive technologies are plotted to define both care and maintenance.

With very recent-model cars, in contrast to seventies and even early eighties models, relatively little can be done without enormously expensive diagnostic equipment and very specialized tools to perform adjustments. For example, one common tune-up job often done at home would involve setting the gap between the breaker points in the distributor, and that would mean the use of a simple instrument called a feeler gauge, which consists of a number of different-thickness blades inserted between the open points to determine the gap. For some time, however, meeting manufacturer specifications exactly has required not only a feeler gauge but also an instrument called a dwell meter, which can measure electronically the number of degrees the distributor cam rotates while the breaker points are closed. No longer prohibitively expensive, dwell meters are widely available and easy to use. They perform the same function, after all, as a feeler gauge. But still newer electronic ignition systems, in contrast, do away with distributor breaker points altogether. Such systems are more efficient, require less maintenance —and are virtually impossible to do anything about at home when, inevitably, they do break down. And that is the key point. It's not that a home mechanic couldn't learn a different and complicated technology; that's happened often enough. It's that there's little to do at all without far more comprehensive and *expensive* equipment than a dwell meter.

In relation to such changes, several things have happened in the literature of automotive work. Much of the space in car magazines that in the past would have been taken up with outlining procedures to get the most out of timing and distributor fine-tuning, as well as carburetor adjustment and refitting exhaust systems, is now given over to "detailing," an almost obsessive involvement in fit and finish rather than performance. Probably the fastest growing discourse about cars, however, involves both books and articles in a wide range of magazines targeted for what their titles "boldly" recognize: auto work for "dummies," for "the compleat idiot," for someone who wants a "greaseless adventure"—and, of course, for women. Along with maintenance in these terms, and consistent with other forms of consumer self-help literature, there is a continual emphasis on self-protection—how not to get ripped off by garage mechanics, used-car dealers, when purchasing a new car, and so on. The shift, in other words, is of both gender and class. The men to whom this marketing is addressed are targeted as middle- and upper-middle-class men used to purchasing someone else's labor to do the work. Detailed instructions for oil changes, for example, seem necessary only for men who've barely glanced at a car's engine before.

For a number of reasons, I think it worth considering this new form of car-maintenance discourse in terms of a more generally pervasive discourse of nostalgia. Most obviously, the appeal—like that of *American Graffiti* and other more recent examples—seems inextricably linked to the re-creation of a moment in the technological past. As a result, the appeal is not just "you can do it," but "you can do it, *too*," where the force of that "too" has nothing to do with people now working as auto mechanics on late-model cars, but with individuals "just like yourself" who some time "in the past" used to spend a great deal of time tinkering with the family car at home. Second, it's a discourse far more overt than other forms of nostalgia about its ostensibly cross-gender implications. Women are invited to abandon their feminized prohibitions against "getting dirty," to learn to love it, and to amaze any prehistoric males in sight with their knowledge. Men are invited correspondingly to be sensitive, caring, and careful workers with their hands, not Camel-smoking punks gearing up for the drag strip. Third, the frontier ideologies of do-it-yourself are at once preserved and updated with a kind of urban guerrilla mythology directed against evil forces lurking everywhere in the jungle (e.g., *Mugged by Mr. Badwrench*). This alignment is then correlated with a notion of similar technological continuity: cars still work in basically the same ways as in the past, only with some new refinements you need to master. Finally, and most crucially, there is—albeit often muted in the midst of all this upbeat advice—a thematic of loss no less pervasive than in any nostalgia production. All the wealth of detailed information can hardly disguise the fact that with newer cars there is very little that can be done at home; there's no obvious labor referent for the information. Donna Sclar, for example, in *Auto Repair for Dummies*, talks at great length about the pleasures of working on carburetors and the gratifying results that follow from the smallest adjustment, and this in a book aimed at owners of newer cars that almost uniformly do not have carburetors, but rather fuel-injection systems requiring a diagnostic computer and expensively specialized tools to perform adjustments. Much of the information then has to do not with your work, but with what to tell your mechanic to look for as a problem: the identification of strange noises, and so on.

Alongside this upscale marketing of car maintenance, however, there exists another kind of discourse, directed at what must be recognized, I think, as the repair of *older* cars; not in that long-familiar sense of restoring "classic" European Jaguars or Mercedeses or Austin Healeys, and so on, but simply fixing up ten- to twenty-five-year-old Fords, Chevys, Plymouths, and cheap-end available VWs, Datsuns, and Toyotas, just to keep them running. Shop manuals, *Chilton* reissues, and specialized manufacturer's instructions (such as those put out by Holley carburetors, for example) are the primary carriers of this discourse. You'll find here no instructions about how to locate the oil filter by color and shape, and the like. A *Chilton* manual's typical procedures for rebuilding an entire engine often take up little more space than instructions for oil changes in upscale discourse. Safety warnings, in contrast, will loom large (they are often the only pages in color) and, unlike the work procedures, may seem insultingly obvious to buyers familiar with upscale discourse.

Such different discourses "mean" in different ways. It's possible without much exaggeration to refine a sense of the nostalgia of an upscale discourse of maintenance into a recognition of pastiche in something like Jameson's sense. Stylistically, the form is a collection of what often seem idiosyncratic accretions—from a whole range of current self-help, fitness and diet, and still vaguely "countercultural" texts such as the descendants of Pirsig's *Zen and the Art of Motorcycle Maintenance*—linked with a curiously empty but nevertheless evocative appeal to artisanal labor and communities of work. All the above then function to obliterate anything like a "real" past or a real history of labor skills, leaving only an empty "look" of the past. Alternatively, that style might be read through Baudrillard's simulation as selling the notion of home labor, home activity itself, as part of what Baudrillard calls a "hyperlogic" of consumption, having reached an extreme point of replacing any signified of production with (literally) the consumption of consumption, as if *that* were productive labor (as indeed it would be in the "obscene" world of "mass" consumption Baudrillard describes). Either way, upscale discourse becomes one familiar version of the postmodern, a perilously unmoored chain of floating signifiers whose combinatory structures yield momentary flashes of what looks like significance, but whose meaning finally strings through an endlessly self-referential circuit of consumption.

While perhaps then epistemologically "empty," such upscale discourse is nevertheless educational, most immediately about how to read what I've been calling repair discourse. This latter will inevitably seem in contrast a more stable, "representational" language, dependent on an assumed security of reference. The detail of instructions in upscale discourse tells you that should you happen to run across instead such things as a *Chilton* manual's abrupt command to "remove the intake manifold," then you're in the presence of the survival of an *older* set of assumptions about discursive signification itself. The instruction, in other words, has to do not only with how to go about changing an oil filter but also with a model of cultural change that would explain why it is that the discourse of *Chilton* manuals and the like now appears remote, opaque, and uninformative. It's a survival from a now obsolete technological past, which will make no particular sense to you facing a new car's engine in the present. The message is a crucial one, for like consumer self-help literature generally, an upscale discourse of car maintenance is not intended to intimidate you with what you don't know or can't do. Thus there's nothing particularly abstract or "academic" about how such a lesson in reading should be part of upscale discourse. It is powerfully functional, alleviating potential anxieties about the performance of maintenance work by turning what could otherwise be felt as a debilitating recognition of lack of resources into an enabling understanding of changing technologies. That is, the discursive "emptiness" of reference supplies an exercise in grasping the conditions of change, and implies that the "performance" at issue here has relatively little to do with work on cars.

In upscale discourse, cultural change, as involving the differences in practices of discursive signification, is not only plotted in direct relation to technological change but also in relation to the social positionalities of those engaged in the work of car maintenance. Such discourse implies that *Chilton* manuals and the like had at one time a generally available field of discursive reference because they addressed technologies generally available to the home mechanic to work with. The nostalgia evoked in upscale discourse's fascination with automobile technologies that existed in the past—carburetors, for example—can be extended easily enough to home mechanics themselves, who in their "natural" surroundings in the past can appear as heroized examples of individual labor skills and resources. But car work isn't simply a thing of the past; while you may never have occasion to remove the intake manifold, somebody may have to. The terms of performance upscale discourse addresses have to do with how you deal with that "somebody." This, then, is where the educational message of discursive technological obsolescence turns into an interventional force in the configurations of social position.

The "somebody" you deal with in the present is not the nostalgically recreated picture of individual labor skills, but what happens to that heroic figure when it "survives" into a very different present. Just as the discourse of a *Chilton* manual will in the present seem uninformative and potentially intimidating, likewise the "survival" to whom that discourse might still make a great deal of sense will seem "awkward" at best, vicious at worst. What the home mechanic "survives" into is the service worker, who is likely to try to "mug" you with price ripoffs for repairs that are "shoddily" done in any case; the occupant of "low-income" neighborhoods, who offends your esthetic sensibilities with trashy yards, car parts, and blocked-up cars all over the place; the "insensitive," who ignores ecological imperatives with polluting exhausts and freeway detritus. The home mechanic survives as a figure who stands as a forbiddingly *masculine* sign of a no longer useful gender economy.

Yet for anyone who *must* engage in it now, car repair work is not so very different from a wide range of traditionally sanctioned women's work. Like women's work, it is repair labor, and is labor intensive, requiring low-tech and often improvisational skills with the relatively cheap materials and tools at hand. It's often performed during time snatched from other and more conspicuously determined concerns. It's almost invisible socially, except perhaps as an "eyesore" when it fails—producing then stalled cars along freeways, or cars blocked up in yards in "poor" neighborhoods and trailer parks. It's unproductive labor, both in a traditional Marxian sense and in the newer meaning of labor that contributes little to a consumer economy. Most important, it's often essential to family and household, when working conditions force people to cope with multiple low-paying jobs in widely scattered locations. My analogy between the necessity of car repair in these terms and the familiar conditions of "women's work" is hardly an exact parallel. Nevertheless, similarities in the qualities, skills, utility, and circumstances of the work do exist, and the recognition of similarities is obscured by the ideological determinations of gender and class positions powerfully reinforced by the ostensibly cross-gender implications of upscale discourse.

When in that discourse women are invited to do their own car work, to cross gender territories, the crossing is imaged as a taking up of new freedom, a refusal of the limitations of a feminized "lifestyle." It should be clear, however, that whatever mobilities this gender crossing might promise to women remain class-specific. While working-class women are certainly no strangers to "getting dirty" or to wearing old and shapeless clothing to do work of all kinds around the house, the shame of exposure in such a state is no mere relic of an older lifestyle, to be happily abandoned for a new, positive attitude toward work, dirt, and old clothing. For working-class women at least, the discourse of upscale maintenance doesn't function as "liberating," but as a vicious reminder of all the conditions of their lives that won't change no matter how much they improve their "attitude."

The male target audience for upscale discourse, in contrast, is invited to learn the patience and care with hand labor that women already purportedly possess, and at the same time to join a long tradition of masculine activity. But in terms of repair labor the class barriers of this gender mobility are almost absolute, for what certain men are invited to engage in as a freely chosen acquisition of new skills and forms of self-satisfaction is for others a grimly imposed logic of necessity. The very possibility of crossing gender territories, in either case, is plotted as strictly as the visibly marked territories to be crossed. You can cross gender territories as a class privilege, as something that comes with upward mobility, which marks your "progress" beyond the hopelessly outdated "traditions" still preserved in the surviving pockets of working-class life.

To the extent that upscale discourse sells an image of performing as a home mechanic, it's no mistake to see that image as an empty one in terms of the semiotic structure of the discourse, and to locate it, as Baudrillard would suggest, within the field of consumer practices rather than the field of work. What I've been arguing is that its conditions of meaning still function as part of an educational process. This car-maintenance discourse is first of all a lesson in how to read, where the immediate reference is not car work but another discourse, that of repair, whose process of signification belongs to "the past." Thus upscale discourse becomes a theoretical model of cultural change, a way of making sense of such changes in signification across the appearance of new, sophisticated automotive technologies. This model is very familiar at that, as, like most theories of the postmodern, it offers signifying practices as the best clue to the dynamics of change and the best available means to "read" the complex of technological innovations that alter the categories and norms of everyday behavior.

As consumer self-help literature, the model of change is then made to address potential anxieties about engaging in the work of car repair, insofar as it restructures perceptions of social position through its narrative of survivals. Those who engage in the actual work of repair at home are positioned not as groups of the population condemned to that work by current conditions, but as survivals from the past. That is, someone employed at Minit-Lube, changing the oil on Accords and Beamers, keeping up perhaps two late-seventies cars for use of self and family members at similar service-sector jobs, and thumbing through whatever literature may be available to guide that repair work, is not seen in terms of a current social organization requiring more and more people to live and work in such conditions.* Rather, that person is positioned as a survival, a once-common figure of home labor now lost in a world where low-tech repair work is only an odd, marginalized pocket in the midst of coefficients of drag and multipoint fuel-injection systems. The "proper" heir to the confident, masculine, self-reliant home mechanic of the past is not really such survivals, but precisely the performing agency of the reader of upscale discourse in the present, empowered with the mobility to move across fixed categories of gender division and with the class lifestyle of the upwardly mobile. Upscale discourse sells an image of performing as a home mechanic, but while the performance has almost nothing to do with working on cars, it's not *just* an empty image. It's part of an educational process of instruction and of social stratification. As a model of cultural change, the educational narrative may have been linked to very different political values than in other forms of postmodern theorizing, where typically it is the "survivals" instead who are focused upon as victims of a relentless march of capitalist "colonizing" now cannibalistically feeding on even its own immediate past in the rush of change. Yet despite the differences in politics, the narrative structures remain remarkably congruent. In whatever political version, there's no room to recognize a sense in which "such people" are not really survivals at all.

II

Obviously the discourses of automobile care and maintenance are only a small part of a much larger configuration, but understanding them in educational terms can help explain a great deal about how the intersections of technological change and ideological change are plotted. Both the automobile and automotive technology have been

*As I argued in chapter 2, what exactly constitutes the "service sector," and the Census Bureau's statistical data used to support the much publicized shift to a "service economy" in the United States, are themselves fascinating issues of social positioning. Early in the century, for example, the Census Bureau classified auto repair work under manufacturing, not under service, as it is currently listed.

so central for so long in the organization of virtually every aspect of political as well as social life in the United States (it was, after all, automobile executives that Bush chose to take on his ill-fated visit to Japan) that it's easy to forget the differential social force of automobile marketing, under cover of that familiar term "mass." Indeed, as Bernard Gendron cleverly suggests in "Theodor Adorno Meets the Cadillacs," the automobile seems the perfect vehicle to explain how earlier theorists such as Adorno understood the logic of mass culture.

Products of standardized design and production lines, cars are distinguished from each other by what Adorno would call a "pseudo-individualization," superficial and stylistic differences that disguise a basic interchangeability of crucial performance components. Standardization and pseudo-individualization would thus mark how the automotive industry solved one of the basic problems of a capitalist economy: standardization meant cheap, efficiently organized and cost-effective production; pseudo-individualization meant the potential to continually expand sales by trading on easily altered features of appearance that didn't affect the basic organization of production. This is indeed the logic Adorno found transposed into the production of popular music in his 1941 essay "On Popular Music." A basic musical core persists through superficial changes in the periphery that generate a hook to sell each new song, without affecting the ease and rapidity of production. Beethoven's music, in contrast, simply can't be understood in the same way, Adorno argues, for there "the detail virtually contains the whole and leads to the exposition of the whole, while at the same time it is produced out of the conception of the whole. In popular music the relationship is fortuitous. The detail has no bearing on the whole, which appears as an extraneous framework" (21).

The problem in the concept of "mass" doesn't lie only in how it accords such an ideologically privileged position to the cultural analyst sophisticated enough to prefer Beethoven to Tin Pan Alley. Baudrillard, for example, as Tania Modleski argues in "Femininity as Mas(s)querade," recognizes not only the elitism of positions like Adorno's but also the often covert gender identifications of "mass" consumption as feminine, the informing values of which he then cheerfully inverts to declare the end of social differentiation in *In the Shadow of the Silent Majority*. As Modleski points out, however, "not the least of the problems involved in equating the masses and mass culture with the feminine is that it becomes much more difficult for women to interrogate their role within that culture" (51). Facing, for example, the upscale discourse of car maintenance I've been describing, a working-class woman won't find much leverage for "interrogation" through Baudrillard's claim that she belongs within an enormous, feminized mass of consumers existing beyond the social differentiations imposed by categories of meaning such as "working class" and "woman." At one level the message of both upscale discourse and arguments like Baudrillard's is roughly similar: everyone is mass, and to imagine that as a woman and as working class you might thereby have distinct reasons to interrogate that mass culture simply indicates your own obsolescence, your persistent clinging to the terms of a now rapidly disappearing social formation. For all that the politics of Baudrillard's account may seem to differ from the educational politics of upscale discourse, the narrative structure of survivals functions no less effectively. "The death of the social," as Modleski argues, "is another of phallocentrism's masks, likewise authorizing the 'end of woman' without consulting her" (51). Obsolescence is rather more easily produced in the present by not "consulting" those to be positioned as obsolete.

In contrast to Baudrillard, Jameson's account of the "colonizing" powers of postmodern capitalist culture retains from Adorno, and more directly from Ernst Bloch, a recognition of what Bloch called "nonsynchronous" change. For Jameson, while the expansion of the marketplace imposes a postmodern cultural "dominant," that dominant culture never completely saturates the field. But while Adorno in "On Popular Music" will continue to privilege the high-culture instance of music like Beethoven's as a source of oppositional critique, Jameson like Baudrillard refuses the autonomy implied by such instances. Thus if in earlier arguments he was relatively willing to supply catalogues "of collective life or collective solidarity [that] have not yet been fully penetrated by the market and by the commodity system" ("Reification," 148), the concept of a postmodern cultural dominant is increasingly used to suggest that even such "pockets" nevertheless exist in relation everywhere to dominant cultural forms. They yield no "outside" on which to ground oppositional critique, although clearly they continue to enlist Jameson's political sympathies, in ways not possible for Baudrillard.

Sympathy, however, doesn't get very far in understanding how mass culture after all doesn't really produce a mass, but rather a newly articulated and mobile system of social differentiation. And without that understanding, potential "outsiders" can only be recognized in terms that suggest an always receding horizon of as-yet "uncolonized" or "unpenetrated" populations, where critique grounded in such an "outside" becomes for Jameson a vanishing and forlorn hope at best. Like public education, mass culture education does spread more and more widely, addressing more and more directly more groups of the population through more of their lives. Like public education as well, however, it will configure that "mass" into sharply differentiated positionalities, where the "outsiders" are not the group still unaffected by the colonizing march of mass culture, but rather the group positioned within the categories of obsolete survivals. Mass culture education, that is, becomes relatively unconcerned with "insiders" and "outsiders" in Jameson's sense, using instead the up-to-date and the obsolete as the key distinctions. Hence the "silencing" Modleski describes is less a matter of preventing speech than of having already assigned it to the categories of obsolescence, as then literally unnecessary to be *heard* in the conditions of the present, yammer away as it will. And while it may be far indeed from Jameson's intention, his sense of the hopelessness of "outsider" critique has something of the same effect; in the newly "destabilized" conditions of shifting social differentiations, such a perception doesn't prevent speech; it just renders it oppositionally nugatory.

Given the social importance of cars, perhaps nowhere is the mass culture production of social differences more pervasive than in the selling of automobiles and the changes in automotive technology. Epistemological constants of description, however, are not particularly useful here; epistemologically, mobile differentiation may seem altogether empty in a contemporary marketplace. The pseudo-individualization that Adorno abhorred has expanded to the point that even more contemporary terms such as "pastiche" or "simulation" hardly appear adequate to describe the marketing of increasingly empty distinctions among makes and models, often "corporate twins"; the interchangeability of parts has gone far beyond what Adorno could have seen; the widespread distribution of production plants makes national labels such as "Japanese" or "American" or

"German" cars anachronistic at best; and of course technologies have become fundamentally similar as well. Thus *Consumer Reports*, for example, can point out the silliness of GM's touting of its so-called quad four engine, when nearly every competitor's engine also has four valves, two intake and two exhaust, for each of its four cylinders ("Five," 191). "Quad four," that is, is a term that logically could be applied to *any* four-cylinder, sixteen-valve engine. Nevertheless, while it's true enough that technologically GM's quad four is little different from a host of available engines on the market, it is significantly different from the four-cylinder engine offered in older Chevy Cavaliers and other J-car models, which has only eight valves, one intake and one exhaust for each cylinder. That's what makes it possible to assign the Cavalier engine to the status of "older" within the terms of GM marketing. The meaning of these marketing distinctions is then hardly empty in relation to the positioning of potential GM buyers, nor are those buyers imaged as merely a "mass."

The marketing is designed to locate a would-be buyer with respect to the owners of older GM cars, as, *unlike* them, capable of possessing technological power equivalent to the purchasers of competitors' cars. That is, the apparent emptiness of the marketing of the quad four nevertheless intervenes toward a profound redistribution of positionalities, not despite but because of the lack of difference with respect to competitors' engines. Further, the marketing is quite capable of supplying an answer to the implicit point of *Consumer Reports'* sarcasm—why not simply buy a foreign competitor's car if you can get a better deal on basically the same thing? The reply is that the U.S. identity of GM is not a reflection of where its cars are made, but a marketing construct of where they are made *for*. The issue, that is, is not a matter of "literal" location in the United States, but a positionally constructed identity of U.S. history and origin. Wherever the car parts may actually be manufactured, in possessing the car as GM-identified the marketing invites you to possess as well a history of U.S. manufacture and purchase, one then available only through GM and other U.S. companies, and not through Honda, say, even though most Accords sold in the United States may be assembled in Ohio.

The potential "dissonance" of meaning here, with respect to social positioning, lies not in the gap between signifier and signified, but in the discrepancy between an invitation on the one hand to *distinguish* a new buyer from owners of older GM cars, and on the other to *affiliate* a new buyer with those owners of older GM cars in a construct of U.S. history and identity. But that dissonance is rather easily, if invidiously, negotiated. Like the discourse of upscale maintenance, what the marketing does is to position owners of older cars as themselves history, so that when they manage somehow to "survive" into the present, they are hopelessly outpowered and outsophisticated by owners of foreign competitors' cars. To be a new buyer is instead to be positioned as boldly carrying forward a necessarily changing construct of U.S. identity and history competitively into a new age. And that positioning comes not at the expense of buyers of competitors' cars—who are playing the same game with "us," only on the other side—but of current owners of older GM cars, themselves now made obsolete by the very history they embody.

Epistemologically, again, all these "constructs" and "identities" and "distinctions" and "affiliations" are no doubt empty enough. But they are by no means empty of social consequences, nor do they function toward the end of "mass" consumption any more than public education functions to produce an undifferentiated "mass" of workers. Marketing depends everywhere on selective distinction, whether under the rubric of "market segmentation" or still-newer methodologies of market research analysis: the intervention in some way in the existing distribution of social positions. Hence advertisers are experts in ideological legitimation, to alter slightly Gramsci's well-known description of the social function of intellectuals generally. But this expertise is not necessarily directed toward "preserving" dominant ideologies in the same forms. In automobile advertising, masculine power, for example, remains a pervasive ideology of advertising constructs only insofar as it remains in control of continually changing positionalities of population groups in relation to the assumed possession of such power. That is, the advertising point is neither to reproduce directly nor to oppose directly masculine gender dominance, but to intervene selectively to distinguish constructs of continually shifting groups positioned as primary carriers of power As a result, the (if still relatively rare) presence of advertising constructs that target women as potential possessors of power in and through a particular car is not immediately a sign of either social "progress" against dominant ideologies, nor a newly refined "trick" to seduce women into playing a man's game. It is first of all an intervention designed to maximize control of the *distribution* of social positions, whatever the continuing effects may be on ideological configurations elsewhere.

III

Rosa Luxemburg argued a long time ago that what is really unique about capitalism is that it can't exist by itself; it needs other modes of economy to feed on. Clearly she was thinking in this context about colonialism, and of the "penetration" into other economies of the capitalist marketplace that continues to concern theorists such as Jameson. But the conditions she describes also suggest another kind of crisis of dependency, to which the resources of educational institutions have been directed no less than to the process of colonizing new territory. An economic system that can't exist by itself is also unable to ensure reproducing itself in the future. So while Marxists have often enough been charged with wildly underestimating capitalism's adaptive powers, its "elasticity" and "responsiveness" to changing conditions, and so on, what Luxemburg's argument, extended in this direction, suggests is that such adaptability is a necessity. It's not some marvelous, inherent virtue of the system, but simply an expression of the uncertainty of the future, of being dependent on what may or may not come to pass. Luxemburg may seem a prejudiced witness, but even relatively conservative educators such as James Conant—in *Education in a Divided World*, for example—have always realized a sense in which education must start over with each new generation. The future is uncertain; it can be guaranteed only by redoing everything again from scratch. That the effects of starting over—and over—will often look "the same" shouldn't obscure how the notion of education as "reproductive" remains a register of effects, a "forever" lodged within the precariousness of "the time being" of the raw material of each generation.

Mass culture as educational seems to have drastically foreshortened Conant's starting over, to the point that even the notion of a "generation" sounds anachronistic, something itself to be conjured up in the midst of the flood of sixties retro. But mass culture education might better be understood as organized toward reducing the uncertainty of the future by working to *eliminate* the reproducibility of the present. That is, while Conant had imagined public education as shaping the raw material of each new generation into the finished representatives of a stable, continuous social order, thereby ensuring that the future would reproduce the present, mass culture education in contrast constitutes presentness as a throwaway. In educational visions like Conant's, no matter what constraints may be imposed educationally to guarantee the success of the process of ensuring the future, it might nevertheless be skewed at any point in unexpected and altogether unforeseen ways. To the extent any present moment can be designed as eminently disposable, however, there's no longer any need for such constraints. Any "time being" will only echo the "forever" of the power of designing. Dick Darman's pronouncement to Congress about Bush's pledge to refuse tax increases, whose terms I've been playing with, is after all a familiar part of almost any new automobile sale. The car being sold is in some form or another always the "latest" and the "best"— for the time being, forever.

In this context of mass culture education, it might then be possible to explain more exactly the sense in which obsolescence is produced in the present, by thinking in terms of degrees of investment in the disposabilities of presentness. The mistake of the "uneducated" is not really that "they" are duped into thinking that the new car just purchased will continue to be the latest and the best. More fundamentally, it's to have misunderstood what the transaction is all about, as if it were just a matter of keeping up with new technologies or new fashions or new conveniences or whatever. This is simply Conant's now itself "obsolete" model of education foreshortened, where each new generation turns into each new model year, and so on. To be "educated" is to recognize instead that the stakes are not at all in the newness of the "new" car, but in the disposability of your "old" car. You ensure your future possibilities not by investing in the newest and the latest in hopes that somehow the future will reproduce those conditions of the present, but by occupying a position that permits your performative participation in *producing* obsolescence. In this sense, so-called planned obsolescence is no longer merely a technique for inducing consumption, but, more important, is an educational invitation for consumers to perform, and to learn the benefits of performing. The "choice" of new car is then hardly incidental to this performance: what that choice announces is less your up-to-date status than your power of investment potential in the production of the obsolete. Crudely, the more completely a new car represents the latest and best of the present, the more disposable cultural as well as monetary income it supplies for your production of obsolescence in the future. What is "reproduced" is thus not the present at all, but the conditions of your production of obsolescence.

Beyond the immediate ends of marketing, such cultural plotting of technological obsolescence also yields a remarkable rationalization for the apparent paradox of what might then be called a continually changing dominance of the same. The obsolescence of older technologies can seem to be what makes them cheaply available to groups of the population who couldn't possibly afford them at their inception, when those technologies were themselves the cutting edge of change. Hence the development of new technologies is very often justified, by a kind of classic rhetoric of "trickle-down," as ultimately benefiting everyone. Without the development of the new quad four engine, for example, used and pre–quad four Cavaliers might not even yet be cheap enough for certain groups to purchase. In this best of all possible worlds, their purchases are "subsidized" by upscale buyers willing to pay out large amounts of money for the latest in new technologies. Likewise, what looks like the same empty story can be projected outside U.S. borders, where such rhetoric rationalizes the sale of older technologies to "developing nations," who then benefit from the same subsidies on their way to eventual independent capitalization.

To ideological critique this justification of technological change may look similarly empty across its coordinated projection of "inside" and "outside," but in terms of social position it functions in very different ways in these two sites. When it is projected outside, it becomes a story of progress, a *bildungsroman* in effect, nicely expressed in the euphemism of "developing nations." But when projected inside it's a cultural narrative of control over "natural selection"; the latter now becomes a process fortunately having been tamed for the benefit of the "unfortunate" by the generosity of the successful. Because everyone inside is assumed to have had roughly the same opportunities, those capable of it will move with the times, and those who aren't will be allowed at least to survive into the present through the subsidies advanced by the others.

In these narrative projections, then, race and class positions are made to intersect very differently. Outside, race is everywhere the primary marker; developing nations are inhabited first of all by other races, with class made virtually invisible, even though with automobile production especially it is these raced outsiders who supply much of the labor force for current production, with profound consequences for insiders as well. The inside narrative would instead assimilate obvious racial inequalities to class as their underlying cause. That is, what used to be a "vulgar" Marxist explanation of racial oppression as ultimately an effect of class structure has now been rewritten and enthusiastically adopted within Reaganism as part of a general attack on affirmative action and other "liberal" legislation. In Reaganism's version of U.S. social organization, class is of course "lifestyle," at best simply an option and even at worst an easily permeable barrier. Anyone who possesses the initiative, intelligence, and desire to work can pass. Those who can't are just survivals from an obsolete past of racial discrimination.

The result is a redistributed configuration of social positions with a forbiddingly balanced symmetry: on the one hand, a racially marked "outside" frozen in adolescence, always "developing"; on the other, a class-marked "inside" of old age, persistent survivals from the past. In order to keep these positions fixed, the cultural plotting of technological change is itself then a necessarily always-changing positionality, always dominant. For the time being, forever.

Politics of Change in Mass Culture Education: Television Programming and Household Flow

Although public education in the United States in the first three decades of this century underwent an enormous expansion at every level, from elementary schools through university, that expansion was not a smooth, uncontested process. Nor was the result—nostalgic reconstructions aside—an institutional formation that perked along quite efficiently until the "upheavals" of the sixties eroded a sense of "mission." As I have argued, its foundational rationale of encouraging and rewarding rising social expectations introduced from the beginning a contradictory set of imperatives. Further, education was surrounded by a rhetoric of crisis throughout its twentieth-century history, in large part because it was expected to intervene in what were already crisis situations, from labor "unrest" to the ideological and scientific battle lines of the Cold War. The integration conflicts of the sixties were in one sense a new kind of crisis, but the perception of education "in crisis" was hardly unfamiliar.

In describing by the example of car-maintenance literature and automobile advertising how mass culture is an educational process, I've proceeded as if, in contrast to the history of public education, mass culture education possesses a massively successful efficiency, relatively free of ideological conflicts and struggles. However, while that assumption is useful enough to explain the sense in which mass culture is indeed educational, there's no real reason to think it free of trouble. Because mass culture is organized altogether differently from public education, and functions in different ways, it's unlikely conflicts and contradictions can be recognized in the same terms. Conflicts over integrating schools are not quite the same as conflicts over integrating commercials. Nevertheless, it's important that oppositional critique of mass culture education should attempt to locate and identify contradictory pressures at work.

Recent studies of mass culture are often useful here, by challenging the assumption that unlike, say, the recognizable postmodern literary text that thrives on contradiction and instabilities of all kinds, mass culture is simple to read because everywhere basically the same, content to remain within the most familiar and conventional forms. Dana Polan, turning to television as perhaps the most pervasive channel of mass culture constructions, suggests how these supposedly simple and banal plot and character formulas can be as great an affront to traditional narrative logic as the most highly wrought strategies of academically privileged postmodern texts:

> For example, what notion of narrative's transparent construction of a diagetic universe could match the strangeness of the fact that the television show *Mork and Mindy*, which is about an extraterrestrial, originated as a spin-off of *Happy Days*, a quaint show about everyday life in the American fifties? . . . Similarly, what notion of the television dramatic series as inheritor of the ostensible narrative and representational grids of the nineteenth century novel could really account for the conceit by which the television show *Dallas*, can substitute one actress (Donna Reed) for another (Barbara Bel Geddes) in the role of a central character (Miss Ellie)? (181)

The implications of such arguments cut two ways. As the boundaries are collapsed between mass culture and postmodern, simple and complex, it doesn't automatically follow that mass culture constructions must then be recognized as contradictory sites of meaning that are potentially subversive politically; you might instead begin to question whether the postmodern is really so critical and "oppositional" as its supporters have often claimed. Yet whether, or in what way, you agree with the argument, it should be clear that what's at stake in Polan's critique of critical reading practices projected by the strict separation of mass culture and postmodern is finally a complex of political issues that makes it difficult simply to write off mass culture as some uniformly imposed ideological manipulation.

In contrast to Polan, Raymond Williams's particular angle of entry into the study of mass culture permitted a search for an explanation of what Polan calls its "fundamental weirdness" (182) in and through the very medium of presentation. Hence his influential concept of "television flow," for example, would suggest that any account of the relation of *Mork and Mindy* to *Happy Days* by analogy to a narrative sequence of discrete texts fails to recognize the way television as a medium dissolves the boundaries establishing discreteness (Williams, *Television*, especially p. 95). Broadly, where Polan's argument works with the ideological intricacies that must be negotiated in reception, Williams's focuses instead on the technologies of production.* Yet Williams is no less critically reflexive in his analysis; television flow as a concept takes on much of its specific meaning in his argument against the conceptual categories of criticism derived from the study of literary texts. Likewise, Williams's argument also points a political lesson: the necessity of attending to the always diverse material conditions of cultural production.

In an essay entitled "Television/Sound," however, collected in the same volume as Polan's, Rick Altman introduces what seems to me an important modification of Williams's concept. Television flow, Altman argues, should not be assigned immediately to some intrinsic characteristic of television itself as medium. The practices of television production differ significantly from one country to another, and flow as Williams explains it is especially relevant to commercial television broadcasting in the United States:

> Either we explain the difference in level of flow [in different countries] by a difference in the stage of development of a particular television system, as Williams does, or we recognize the extent to which such differences in flow correspond to differences in the function of television as defined by a

---

*There are an increasing number of studies of television audience, often far more directly concerned than is Polan with how different audiences make meanings from television programming very differently. Ien Ang, for example, has contributed a lengthy study of *Dallas* itself. In relation to my focus on households in this chapter, however, the recent work of David Morley and Roger Silverstone is particularly crucial, for they emphasize—rightly, I think—how any study of audiences must recognize the complexities of the domestic context (which includes other technologies such as VCRs, radios, and computers) in the analysis of meanings television audiences construct. Further, and in contrast to how critics such as John Fiske construe the creative power of audiences to make different meanings, they distinguish carefully between what they call "power over a text and power over an agenda" (34), where the examples Fiske can cite of the former nevertheless do not translate neatly into the latter. In this terminology, my concern here is primarily with "agendas" rather than "texts," and in showing how television programming itself can involve different and even conflicting agenda directions.

particular culture. Provisionally, I would suggest the following hypothesis: flow replaces discrete programming to the extent that (1) competition for spectators is allowed to govern the broadcasting situation, and (2) television revenues increase with increased viewing. In short, flow is related not to the television experience itself—because there is no single experience—but to the commodification of the spectator in a capitalist, free-enterprise system. (40)

If Polan's argument can be understood as concerned primarily with reception and Williams's primarily with production, I would suggest that Altman's hypothesis directs attention instead to circulation. What he calls, perhaps over-hastily, "the commodification of the spectator" is largely a function of rating surveys such as the Nielson and Arbitron systems, which measure not "the number of persons actually watching television but . . . the number of sets turned on" (43–44).* That is, they are a measure of circulation, of how well television flow is coordinated with the flow of people in the household, not of what happens or doesn't happen in reception. By "household flow," Altman means quite simply who goes where in the house, in and out of the house, when, how often, and so forth. Such movement obviously will be determined by a great many things: the size of the household and the physical size of the living space itself; the income levels of its members; the relation-

*In "Why We Don't Count: The Commodity Audience," Eileen Meehan recounts the history of rating services in the United States, from CAB and the "Hooperatings" to "people meters." What Altman refers to as "the commodification of the spectator" is crucial to her argument, for the economics of rating services is to some very great extent a matter of television's selling an audience to advertisers, as Altman implies. Ratings are one obvious "agenda"—borrowing Morley and Silverstone's terminology—that drives television programming, insofar as the numbers supplied by the rating service occur at the crucial intersection of the size of the viewing audience and rates that can be set for advertising time on specific programs. And as Meehan points out, network interest and advertiser interest in how audience numbers are determined are by no means congruent. Generally, networks will want measurement indices that skew the figures toward as large as possible a viewing audience, in order to justify higher rates; advertisers in contrast want indices that minimize audience size, to justify lower rates. While obviously important to any consideration of television programming, however, ratings are not the only agenda that determines programming, as Meehan's argument sometimes seems to imply. As I will emphasize, programming decisions always occur at specific intersections of economic, technological, and ideological factors, which doesn't mean ignoring the economics of ratings Meehan discusses, but does question the overwhelming priority she assigns to "the numbers game."

ships existing among them; the relations each of them may have with other locations outside the household (work, school, shopping, entertainment and leisure activities, friendships); and the specific household activities in which each person engages. But television always intervenes in this flow of people's movements as a potential focus of attention, and for Altman television programming is then "fragmented into short segments which reflect the continuous viewing time of anyone caught up in the household flow" (44).

Altman's emphasis is important, for while cultural reception no less than production have become increasingly familiar subjects of complicated critical analysis, perhaps nothing so clearly marks the distance of academic criticism from the vast business of mass culture as the relative lack of interest in the complexities of circulation. Obviously no one working in television programming in the United States is likely to forget circulation for a moment, and if criticism is to understand very much about mass culture it seems a good idea for criticism not to forget it either. After all, from a television programming standpoint "How do I preserve the narrative continuity of *Dallas?*" is not nearly so crucial as "What will retain and potentially expand circulation figures for *Dallas?*" If, in Polan's example, you imagine a range of possibilities—killing off Miss Ellie, say; giving her an incurable disease requiring she stay off-camera for an indeterminate time, and the like—substituting another actress for Barbara Bel Geddes will emerge within this range as the most attractive option if it will seem the best opportunity to expand circulation. Insofar as narrative continuity (or the lack of it) may become a problem, it is within the context of circulation, as that is where all the interests converging on the issues of production and reception must for the moment hang suspended, dependent everywhere on the possibility of integrating the movement of television programming into the patterns of movement among the members of the household—television flow and household flow. Unless in some way that integration completes the circuit and permits circulation, whatever went on in production and whatever may have resulted from reception turn into merely matters of disinterested curiosity.

Altman's conception of television flow plays off and against earlier directions of analysis, and thus in one sense his essay is critically reflexive in ways very like Polan's. What I've implied, however, is that it can be made to function as a rather different order of reflexivity, directed not at the conceptual inadequacy of critical categories, but toward the end of recognizing more clearly the social position occupied by the academic critic of mass culture. It seems obvious enough that working in television programming you might have a powerful interest in what will expand circulation figures for *Dallas*. But it should seem no less obvious that working as a critic within the university you might have an equally powerful interest in understanding narrative continuities and discontinuities. It won't occur to just anyone anywhere to question "narrative's construction of a diagetic universe" by pointing to the spin-off of *Mork and Mindy* from *Happy Days*, nor to use the substitution of actresses on *Dallas* as a critique of the notion that television programs inherit "the ostensible narrative and representational goals of the nineteenth-century novel."

These aren't neutral inquiries, as the political context of Polan's argument is intended to demonstrate. But no less than the television programmer's concern, they are also location-specific, having to do with a particular kind of work in a particular place. Thus if I assign the viewing of *Dallas* episodes to a class of students, the politics of a decision to devote class time to an analysis of their relation to the nineteenth-century novel will differ, perhaps dramatically, from a decision to devote class time instead to collecting their "weird" effects in relation to the postmodern novel. Nevertheless, to some very great extent both these directions of classroom work can be made to seem "plausible," "worthwhile," "intellectually defensible," or whatever, because both observe a certain obvious congruity with their location, and with the kinds of work typically carried out in an English classroom in the university. As a result (except perhaps for the inevitable percentage of "bored," "anti-intellectual," "ideologically duped" students who persist in wondering why they have to do this) location becomes largely invisible.

But if I chose instead to devote class time to a discussion of what might expand the circulation of shows like *Dallas*, there seems something immediately odd. Clearly such a discussion couldn't be for the purpose of changing the production of *Dallas* to generate wider circulation. It won't function anything like a discussion among programming personnel connected to the production of *Dallas*. In contrast to the former directions of classroom work, this discussion would raise the issue of location almost unavoidably. While it can be reduced to merely a stratagem, an indirect way of returning to

familiar classroom issues, at best it yields another kind of question altogether: not "What are the politics of critical analysis?", but
"What political effects are possible *to* critical analysis?" across the distance between its location within an institutional formation of education and the mass culture constructions studied. That distance is
not just a matter of the academic and the educational on the one hand
and the business of buying and selling on the other. But while mass
culture constructions also function educationally, Altman's emphasis is a reminder that whatever similarities may exist in reception—
as Polan argues—and even in production, the process of circulation
is organized very differently. Television always goes home, and its
programming is in direct relation to the movements of people in the
household. Those relations are hardly "simple"; their complexities,
however, involve another register of operation than the complexities
of postmodern literary texts.

The immediately crucial point in this context is that the very
notion of the household *as flow* is not "simple," just "natural" or
"obvious." In the history of capitalist development, the household
has been imaged in a great many often competing ways. With the
massive transformation of "unproductive" to "productive" labor,
for example, the household was identified as a primary location for
the reproduction of labor power. But from a marketing standpoint,
this transformation meant the household could be understood as the
place where consumer goods were purchased in enormous quanti-
ties, and these images were not necessarily congruent. The distinction Michèle Barrett emphasizes in *Women's Oppression Today*, for
example, between "household" on the one hand and ideologies of
"the family" on the other, has to be read in relation to this dissonance. In terms of how the household functioned, it might almost
be said that the transformation from unproductive to productive
labor involved two very different processes rather than a single phenomenon. And ideologies of consumption, of work itself, and of the
gender relations among members of the household shaped and were
shaped by the very different demands of production and marketing
to position the household as an important site.

However, if for television programming the household has
emerged as a system of movements, of "flow," this marks another
kind of change, a shift from a relatively static to a relatively dynamic
understanding. Rather than being a fixed site for either the reproduction of labor power or the expansion of commodity purchases, the

household becomes a dynamic pattern of intersecting movements. As Altman argues, television programming may often then find itself in competition with household flow patterns for organizing attention. More important, however, because the selling of an audience to advertisers depends on flow, programming must actively work to *produce* a concept of the household as flow, against what will now seem for marketing obsolete, no-longer-useful assumptions about the household. This image of the household as flow is an image of circulation, of people's movements—but circulation in this sense is necessarily also a matter of social mobilities, of an individual's range of movements and power to determine patterns and changes.

In relation to "older" conceptions of household function, the household as flow generates a whole sequence of potentially destabilizing and antihierarchical effects. It dislodges the power of movement from the determination of fixed position within the household. In so doing, it intersects in different ways than "older" conceptions with ideological constructions that determine configurations of social position generally. That is, it affects a great many otherwise very different ideological indices of social position by altering possibilities of social mobility. As a result, in competing with "older" ideologies of household function, it also disrupts the complex ensemble of relations between those "older" conceptions and other indices of position, in particular what Barrett would identify as ideologies of "family."

There is no reason to assume that the historical development of mass culture education was any more free of conflicts and contradictions than the history of institutional public education, and thinking of household flow in these terms can begin to suggest something about the conflicting pressures and imperatives that marked that history. Further, household flow affords a particularly useful angle of entry, because to the extent it is a function of *television* flow, it brings into focus not only ideological pressures but also the economics of selling an audience to advertisers (as Altman reminds us), and (as Williams argues) the specific technologies of television as a communication medium. Indeed, it may be possible to argue that the constructions of television programming have less to do with any inherent characteristics of the medium than with its functional role in resolving emerging contradictions in the history of mass culture in the United States, by means of exactly how television technologies were developed. The next section of this chapter will sketch out the conjunction of ideological, economic, and technological factors in emergence of household flow as a marketing conception, in order to return in the third section to the larger issue of its educational role with some sense of how such flow affects configurations of social position.

The importance of household flow in marketing; the way in which it competes with what must then seem to be "older," obsolete marketing conceptions; the destabilizing of fixed positions in the household and the correlative emphasis on movement and change—all these suggest a certain congruence with the social organization of class-as-lifestyle. Thus it might be anticipated that television circulation, as it produces a conception of household flow, functions educationally to produce as well promises of social mobility within the field of consumer practices that locates the terms of class-as-lifestyle. On the other hand, however, the very notion of "household" figures prominently in the whole range of so-called social issues high on the agendas of conservative politics. That is, "household" names the privileged site where the importance of "the family," the stability of patriarchal relations, and the value of white culture norms must be defended. In chapter 2 I emphasized the effects on those groups of the population condemned to obsolescence by class-as-lifestyle division; now, by means of this focus on household flow, it becomes possible to recognize potentially contradictory pressures existing *within* dominant, organizing ideologies of class-as-lifestyle. Such recognition is not important because as academic critics we might then be able to read mass culture constructions critically in new, more complex ways. It's important because knowing where and how contradictions complicate the process of mass culture education helps identify as well where and in what ways institutional public education will be expected to compensate, to intervene for the resolution of those contradictions. Recognition of contradictions in this sense begins to answer the question of what is possible politically to critical analysis across the locational distance from the mass culture studied, and in opposition to that expected resolution.

I
———

Advertisers long ago recognized the household as a primary site of consumption. But households differed in size, relationships among the members living in a household, income levels, geographical location, accessibility to advertising, and so forth. Perhaps more important, from an advertising standpoint there seemed a pervasive indeterminacy about what exactly in a given household occasioned the purchase of consumer goods. And in determining how to target advertising constructions, marketing on a large scale in the twentieth century could not afford a relatively inefficient and time-consuming process like that of the door-to-door salesman canvassing each specific territory. The far more efficient strategy would be some way of designating one member of *any* given household, no matter what the other variables involved, as "in charge" of household consumption. Gender-marked divisions between "work" and "home" were immediately available not only to identify "household" with "family" but also to isolate the "housewife" as the person in charge of household consumption. Thus advertising early in the century began to take great leaps in relation to this positioning of the housewife as a target. The increasing reliance of marketing on large-scale advertising campaigns by means of mass communication media simultaneously made use of already existent and familiar ideological attitudes, and redirected their force toward a certain stabilization of the household. Advertising could not control such things as household income level or the geographical distribution of households. But it could work powerfully to reinforce ideologies useful for centering the patterns of household consumption around the crucial figure of the housewife.

Carol Ascher's survey of earlier twentieth-century advertising in "Selling to Ms. Consumer" suggests a great deal about how advertising aimed at the housewife altered fundamentally certain long-standing practices of household work. The marketing of vacuum cleaners, in a now classically familiar example, presented a very different image of what household cleaning looked like. While in the past, the effort of sweeping, of cleaning rugs, and so forth, had been accompanied by clouds of dust as a sign of work under way, advertising of vacuum cleaners had to transform this image into clouds of noise. The vacuum was a noisy machine, and since it functioned by sucking up dust rather than throwing it around, the advertising picture of household labor was conformed to this new process (Ascher, 43–44). While the skills needed to run a vacuum cleaner were significantly different from the older skills of housecleaning, there's no intrinsic reason why men or children couldn't have been targeted by marketing to learn these skills. Indeed, as a machine it might seem at least plausible ideologically to picture men as appropriate users, or, since ease of use was a primary selling point, children as users. For advertising, however, the immediate issue wasn't who used the machine, but who bought it. Thus housewives remained the target of advertisers, because the identification of household and housewife had been developed as an efficient marketing strategy to take advantage of the household as a stable location of consumption. Ideologically, the housewife was to be responsible not only for household cleaning, but for purchasing whatever technologies might be made "necessary" for the work.

Yet as more and more women entered the work force outside the home, as the continual growth of public education meant that schools rather than home life organized more of children's time, and as mobility generally became easier for at least some more people, this stabilization of the household began to seem for marketing a grid of limitations rather than an efficient strategy. The identification of household and housewife left as random variables a remarkable range of other occasions and other targets for potential consumption. In these new circumstances, to channel advertising campaigns toward the household as a stable site meant to circumscribe opportunities for selling. In post–World War II advertising images of "the modern household," the housewife remained a crucial figure, but more often than not, it was now as a kind of business manager, someone who regulated the movements of other household members in ways that would ensure the most productive and pleasurable uses of their time both in the home and elsewhere.* Such images, by ideologically re-

---

*The succession of advertising images of "the housewife" has a fascinating parallel to changes in production work and office organization for men. Ascher quotes Christine Frederick's 1929 book, *Selling to Mrs. Consumer*, to the effect that housewives early in the century were made to feel that they, as housekeepers, had become like machine operatives rather than hand laborers (Ascher, 44). It was roughly at the same time as Frederick's book that Alba Edwards, working for the Department of Labor, was transforming older statistical data about occupations into a new set of indices that recognized the category of "operative" as separate from and more highly skilled than hand labor. Correspondingly, later images of the housewife as "business manager" paralleled the spectacular growth of middle layers of management and the emergence of the so-called efficiency expert in large corporation offices.

defining the duties of the housewife, also made it possible to extend the conception of the household as a primary location of consumption. Rather than being a simple, stable site for the purchasing of goods and services, the household began to emerge as a point of interchange within an increasingly complex network of movements of household members. It was where all these movements intersected, regulated by the household business manager who held the purse strings.

The next step was to see the household itself as a pattern of movements, a flow of people interacting with one another both as they moved through their dwelling and in their myriad relations with other locations. The advantage to marketing is obvious. Insofar as the household was at once a location for the distribution of income available for purchases and at the same time an integral element in a much larger network of people's daily activities and movements, it became possible to regulate advertising strategies with some precision across an immense range of variables. While consumer "demands" for goods and services might emerge from a thousand directions at once, they would appear in ways already reflected in the proliferating movements of household members. Household flow became an available index of visibility to help construct the details of market segmentation, lifestyle analysis, and so forth, now so familiar in advertising work.

I've made a conception of household flow seem simply the result of a logical progression of mass marketing practices, but in fact the issues were considerably more complicated. The development of this dynamic picture of the household as little more than a distributor firing the engine of consumption across more and more moving cylinders also threatened a whole range of ideological constructions that had been left relatively undisturbed by earlier marketing strategies. Indeed, there is a sense in which marketing aimed at the household as a stable site of consumption helped make such constructions invisible. Everything conspired to locate not only the household but fixed positions within the household as "natural," "obvious," a result of the timeless verities of family structure. The marketing development of household flow, as it alters a conception of the household itself, breaks with this assumed system of family relations, such that "family" emerges in all its distinctness as a "problem," a henceforth precariously poised unit, something whose representation in mass culture now had a nervous urgency and insistence.

It should then be no surprise that the most powerful television representations of the stable identification of household and house-wife, for example in fifties sitcoms, occurred during a time when proliferating patterns of movement were rapidly becoming a visible and, for many commentators, worrisome sign of family "fragmen-tation" and "decline." Rather than trying to compete directly with ideologies that had reinforced older conceptions of household func-tion—obviously a losing game—television "preserved" them as an ideological content in the process of contributing to and taking ad-vantage of what the new situation afforded for marketing. The con-tinuity of television *programming* strengthened the new marketing strategies aimed at maximizing household flow, while the ideologi-cal content of *programs* reinforced the importance of ensuring the stability of the household as a static nuclear family unit. Such sit-coms habitually turned on the threat of intrastructural disruption, from Lucy's high-energy attempts to invade show business to Ralph Cramden's titanic explosions and the Nelson boys' habit of forever dragging home troubled situations from the uneasy flux of their outside world. The inevitable containment of disruption thus can appear to slip seamlessly into the commercial flow of programming relations that were in fact one agent of disruption in the first place.

But before moving directly into the role of television in a mar-keting conception of household flow, it's necessary to back up a bit and recover still another aspect of the complex ensemble of adver-tising changes sketched in here, involving the development of new media technologies. The shift of marketing from a labor intensive process of individual "salesmanship"—one-on-one with prospec-tive customers—to the advertising campaigns of major agencies not only necessitated a reorganization of the work of marketing and new uses of available communication media, but also generated a powerful incentive for development of much more technologically sophisticated media. What miracle of communication, the J. Walter Thompson *Blue Book on Advertising* had asked rhetorically in 1909, could inform potential customers in Ohio of the attributes of chairs made in Connecticut (Aaker, 17)? The answer, of course, was the resources of an agency such as Thompson. Advertising, according to the *Blue Book*, could revolutionize marketing in the same way modern manufacturing had revolutionized production, by utilizing machinery to do the job. Magazines, bill posting, newspapers, the centralization of publishing, and so forth, had all contributed to the potential for advertising to reach millions of different households, millions of geographically scattered sites of consumption.

The development of radio, however, marked a fundamental change for advertising. It meant that you could reach millions of households simultaneously. Time as well as space became a variable that could be controlled. The *Blue Book* had imagined modern advertising as able to leap across vast spaces to contact potential customers, but radio made it possible to coordinate contact temporally. As a result, the so-called turnover time of advertisements, and before long of products as well, became the crucial factor in marketing as well as production. The technology of radio thus advanced dramatically what was already well under way: the determination of production, and hence of work and the organization of work, according to the requirements of marketing, rather than the other way around, as the *Blue Book* had assumed (Braverman, especially pp. 265–67). Radio did not cause these changes; there is nothing inherent in radio technologies that "naturally" leads to the enormous changes in production and work occurring after World War II. More accurately, the ways radio technologies in the United States developed should be understood as in part a result of radio's use in the practices of marketing.

Radio could circulate messages very widely indeed, to millions of households simultaneously. And it very soon became a mobile technology as well, which then contributed in a number of ways to the initial emergence of conceptions of household flow. Yet in another sense, radio technology was embarrassingly mobile. It seemed impossible to monopolize where radio's messages *circulated from*. That is, while radio had made possible for marketing new kinds of intervention in the household, the technologies involved in transmission—despite the legal apparatus soon put into place to regulate the licensing of stations and such—were simply too easy to construct, too inexpensive, to prohibit the rapid dissemination of ownership, which then became difficult to control from any central source.*

---

*Morley and Silverstone suggest how with the development of television particularly, government intervention has functioned not only in the licensing of stations

There was network radio, but buying an advertising spot on network radio did not guarantee the kind of circulation—potentially millions of households—that the technology promised. At this historical juncture, the development of radio was for advertising a double-edged weapon.

Television, however, was another matter. Television largely supplanted radio in the United States not just because it was a more "complete" medium, involving black-and-white and then color images as well as sound, but because it was developed into far more elaborate and *expensive* technologies, making possible the centralization of transmission that radio, for all its promises to advertisers, had not.* Arguments that try to read off effects from some assumed "intrinsic characteristic" of various media usually, as in this case, fail to account for how the characteristics appear in the first place. That is, the monopolized control of transmission isn't an effect of the essential nature of television as a medium. The specific developments of television technology in the United States proceeded to ensure precisely that control. In the medium of television, marketing then had what was necessary on the one hand to intervene simultaneously in the flow patterns of vast numbers of households, and on the other to direct transmission from relatively few centralized sites. Commercial television was in a position to capitalize as fully as possible on multiplying patterns of household flow, on "producing" the household as flow.

Now it would seem that from a programming standpoint, ideally a household will make available a maximum number of coordinated flow charts and minimize "random" movements among house-

---

and so on but far more importantly within the ostensibly private, domestic space of viewing itself: "Paterson (1980), drawing on Donzelot's (1979) analysis, points to the state's increasing regulation of the domestic sphere, through its various welfare agencies, as the broad framework within which to situate an analysis of the significance of censorship and scheduling as specific modes of regulation of domestic media. . . . The point, from our perspective, is that this includes children's viewing of TV, as a key focus of the state's concern with the moral welfare of its (future) citizens" (39). I will argue in my concluding chapter that the Bush administration's development of Reaganism has indeed made concern for "the child" a primary rationale for a kind of interventional cultural entrepreneurship of the state in "family affairs."

*My continual qualification—"in the United States"—is important because in other countries, as Altman could point out, the relations among different technologies often do not follow the same patterns as in the United States.

hold members. That is, the ideal circumstance would seem to be a whole series of times when every member of the household would be glued to the TV set, attentive to every commercial message coming down the pike. As Altman suggests, in such ideal terms the flow of television programming would compete with other directions of household movement, toward the end of harmonizing these potentially very different kinds of circulation—programming and people—around the television. Yet as a conception of household intended to increase consumption and the occasions for consumption, household flow "works" only insofar as it capitalizes on the *multiplication* of relations of movement in the household, thereby multiplying occasions for consumption. From this perspective, the "ideal" terms above are perhaps not so ideal after all.

The issue isn't finally a matter of how to regulate people's movements around the television set, but of how to use television most effectively to sell products on as many occasions of consumption as their movements might permit. We might then add to Altman's recognition that commercial television sells an audience to advertisers the corollary that a sale of an audience promises neither an "ideal" coordination of household flow nor the power to directly induce consumption of specific products, but rather a means for predicting patterns of intersection. The difference is crucial, for television programmers no less than advertisers know well enough that television cannot reliably deliver on either of these promises of control, nor is modern marketing directly organized around such manipulative powers (Watkins, especially pp. 165–82). Television "competes" with household flow only in the sense of having to accumulate the data-base projections of information that enable the prediction of patterns of movement and intersection, not by claiming to determine these patterns toward the end of inducing consumption.

Here it is useful to return to Polan's question regarding the *Mork and Mindy* series in the context of the more general issue of spin-offs. Considered as a question of circulation rather than of narrative logic, any spin-off is a predictability gamble. Like the apparatus of test marketing for advertisers, a spin-off is an attempt to generate the boundary conditions that would permit the calculation of predictability as precisely as possible, while still respecting (in this case) the necessity for multiple movements in the household. Thus it would build household flow toward the possibility of *repeated* intersections

rather than the stability of continuous viewing. For television programming, it is the length of time the television set remains on that
is crucial, and household movements that result in intermittent attention, even VCR taping of programs for delayed viewing, are not
a problem unless they jeopardize the use of the set(s). Indeed, as I
have suggested, it is such movement—signaled often by intermittent attention and the like—that can actually increase the potential
for consumption. Very simply, even if television could somehow
force people to sit still and watch commercials, that would do little
toward "producing" the movements of people that are necessary to
consumption.

In a certain sense, then, obvious narrative continuities of programs become a liability rather than an asset. So long as the primary
question is imagined as how an audience for an 8 P.M. show might
be manipulated into remaining an audience for an 8:30 P.M. show, the
ostensible narrative continuity afforded by spin-offs offers a plausible
answer. But when you recognize the issue as a matter of maximizing the occasions for consumption by *maximizing* household movements, then such continuities supply at best only half an answer.
Just as in advertising itself, where the calculation of predictability
replaced older models of manipulation, for television programming
what is wanted is a way of predicting the likelihood of continual
household movements intersecting again at some future time. Thus
while spin-off takes its name from what looks like a form of narrative continuity, it really names the projection of probable repetitions
of circulation. That Mork first appeared as a character on *Happy Days*
becomes the after-the-fact rationale for a completely different order
of decision. And trying to make sense of that after-the-fact rationale as though it were part of some basic narrative logic will always
make it appear to be—as Polan rightly perceives—"fundamentally
weird." Narrative continuity, like the identification of household
and housewife, has been preserved as part of the ideological content of programs, but with the sequence of programming directed
at other ends altogether, which inevitably exceed what is implied by
that ideological content.

In this context, however, the relative failure of substituting
Donna Reed for Barbara Bel Geddes on *Dallas* serves as an instruc-
tive reminder that ideological pressures displaced into the content of

television programs nevertheless continue to exert a certain force in the determination of television programming as well. Programming has had to learn what advertisers have institutionalized in the apparatus of test marketing, that "failure" in one sense at least is always part of the game at the point when you recognize ideological factors necessarily at work in the calculation of predictability. That is, if television programming were out to manipulate household movements, it would locate failure as a direct result of a misplayed attempt at manipulative intervention. But when you assume instead that programming seeks to capitalize on household movements rather than manipulate them, then failure has to be read two very different ways. On the one hand, it implies nothing more than a means of registering a still further potential for consumption, as yet untapped. Test marketing "failures"—which far exceed "successes" for any major corporation—in this sense then contribute to the amassing of information, necessary for the next projected advertising construction. Failures make boundaries visible, and are thus an integral part of marketing as an ongoing, expansive operation.

On the other hand, however, failure can mean instead the *collapse* of boundaries, of those terms that permit the recognition of ideological factors and how they are distributed. Without the clear demarcation of programming decisions from the representations constituted within the program itself, there is no way to calculate in advance the potentially positive effects of such decisions. Failure in this sense is then less a matter of relative conformity or challenge to the perceived norms of dominant ideologies, than a loss of the means of maintaining the distinctness of the program field of representation, on which predictability calculations depend. (That field may include ostensibly self-reflexive reference to programming decisions, as has become quite common in recent commercials and in programs such as *Saturday Night Live*, without in any way jeopardizing the distinctness of the field, any more than the self-reflexivity of many postmodern texts yields anything at all relevant to their actual conditions of production.) The substitution of Donna Reed was then not merely an "ideological" mistake that might have been avoided by the choice of a different actress, but a failure to preserve the field that permits decisions about what might or might not be a disruption of the continuity of representation. Unlike test marketing failures, which do yield information, failure in this second sense threatens the very basis of determining what counts as information in programming.

Programming decisions are never merely a lever to gain advantage in a competition going on somewhere else—among programs, networks, sponsors, and so on. As I have argued, programming itself produces a marketing conception of household flow in competition with other conceptions of household function and organization, where it's then clearly to the advantage of programming decisions to appear second order and reactive, less a source of change than simply a response to what has already changed. Thus programming must contain, but not seem to interfere with, the ideological content of programs. In relation to programs, programming decisions are always excessive, by functioning to make available program content as indeed content, a clearly demarcated field in which to register how ideological pressures are distributed in any given case. The collapse of boundaries marked by the programming decision to substitute Reed for Bel Geddes had the effect instead of making programming itself visible, as part of the ideological competition. That is, the "problem" didn't necessarily lie in how viewers refused to accept Reed in Bel Geddes's role; it's that *there was no way of knowing* whether viewers had rejected Reed or simply the visible interference of a programming decision within the frame of the program. Thus even if things had instead "worked out," if the viewing audience had expanded, explanation would still have been available only in retrospect, defeating the whole purpose of predictability calculations. Programming decisions compete successfully by never appearing to compete at all.

II

"Okay, motivate the spider."
—(from a National Geographic Special, a behind-the-scenes
look at the filming of *Arachnophobia*)

I've tried to indicate in my account something about the changing intersections of economic, technological, and ideological factors involved in the circulation of commercial television broadcasting in the United States. I've done so in ways that suggest a congruence between the specific destabilizing effects of the household as flow and the workings of technoideologically coded class-as-lifestyle generally. But on the other hand, there remains a certain dissonance within that congruence, which appears most obviously in a New Right politics of "social issues" with its defense of "family" and "family values" centered around the now "older" conception of the stability of the household. It's worth pursuing what opportunities the dissonance that appears across the projection of household flow might make available to oppositional politics. The characteristics of desirable class-as-lifestyle are realizable only for a few; and while the New Right has any number of highly visible, "prominent" spokespeople, it is also a politics of the downward trajectories of lower-middle-class life for white people, groups of the population for whom the ideological plotting of now obsolete survivals makes all too much sense. New Right politics expresses the anxieties generated by the felt slippage and erosion of the purchasing power of their cultural, as well as their economic, resources. In other words, support for New Right politics very often derives from fears of being made obsolete in the ongoing process of social change.

The notion of a "proletarianization" of groups of the middle class has often fascinated left politics with the promise of a subsequent "radicalization" if these newly proletarianized workers could only be made to see their "real conditions." But in the class-as-lifestyle–organized social positionalities of a service economy / consumer society, it's hardly likely a sudden openness to what it means to be exploited as a newly proletarianized "working class" can be encouraged by immediate reference to the organization of work and deteriorating conditions of labor. This is so for the perfectly good reason that downward mobility will not be perceived immediately in work-oriented terms. New Right politics offers rather what might be called a theory of *cultural* exploitation, which takes account of the valorized performative agency of class-as-lifestyle. Within those terms, downward trajectories can only be seen as the result either of individual failure or of some systematic "exploitation" by institutional legal, educational, political, and economic constraints on realizing the powers of performative agency for oneself. That is, to the extent that "class" is the preferred social category of technoideological coding, then a preferred explanation for social inequalities and disequilibriums can best appear in terms of class exploitation.

Likewise, if desirable class position depends on the individual agency successfully realized through lifestyle performance, then "exploitation" can name any system of cultural practices that seems to limit or constrain performance.

Not surprisingly, exploitation in this sense supplies a more attractive answer to downward mobility than individual failure, and New Right politics addresses its white, lower-middle-class constituencies as victims of exploitation that is institutionally enacted through such things as "favoritism" to women and "minorities" *as groups*; the benefits of "family" being extended to all kinds of living arrangements, including homosexual marriages; educational funding and educational programs that stress "multicultural literacy," "alternate" culture canons, and class, race, and gender issues; tax structures that commit large percentages of funds to "social programs," and so on and on. Downward trajectories, according to the New Right, result from such forms of cultural exploitation.

However bizarre or incoherent this logic may seem from the outside, it works as all ideologies work, because the story "fits"—fits in this case the immediately visible circumstances of disequilibrium, erosion, and loss. Against this it does relatively little good to point out the "obvious": how New Right politics legitimizes a whole complex of classist, sexist, and virulently racist practices. Within the terms of class-as-lifestyle, such critique can only be heard as yet another way of identifying individual failure, as if such groups of the population are responsible not only for their own downward trajectories, but for viciously oppressing others in the process. Given what seems to be a choice between this accusatory critique and a New Right theory of cultural exploitation, the latter will make considerably more sense. This being so, I want to suggest, rather than trying to expose the practices of exclusion disguised through the incoherences of New Right politics, an alternative means of political countereducation: asking what a New Right defense of the "stable household" *makes visible* about the organization of class-as-lifestyle. Clearly it does address, for any number of people, an intensely felt perception that the effects of "household flow" are far from benign— and there's no reason to leave such perceptions to the explanatory powers of Reaganism.

In ideologies of class-as-lifestyle, with their consumer-oriented positioning of occupation as a matter of instrumental choice, labor disappears into the category of occupation. That is, work and the social organization of work are identified within the armature of occupational "options" and "choices." Occupation is understood as merely one (if a crucial) resource to be deployed in consumer performance. Under the banner of so-called methodological individualism, even some directions of Marxist critique have succumbed to these ideologies of performance. Within Reaganism, however, an overtly New Right politics of social issues, while preserving the emphasis on occupational choice, nevertheless also maintains a certain vexed, uneasy attention to work itself. Even if most often expressed in the familiar pieties of a "Protestant work ethic," the fact that labor remains an issue at all suggests a disturbance in the valorization of performative agency through the organization of class-as-lifestyle that is worth pursuing where it appears most obviously: in New Right defense of "older" notions of the household.

In my sketch of the emergence of a conception of the household as flow, I emphasized its importance in marketing, but it also affects the perception and organization of work. Marketing that positioned the "housewife" as a stable center of household consumption functioned also to make her work within the house invisible. Even as an increasingly wide range of products were sold to the household as "labor-saving" devices, it was far from clear that what was being "saved" was in any "real" sense labor at all (a perhaps necessary "confusion," since most of the devices marketed in these terms created new forms of work rather than "saving" labor). Household flow, in contrast, recognizes that not only adults but often older children as well are likely to be working members of a household, people whose flow patterns will include leaving for and returning from a range of jobs, multiple work activities within the household such as housecleaning, child care, schoolwork, and buying and using consumer goods. And in any case, the household as flow is not necessarily equivalent to the family unit at all. While not every form of work is then directly linked to income by marketing assumptions about flow patterns, it is in any case the relation between work and *spending* rather than work and income that is crucial to a conception of household flow. Thus insofar as they involve people's movements, all forms of labor—whether income-producing or not, culturally valued or culturally ignored—are equally relevant to flow. Among other effects, this assumption of equivalence permits, for example, the marketing of "labor-saving" devices far more widely. Car phones, call waiting, educational software programs and link-ups such as Prodigy, even burglar-alarm systems can be marketed in these terms. Household flow, that is, cancels an "older" set of boundaries between invisible and visible labor by rewriting all labor into a function of flow patterns keyed to consumer possibilities.

For New Right politics, however, any assumption of labor equivalencies like those that emerge across the coordination of flow patterns is perceived as breaking the identity of household and family, and as a subsequent devaluing not only of the occupation of the male "head" of the household but of what in retrospect is also made to appear an occupational choice: the role of "housewife" and "mother." Thus the housewife who had been imaged in mar-keting conceptions as the central agency of household consumption here reappears as also engaged in an occupation, and this occupa-tional choice is to be cherished against the threat of forced disappear-ance in the present. By extension, it is precisely these occupational choices that can be made to look "exploited," culturally devalued, and mocked, when their practitioners are constrained to pay taxes that support color TVs for welfare mothers, family counseling ser-vices and welfare for homosexual marriages, university salaries for people to teach "subversive" literature instead of "basic" values, and so on.

Yet once pushed to this extent by the logic of New Right poli-tics, the governing category of occupational choice itself, in a kind of return of the repressed, comes to mark instead the intensities of *labor* as value. Exploitation can appear in just these terms only by means of a powerfully nostalgic reconstruction of the importance of certain very specific "occupational choices" as finally a function of the value of the labor they entail, where that labor is assigned value in some other way than through the choice of lifestyle options. That is, a New Right theory of cultural exploitation must nevertheless return at this level to conceptions of work, of labor, as the ultimate measure of what exploitation is all about. Household flow thus itself emerges as a threat to the value of work, as imaged through these nostalgic lenses as "the work of the family unit."

Marketing conceptions of household flow, however, not only can but must *continue* to compete with such "older" conceptions of the household. In this form, the visibility of labor is not a matter of some deconstructive "accomplicehood" of a conception of household flow with its ostensible competition, but rather, and quite simply, what I argued in chapter 2 to be the inability of mass culture education, in isolation from the school system, to produce the present supply of labor on which the social organization of class-as-lifestyle depends. In larger terms, a New Right defense of stable household and family has something of the same strategic usefulness to a conception of household flow as television programs have to the flow of television programming. The New Right is useful precisely in its nostalgias, in how those nostalgias, like television programs, preserve the distinctiveness of a field of representation. Rather than looking at the inadequacies or deceptions of mass culture education in relation to a present social organization of work, New Right politics after all focuses attention on labor only in and through the nostalgic valorization of certain privileged forms of work. That is, it preserves a distinct field of representation.

If work and the social organization of labor were to be dislodged from the nostalgic reconstructions of the New Right, as no longer a "thing of the past" but of the present, then household flow could itself be understood in rather different terms than the consumer choices of lifestyle through which it functions as a marketing concept in mass culture education. It would appear instead as the present, daily, grinding necessities imposed on any number of household members juggling the demands of (often) two or more part-time jobs in multiple locations; scrambling to repair the always deteriorating house and its likewise deteriorating technologies, from "obsolete" car to refrigerator to washing machine; sending young children to day care in order to earn an income caring for the children of others in "spare time"; buying food and clothing based on which purchase is cheapest and quickest. That, after all, is "household flow" for many people most of the time.

The ideological danger of a New Right politics of social issues is not only that it actually produces the deeply racist and sexist determinations of class-as-lifestyle's labor requirements that condemn people to household flow in these terms. It is dangerous because it's a politics that creates conditions permitting these determinations to be continued, by absorbing possible alternatives into the nostalgic reconstructions of the household and its intrinsically dignified labor.* A marketing conception of household flow thus not only *can* compete with an "older" conception valorized by the New Right, but again, it *must continue* the competition.

The presence of New Right politics suggests well enough how the organization of work cannot finally remain invisible within the interstices of consumer occupational choices. New Right nostalgias, however, conveniently focus the visibility of work in such a way that only certain forms of labor are privileged, in ways surrounded by a whole complex of social values attributed to the work—"being a mother," for example, or "being a breadwinner." Those groups of the population who actually perform the primary "dirty" labor of a service economy, and whose "lifestyles" as a result often fall outside the range of such values and their identification of privileged forms of work, can then be targeted as the assumed beneficiaries of public welfare policies, and blamed for how lower-middle-class whites are being continually driven into the labor pool of a service economy as well. New Right politics, that is, generates an explanation that would account for disequilibrium and loss in and through its selective reconstruction of the value of labor, subjected to cultural exploitation. And that explanation must be sustained within and by the marketing conception of household flow itself.

Public education has always "educated" people for work, supplying a population "suited to" the demands of a specific organization of labor. Given the inability of mass culture education to provide this labor pool, schools must now do so, and must do it largely without the supporting rationale of rising social expectations that has been relocated to mass culture education. With that relocation, however (as I will argue in my concluding chapter), schools then become a

---

*In her chapter entitled "Playing House" in *A Primer for Daily Life*, for example, Susan Willis argues powerfully for alternatives that appear in recent novels such as Toni Morrison's: "I have argued that the 'three-woman households' that occur throughout Morrison's writing enable the author to reconceptualize social and sexual relationships along utopian lines (Willis, 1987b). These involve heterosexual relationships that are not oppressive, and relations between women across generations that do not obtain in male-dominated nuclear families" (106). That is, Willis is speaking to the possibilities of rethinking the very social organization and value of "domestic labor" that marketing concepts such as household flow on the one hand, and New Right nostalgias on the other, function together to make invisible.

particular institutional target of New Right politics, by which they are understood on the one hand as "keeping alive" an obsolete emphasis on race and gender as fundamental social categories, and on the other as depriving individuals of the resources they need to become productive, rewarded, working members of society. In parallel fashion, nostalgic New Right reconstructions of the intrinsic value of certain forms of *labor* appear in educational terms as the intrinsic value of resources of *knowledge*. And where the former deflects attention from the presently necessary labor of a service economy, the latter likewise deflects attention from the present role assigned to public schools, which is not at all to transmit the resources of specific knowledges but to produce the labor force of a service economy. Public education "resolves" the contradictory impasse of mass culture education by at once compensating for its fundamental inability to supply an "adequate" labor force, and at the same time taking the brunt of criticism for that inability. Educationally then as well, the danger of New Right politics is not that it produces the role of public education in these terms, but that its nostalgias create conditions for the role to be perpetuated by absorbing alternatives.

One obvious alternative would be to take advantage of how public education is positioned as necessarily compensatory, in order to educate about how it is *mass culture education* that helps position public education as compensatory. This is less a matter of "reading differently" mass culture ideological constructions, or of celebrating its frequent burlesques of New Right politics and constituencies, than of pursuing in different terms the opening made available by New Right politics itself. That is, New Right ideologies, if nostalgically, nevertheless make work and categories of labor visible within the very interstices of conceptions of performative agency and lifestyle "options" and of such crucial marketing concepts as household flow. To the extent they make labor visible, however, they also create a space of visibility where it becomes possible for an educational process in the schools to include perceptions of labor as it occurs in very different forms than in nostalgic reflections on "breadwinners" and "mothers." And looking at what much service work, for example, actually involves—apart from such nostalgia—likewise permits constructing explanations very different from a New Right version of "cultural exploitation" for who does what work and why.

In looking at MTV, for example, that available space permits a focus on the "behind-the-scenes" construction of performance as students view it, on what makes possible the center-stage positioning of a band such as Guns N' Roses. That positioning, after all, is considerably more than the semiotics of camera angle, shot frame, lighting, intercutting, costuming. There is also the organized if invisible work of any number of people, the whole ensemble of specifically social relations of work that make performance in this or any other sense possible. That the lead singer of Guns N' Roses might "simulate the feminine" in the very midst of "heavy metal thunder" is an important emphasis for would-be countereducational practices. But it is surely no less important to emphasize how many women and men must operate the cameras, edit footage, clean up the stage afterwards, sell tickets, staff telephone lines, and so on, and how it is that they are tracked into this and similarly invisible work.

In commenting on Manuel Puig's novel *Kiss of the Spider Woman,* Tania Modleski questions whether social "power dynamics" can ever really be changed simply by adopting new consumer strategies: "Despite the suggestion in *Kiss of the Spider Woman* of a role reversal and a shift in power dynamics—with Molina temporarily in the ascendancy as a result of his feminine strategies, which are also the strategies of the consumer—nothing much ever really changes" (51–52). And the "power dynamics" involved in the occupational tracking I've been discussing are not a matter of consumer strategies. Unless those forms of tracking are changed, however, their dynamics will determine what's all too likely to happen to most of your students for most of the rest of their lives if Reaganism continues. They will be out of sight and out of mind, existing somewhere way behind even the command to "motivate the spider."

In its nostalgias for the stable family household, the patriarchal dignity of the work of the "head" of the household, the "sacred duty" of motherhood, the value and importance of "traditional" educational knowledge, and so forth, New Right politics speaks directly to those who feel themselves already slipping out of sight and out of mind. It is precisely as nostalgic reconstructions that such New Right ideals then remain necessary to the organizing terms of class-as-lifestyle, something to be at once satirized and yet scrupulously preserved. But the dissonant space made available by this necessary presence of the New Right is also an opportunity for a countereducation about mass culture from within educational institutions; it is one way of finding an answer to the question of what politics are possible *to* critical analysis. And for any viable politics of the future, that opportunity cannot be quietly, conveniently ceded to the nostalgic terms of explanation the New Right will continue to supply.

FIVE

When I Win the Lottery:
Educating Taste in a Consumer Culture

To the extent lifestyle identifies social position, taste becomes both an "expression" of lifestyle and a vehicle of social mobility. Taste names how you get to a position as well as its performative expressivity; it is a matter of lifestyle *education*. In his attack on the "tenured radicals" he sees as now in charge of university education in the humanities, Roger Kimball complains that the very "idea of literary quality that transcends the contingencies of race, gender, and the like or that transcends the ephemeral attractions of popular entertainment is excoriated as naive, deliberately deceptive, or worse" (xv). But he only exposes thereby the lifestyle sensitivities of the would-be "natural aristocrat" whose tastes suggest that race as well as entertainment should properly belong to the contingent beach curiosities of summer vacation. Indices of taste can indeed seem at home in this fluid of "natural" qualities, "inherent" sensibility, the graceful outer expression of inner nature. In the logic of lifestyle, however, taste has become amphibious. It is equally at home on the immediate landscape of technoideological coding of position, gill rhythm mutating into expansion slots of connectivity linking the organism to whatever available ledge it finds for itself, Kimball's flailing sea fins becoming the chips and motherboards that give purchase on airy nothings, commanding endless sparkling pixels to knit in the spaces and move. The education of taste must then occur in an intertidal zone, registering the continual shock of contact felt all across the borderlands, altering the scene before one's very eyes. Everyone knows by now that such zones are "environmentally sensitive"; it should be no surprise therefore to find in the processes of educating taste also a clash of sensitivities as whole fields shift, exposing their inhabitants—Kimball no less than "tenured radicals"—to different pressure and intensity levels. "Ephemera," after all, is just another name for taste's intertidal environment, the sensitivities of its amphibious inhabitants.

Pierre Bourdieu's exhaustive analysis of indices of taste in *Distinction* is beginning to be recognized as an invaluable field guide to the politics of educating taste, even with the difficulties of translating from a French to a U.S. context. But there's a great deal more to be found in *Distinction* than support for various current projects to "expose" standards of high-culture taste such as Kimball's "literary quality." Bourdieu makes available more than the networks of correspondences between "natural" sensibilities and the pressure-sensitive accumulations of "cultural capital" that reveal high culture. If not always foregrounded explicitly in his analysis, it seems clear that the politics of educating taste that emerges across these correspondences everywhere involves issues of *field constitution:* of what counts as a "field" where expressions of taste are recognized and find their force. Kimball's "problem," after all, lies in the proliferation of fields of taste other than the "literary," as well as in the "demise" of a concern for "quality."

For Bourdieu, differential indices of taste ultimately mark distinction as freedom from what he calls a "logic of necessity," and as the social distance from those who are condemned, in contrast, to operate by that logic. The education of taste must then be a process that not only instructs behavior within recognizable fields of taste, but also produces continually shifting boundary conditions that demarcate zones of *necessity.* Taste can change only as necessity changes, for if taste always identifies a distance from the necessary, shifts in taste simultaneously involve shifts in what counts as the necessary. The relentless anti–avant-gardism of *Distinction* is simply a matter of having understood how completely avant-gardism also depends on engineering this proliferation of the necessary, it being indispensable to the emergence of "new fields" and "new tastes." Intellectual and artistic movements are not thereby reduced to nothing more than the parade of fashion. Rather, the ephemera of fashion can be recognized as likewise belonging to and helping to define the pervasive educational processes of a politics of taste.

More generally, however, the academic study of "popular entertainment"—even when it is, to Kimball's dismay, linked to "race, gender, and the like"—itself often trails the vacational mentality of "slumming," and, as Bourdieu warns, a politics of location. The sensitivities of academic study are trained to positional indices that continue to respect specific principles of field constitution, even as they focus the deployment of multiple countertastes challenging received notions of transcendent "quality." Unlike Kimball, such studies may have no difficulty at all looking to Camper Van Beethoven as well as Beethoven, and in understanding how the former can function in both the pleasures of a certain kind of taste and the politics of a countertaste in its disrespect for high-culture standards. But the perception of conflict here, the political clash of differently educated sensitivities, remains securely within the field of music; what's at issue is which music, for whom. Without denying the importance of such conflicts or their political stakes, I want to describe the education of taste in ways that recognize not only such intrafield conflicts but also the conflicted positionalities at stake in field constitution. Educating taste is a matter of social mobilities, of technologies of motion as well as felicities of expression, and mobilities in this sense involve the always changing borderlands of any possible field.

From within positional dispositions other than the academic, rock may appear as a subcategory of the technologies of sound (not quite the same thing as "music"); from somewhere else it may seem a virulent pedagogy of sex education, and from still another disposition it will be a primary *narrative* scenario of play with dolls, as in the recent "tot rock" event where Barbie arrived to premiere a new song and Hammer a new doll. These aren't simply different ways to think about or to assign a taste value to rock music; rock appears differently as a field to the extent that the indices attached to its "musical quality" are made secondary to other and more fundamental indices of taste. If you understand rock as encouraging "sexually deviant" behavior, your counterstrategy won't necessarily be getting teenagers interested in symphonies instead. For Christian fundamentalists, for example, "heavy metal" is first of all an expression of "perverted" sexuality, its rhythms first of all sexual rhythms, and any claim that metal is legitimate music wouldn't look like an outrage to musical taste, but simply a stupefying inability to understand the real issues. From this perspective, "intellectuals," as usual, just don't have a clue where they are, what field they're in.

Thus "field" as I will use the term designates less where conflicts
of taste are located than what conflicts of taste produce as a politics
of location, of field constitution. Conflicts have to do with what
counts as a field, not only with standards of quality within fields. As
Bourdieu suggests, field constitution then inevitably registers the
intersections of "necessity" and "freedom from necessity"; fields are
produced as those intersections are redefined and deployed differently across the mobilities of location. Taste may then seem everywhere a matter of leisure-time luxury, a function of the freedoms
of consumption, but, as Bourdieu also remarks, "the consumption
of goods no doubt always presupposes a labour of appropriation,
to different degrees depending on the goods and the consumers, or,
more precisely, that the consumer helps to produce the product he
consumes, by a labour of identification and decoding which, in the
case of a work of art, may constitute the whole of the consumption
and gratification, and which requires time and dispositions acquired
over time" (100).

Consumption itself is work, and no less than "real work" can demand the investment of time "and dispositions acquired over time."
Yet it can afford pleasure as well, and, like many academics study-
ing "mass culture," Andrew Ross would mark a certain "disrespect"
in popular tastes for the "serious intellectual labor" commanded by
the consumption of high-culture artifacts Bourdieu describes (Ross,
59; after quoting the passage above from Bourdieu). The consumer
intersections of labor/pleasure, that is, like the intersections of ne-
cessity/freedom, function everywhere in the processes of field constitution. This is a rather different matter than the assumption of
already existing fields that would yield variable measures of work
and pleasure. Despite Ross's suggestion, mass culture education of
taste doesn't simply privilege pleasure over work, in reverse symmetry to the typical academic valorization of the labor of appropriation.
Field constitution itself is a different process.

You can begin to get out of that reversal schema of labors and
pleasures when you forget for the moment things like rock con-
certs and midnight *Rocky Horror Picture Shows* and Cindy Sherman
photographs, and think instead of something like buying over-the-
counter cold medicine or kitchen cabinet hardware. These activities,
after all, are no less a part of mass culture consumption and yield
no less significant indices of taste, even if from within academic

principles of field constitution consumer practices here don't really look like they involve fields *of taste* at all. In whatever variable ratios, however, both labors and pleasures function also as promise, and it is in terms of promises that mass culture field constitution can perhaps most easily be understood educationally. What Bourdieu might call a disposition to seek esthetic gratification from reading "high" literary texts is obviously learned, but learned in a context where the foregrounded valorization of labors and pleasures in the reading depends on the implicit promise of functionally isolating "literature" as a field from other activities. The labors *and* pleasures can be foregrounded only because academic principles of field constitution designate "reading literature" as so clearly and "naturally" a field of taste (however contested its borders) that its constitution as a field can be ignored and attention focused instead on the time necessary for appropriation and the multiple, often conflicting standards that command the field.

In contrast, cold medicine advertisements set nowhere near the same value on the time of appropriation, and often hype the pleasures of the product only tongue-in-cheek. It may "taste" better than other medicines, but it's still medicine. What such advertisements promise instead is a far more directly visible isolation of field constitution as itself an important process. You will be able to make it through work tomorrow, and remain congenial to your associates, because of your wisdom (or more likely that of your loving spouse) in having learned to isolate as special in the midst of all your activities the short time it takes to hit the drugstore and get the medicine. The education, that is, has to do in part with how and why to recognize buying cold medicine *as a field of taste*, and that education may well involve a certain contempt for what then appears to be the intellectual lack of respect for the field as a field. It's a field such as over-the-counter cold medicine that may be the Rodney Dangerfield—the title character, as it were, of Ross's *No Respect*—of *both* labors and pleasures in comparison to a highly valorized activity such as charting the punned intricacies of *Finnegans Wake*. But then again, snot-dribbled puns don't help much to establish you as a "person of taste" at work. What is promised is a different kind of gratification predicated on different principles of field constitution, and which evidences a "disrespect" not only for socially certified intellectual guidance systems of taste, but also for the very fields of academic taste where they are exercised and determined. In *Caddy-shack* Dangerfield, after all, played an earlier and much more raucous version of the "back to school" character Ross discusses.

In previous chapters, I've often focused deliberately on what in the context of taste are likely to seem odd, peripheral sorts of things such as car maintenance literature. Even if it is easy enough to recognize, for example, the "choice" of a BMW over a Ford pickup as no less an expression of taste than the choice of a Puccini opera over Dwight Yoakam, questions about car *maintenance* don't seem central to issues of taste in the same way. What I want to argue now is that the "odd" and "peripheral" are often crucial to a mass culture education of taste, insofar as they function in a redefinition of categories of taste; that is, they constitute fields of taste across very different indices than established academic field schemas. Thus so-called popular taste as it exists in relation to mass culture constructions is not just a matter of opposing Camper Van Beethoven to Beethoven, or Public Enemy to Mahler or *Doogie Howser* to Proust. "Popular taste" in all its multiplicities takes advantage of the educational promises of mass culture in terms of the instabilities of field constitution as well. The "disrespect" for "intellectuals" may take the form of a challenge to what is perceived as an "intellectual" interest in *either* Camper Van or Beethoven, and correspondingly, a challenge to an "intellectual" disregard for things like buying over-the-counter medicines, as if such buying decisions didn't figure in any crucially important field of taste.

As they saturate more and more aspects of "daily life" with their powers of educating taste, however, odd and peripheral fields of mass culture also begin to make visible a sense in which taste is never only a matter of consumption. The intersections of the labor and pleasure of appropriation in advertisements for cold medicines, as my example implied, are extended to include as well the intersections of labor as job, as occupation, with the practices of consumption. Thus while within the social organization of class-as-lifestyle, taste does identify specific performative powers within the field of consumption generally, it also and everywhere mediates the transformation from social distinctions plotted across occupational stratification and the organization of work to the rearticulation of such distinctions across consumer performances. More or less explicitly, more or less visibly, indices of taste continue to carry a residue of that directional process of transformation. In odd and peripheral fields, the relative importance of time signals, precisely, the visibility of the residue; it marks consumption as always looking over its shoulder at the pressures of time demands imposed by work. Hence direction and duration themselves become conflicted issues in the politics of taste. As Bourdieu often emphasizes, not only must tastes be learned (and the learning itself takes time) but the exercise of taste involves a certain duration as well, which in many cases must be wrested from work pressures.

High-culture taste is likely to dismiss the "popular" as merely a demand for "instant gratification." A "high" theory of "low" taste, however, is just as likely to mystify that demand in the metaphysics of "distracted" gratification in a temporal grain of sand. In "Banality in Cultural Studies," Meaghan Morris argues that ostensibly "anti" academic attention to "the popular" and its "distracted" gratifications in these terms has the paradoxical effect of returning cultural studies to the very thesis of "cultural dopes" that informs high-culture theory:

> The problem is that in antiacademic pop-theory writing . . . a stylistic enactment of the "popular" as *essentially* distracted, scanning the surface, and short on attention span, performs a retrieval, at the level of *enunciative* practice, of the thesis of "cultural dopes." In the critique of which—going right back to the early work of Stuart Hall, not to mention Raymond Williams—the project of cultural studies effectively and rightly began. (Morris's italics, 24)

In emphasizing the connections between taste in consumption and working conditions, I want to suggest that the so-called distractions of "the popular" are instead part of a complex process of negotiating such connections. What's "distracting," in other words, are the continually intrusive demands of working conditions on the "leisure time" of consumption. "Intermittent" viewing and the like is not by any means always a restless search for instant gratification. So far from being "distraction," it can and often does register instead the pressures of working conditions very different from the conditions of academic work.

In contrast to academic study, however, mass culture field constitution often simply ignores gratification, to focus on the importance of the very possibility of duration. Pleasure, that is, doesn't come from the promise that *gratification* might be instant, but that *whatever* arrives, whether particularly gratifying in itself or not, will at least arrive within the parameters of available duration. Taste as it appears in such odd and peripheral fields, emphasizing duration, then reveals much more clearly than elsewhere the ensemble of relations linking consumer practices to working conditions, in ways I will explore in some detail in the next section. The speed in which cold medicines, for example, can be advertised, purchased, consumed, and "put to work" openly acknowledges the demands on time imposed from elsewhere. In fact, however, a taste for high-culture novels is no less involved in that ensemble of relations. Emphasizing the labors and pleasures of appropriation is important not only in itself but also in order to signal the distance from time demands, to show just how far taste has traveled from any such temporally imposed necessities as are evident in cold-medicine advertisements.

The dynamics of mass culture education of taste, unlike more or less "traditional" practices of an academic education, thrive on the instabilities of field constitution as much as on intrafield change. For reasons I'll suggest later, such instabilities are fundamental to the performative indices of class-as-lifestyle social organization. Because it makes available different possibilities of field constitution, however, mass culture education opens up not only the possibility of multiple forms of countertastes but also ways to renegotiate the always present linkages of working conditions and conditions of consumption across the mediating powers of taste. For it's not only the case—as the work associated with the Birmingham Centre in England has emphasized—that various subcultures might alter in their responses the ideologies coded into mass culture constructions. There's also a sense in which "resistance" has to do with refusing the distance between consumption on the one hand and working conditions on the other. That is, resistances in these terms are not so much expressions of countertaste: challenges to normative determinations of taste within fields. They contest the very *direction* of taste, construct what might then be called in contrast a *counter-taste*, a challenge to taste's mediating direction of movement from work and the organization of work to the conditions of consumption in the terms of class-as-lifestyle. Counter-taste runs counter to the logic of lifestyle education itself. Thus resistances as counter-taste bear little relation to either the blurring of stratified categories of discrimination within fields or to the "radical" textual play valo-

rized in familiar postmodern notions of resisting countertastes. As
I will argue, they work with odd and peripheral fields not as some
postmodern "marginal," but as transitory, throwaway, obsolete. By
analogy to what I have been calling the repair work on obsolete
technologies, resistances here might be understood as a similar kind
of repair of obsolete *ideologies*.

Fields of taste are produced at the always shifting intersections
of necessity and freedom, of the consumer labors and pleasures of
appropriation, of the demands of work and the "leisure" time of
consumption. While within academic principles of field constitution, Kimball and his antagonists might worry about or applaud the
"collapse" of intrafield standards of quality, mass culture lifestyle
education not only acknowledges but often encourages the field instabilities that appear across all these intersections. In what follows,
I'm relatively uninterested in trying to "side with" some imputed
popular taste and its "disrespect" for academic standards and for
"intellectuals." The resistances I will focus involve instead the survival skills of survivals, the cultures of obsolescence that, in the very
midst of educative taste and its mobilities, have learned to read the
tidal shifts of field instabilities, collect and use the leftovers of academic conflicts to construct shelter. Even in the worst of times such
survivals can exert the pressures of directional counter-taste as also a
counter-education, a challenge to the social organization of lifestyle
and its pedagogical powers of educating taste.

I

Adorno's well-known essay "On Popular Music" seems an unlikely source to learn anything much about popular taste or about
conflicts within mass culture education of taste. Critics of the essay
have pointed quite rightly to Adorno's nostalgia for the "organic
wholeness" of Beethoven, to the fact that he knew little about jazz or
even Tin Pan Alley music, and even less about the conditions of their
production and reception. The essay is built on the relatively simple
premise that the modern organization of labor requires a mass culture that will both stimulate workers and "distract" them from the
repetitive, boring, mind-numbing conditions of their work—that
mass culture is only a spectacular adjunct to the control of work in
a capitalist economy. It seems to me, however, that what this prem-

ise recognizes as a profound connection between the conditions of work and the conditions of cultural consumption makes a great deal of sense. The immediate problem in Adorno's use of the premise lies less in the way it kept him aloof from any knowledge of mass culture consumption—free to rhapsodize over Beethoven—than in how it skewed what relatively little he knew about actual working conditions for most people.

So much sociological study, like that of Adorno, has accepted (with variations) the litany of "repetitive," "mind-numbing," and so on, that by means of what Bourdieu calls "theory effects" (the repetition of such theoretical constructions as they circulate in other contexts) workers themselves may often repeat the same litany, in interviews such as those in Terkel's *Working*, for example. But try to read between the lines of "theory effects" in such interviews and imagine to whatever extent possible these descriptions of the routine even of an assembly-line job apart from the familiar categories supplied by theory. I think it likely then you might recognize a sense in which the job in fact requires a prodigiously concentrated intellectual attention, where the very repetitiveness of the tasks constitutes a clear and present danger in "letting your mind wander" or "becoming bored" or whatever. The tasks may be repetitive, but that also means they must be done in exactly the same way each time, or there is risk not only of disrupting the process but often of physical injury as well. From the outside, that may look like becoming a mind-numbed robot, but as you're doing the work it feels like a continual, pressured intensity of focus, which it is necessary to sustain all the time.* As a result, at the end of eight hours it's your *mind*, not just your body, that's dead tired. Secretarial work, for example—and most service work—is if anything far more mentally demanding than the assembly line. No one actually serves McDonald's hamburgers for a working day with an "automatically" glued-on plastic

---

*The most serious work injury I've ever observed was at a flour packaging and distribution warehouse. All the victim's co-workers, myself included, suggested immediately that the victim "just wasn't thinking about what he was doing" for the bare split second in which it happened. Doubtless had any of us been interviewed at some other time—for the purposes of sociological study—about the process of work, loading hundred-pound flour sacks onto boxcars, we would have faithfully repeated that it was a mechanical, boring routine. But in the event, we reacted immediately to what we knew in fact to be a necessity for constant, focused attention.

smile. It's an intense mental effort to sustain it, and it wears people out to do it.

Now if you can imagine a work day spent in such intensities of intellectual effort, and imagine it as a work day that happens every day, you might also be able to imagine not only the "disrespect," but the utter contempt you might often feel for an invitation either to think carefully about Beethoven's surprisingly intricate counterpoint or to enjoy the pleasures of the counterhegemonic insouciance of Camper Van Beethoven's electric violin. That contempt doesn't come from having been so immersed in some nonintellectual immediacy of the body that you can't turn your mind on, nor from having been bored all day at work and just wanting some excitement instead of all this heavy stuff. It's a result of busting your mind as much as your ass all day long, with no control whatsoever over the demands to do so. Thus an invitation from somewhere else to whatever labors or pleasures looks like nothing so much as itself an expression of contempt directed at you. That is, the disrespect that "intellectuals" are likely to find so much a part of "popular taste" is all too easy to misrecognize as having to do with the qualities of a particular field of taste. Rather, it can involve first of all the relations between working conditions and conditions of consumption, and second, a reaction to what is perceived as "intellectual" ignorance about that relation. The issue isn't really a matter of field qualities but of field constitution, and of how that constitution negotiates the boundaries between work and consumption.

Temporal duration, or more exactly possibilities of control over duration, play an obviously crucial role in that negotiation. The relevant characteristic of the working conditions I'm assuming is not that the tasks are repetitive and hence boring, but that they require a continuous mental attention. As a result, the promises of the field will seem most attractive when, regardless of the labors or pleasures "intrinsic" to the field, the field itself is constituted in such a way that, utterly unlike work, it permits some control over the duration of attention. That is, the contrast at stake here isn't between, say, a long, comfortable, and leisurely evening absorbed in television programs with all their pleasures, and on the other hand having to dress up, go to the opera, and prepare for a careful discrimination of the performance of this mezzo-soprano and the one you heard last year. What seems available from television—and what you would know better than to expect from opera—is the possibility that you can tune "in" or "out" at will with no penalties attached. Thus, rather than some gratifying "appropriation" of and "identification" with what you see, the pleasure lies in your control over the duration of seeing, because this control is likely to be unavailable altogether at work, in lower-level service-sector jobs especially.

From this perspective, what marks "intellectual" taste is a process of field constitution that takes control for granted, and hence a social location where you can assume as a given the freedom to engage in appropriation and identification, and read off indices of taste from the process. Such "intellectual" taste may of course valorize soap operas rather than opera, or effect some collapse of the lines of distinction that separate the two forms. But when that happens, it is perceived from elsewhere, from other locations, as "slumming." And the perception of slumming isn't just a matter of objecting to a "simulated" identification with a taste "intellectuals" don't really possess. In some sense whether the identification is real or simulated isn't an issue. Slumming involves a more fundamental error in understanding what's at stake. Mass culture constructions can then seem more attractive than what is highly valued in the organization of an academic education—even when the latter might often involve those very mass culture constructions—because mass culture field constitution does not necessarily take freedom of control for granted. Thus fields that look "odd" and "peripheral" to academic education become crucially important to a process of mass culture education that recognizes the importance of achieving freedom of control.

It's perhaps necessary at this point to raise in more detail the question of whether the odd and peripheral in this sense can be understood as fields of taste at all. If, as I've suggested in my example, the "pleasure" of TV viewing may lie simply in phasing in and out when you want to, then what's on the screen would appear virtually irrelevant. And while such viewing may be an appropriate enough subject for the sociology of work, the irrelevance of viewer program choice would make it hard to recognize any sense in which taste is crucial here. Yet it is viewing. And it does involve at some level a "choice"; it's not likely to be replaced happily by a night at the opera.

I think it's possible to cut across the dilemma by recognizing taste as never *only* a matter of consumption, but as directly or indirectly mediating the intersections of working conditions and conditions of consumption. Assuming that taste begins somewhere on the far side of "mere" control over duration makes that process of mediation invisible, but it doesn't break the connection. The assumption simply implies that certain working conditions are also a precondition for the exercise of "real" taste, in whatever form. That is, the demands necessarily imposed by working conditions can be put at more or less distance, can appear more or less directly relevant to fields of taste, but some connection is always inherent in *any* expression of taste. If, as in my example, the "pleasure" of viewing comes with control over duration, that's certainly a different expression of taste than rapt attention to soap operas, than scorn for their banalities, or than re-working them into instances of postmodern textuality. But all four of these possibilities represent specific deployments of taste across the intersections of working conditions and conditions of consumption. As I suggested earlier, odd and peripheral fields emphasize these connections rather than valorizing distance and freedom from necessity by effacing them.

What's on the screen as a focus of intermittent or ostensibly "distracted" viewing is then not irrelevant by any means. If there is to be any pleasure from the control of duration, the exercise of that control has to occur without penalty. It wouldn't after all be control if, having phased out for twenty minutes, you come back to find yourself completely at sea about what's going on. While that might not be quite the same "penalty" you would incur by failing to log a rotation of goods on the assembly line or having the manager catch you badmouthing a McDonald's customer, it's nevertheless in its own way a certain threat to control. Principles of field constitution that permit intermittent viewing can then result in things like advertisements for over-the-counter medicines and the like, which neither last very long nor promise a lengthy duration in realization. The fields that result can seem indeed odd and peripheral through and through. But while soap operas are often also viewed intermittently, in this context their most obvious characteristic is the length, the way in which they go on and on and on. Soap operas can be viewed intermittently, yet it's no less true that they are often viewed in their entirety. Indeed, the viewing time can even be extended into reading soap commentary such as that in *Soap Opera Weekly*, much as your reading of Proust might extend into *PMLA* commentary. Soap operas, that is, afford a particularly good example of potentially very different tastes across the variables of temporal duration as those variables function in the constitution of fields. Surely the question of exactly what kind of field it is is open, when you can snatch it up as quickly as buying cold medicine or take as long with it as a Proust novel.

II
_____

Tania Modleski and others have argued that soap operas seem interminable in their weaving and unweaving of narrative, and hence likely to frustrate expectations of closure, of the "well-made" plot. Likewise, although the grid of character positions in soaps may appear the most banal division of heroes and villains, angels and whores, in fact viewer identifications rarely observe such convenient ideological distribution. Not only do characters often obligingly change position, but the positionalities themselves can be invested with considerable counterenergies and excesses that disrupt ideological schemas as much as the narrative frustrates closure. Before turning to these elements of narrative form and ideological representation, however, I want to focus first on the complicated interplays of duration that occur in what soap operas promise as a field of mass culture. The instability that at the level of narrative form appears as a potentially interminable plot structure, and at the level of ideological representation as a continual process of collapse and reshaping, also disturbs the very constitution of soap operas as a field. As I suggested, on the one hand, and similar to "peripheral" fields such as buying over-the-counter medicine (something in fact likely to be advertised during commercial breaks in soaps) soaps permit the promise of a certain intermittence. It is possible to tune "in" or "out" and still keep up with what's going on, to miss whole episodes and even groups of episodes and return successfully. On the other hand, however, they promise as well the possibility of sustained absorption in the program, the extended duration of labors and pleasures of identification.

It's true enough that soap operas don't pretend to be "high culture," and in some sense even define themselves against perceived norms of high-culture taste. But that recognition won't get very far in understanding either the logic or the possible effects of this double promise of field constitution. Most obviously, the doubleness of promise situates soaps as a field that can function in different ways within specific constellations of relations among fields. If, for example, you're typically an intermittent viewer, that doesn't preclude the possibility that soaps might nevertheless rank very high within the range of fields of taste that seem for whatever reasons especially crucial. Because in terms of some absolute percentage relatively little of your time is spent in viewing soaps doesn't mean that their importance is therefore diminished in relation to other fields. Conversely, the promise of absorption doesn't mean necessarily that soaps will rank highly. You may even recognize soaps as a particular addiction and still assign little value to the fact. On this level, the doubleness of promise thus permits what, in contrast to a high-culture taste for reading Proust novels, say, is a remarkably casual relation between value and time investments. Because reading Proust seems always to require a considerable investment of time, it's much more likely than with soaps that the time set aside for reading will always be valued highly.

However, on another level the promise of intermittence locates a negotiation between working conditions and conditions of consumption that situates time itself in a very different schema of values. Intermittence assigns a taste value, as it were, to time, in direct opposition to what will then in contrast seem the luxury of "intellectuals" able to spend their brains and time knocking about with untranslatable French expressions in Proust and the like. For "ordinary" people working "ordinary" jobs, such "intellectual" taste and its imperatives become just a pain in the ass. Like intellectual taste, however, and unlike intermittence, absorption also depends on an extended temporal duration. Thus rather than challenging the luxury time of intellectuals, absorption instead can be understood to challenge the completely different demands imposed by "ordinary" working conditions. Absorption affords an opportunity to at least imagine that you can "shove the job" and extend yourself instead into the identifications with the soap-opera world, just as intellectuals absorb themselves in whatever stuff they read. That you do so with soaps rather than with Proust is to be sure a powerful index of taste. But within the logic of the double promise of field constitution in soaps, it occurs across a particular negotiation with working conditions that remains invisible so long as the focus stays simply at the level of contrasting a taste for soaps with a taste for Proust.

Finally, and thinking now about both points together, the doubleness of promise makes possible for at least certain viewers a way to negotiate what look like utterly different, if no less equally formidable kinds of impositions: on the one hand, the demands of working conditions that extort a toll on intellectual resources as well as on physical resources; and on the other, the imperatives of high-culture taste, from which, as Bourdieu's analysis reminds us, no "subordinate" taste is ever completely independent. Very simply, in taking up a promise of intermittence, you must also acknowledge the necessities of working conditions that permit only scattered and discontinuous viewing time. But that acknowledgment, as I argued, can also function as a challenge to the very principles of high-culture field constitution, setting a very different value on time and temporal duration, so that high-culture taste will appear merely an intellectual luxury. Conversely, in taking up the promise of absorption, you enable a certain challenge not to intellectual taste but to the necessities of working conditions; in effect, again, you "shove the job" and its demands for the duration. In that sense, however, you also acknowledge the principles of high-culture field constitution, which always require an extended duration for the labors and pleasures of consumption. In playing these combinations against and with each other, the shifting terms of acknowledgment and challenge can function as a means to preserve a certain openness of possibility against impositions of *both* kinds. That is, the instabilities of soaps as a field make available, at least potentially, a multiedged weapon of defense, a way of warding off both the necessities of working conditions and the imperatives of high-culture taste.

Those instabilities do permit a certain strategic shifting on the part of viewers, a relative power of control over *intermittence and absorption themselves*, depending on the circumstances. While intermittence may force the acknowledgment of working conditions, the ability to shift strategically to the promise of absorption is available to counter that acknowledgment, just as the ability to shift from absorption to the promise of intermittence counters the implicit acknowledgment of principles of high-culture field constitution. With such shifting, you don't thereby "escape" the field of soaps, nor would you want to, for you learn instead to make use of its instabilities strategically, to control passage through the field on your own terms, deploying its promises where they do the most good in specific circumstances. Soaps become a weapon to use rather than simply a field of taste.

I'm not suggesting that soaps are produced to facilitate this operation of strategic shifting. I will argue in the next section that educationally (and like self-help literature) soaps model performative strategies, educating taste in relation to the social organization of class-as-lifestyle. The immediate point, however, is twofold. Whatever educational functions soaps perform do not preclude the strategic shifting I've been describing, insofar as such shifts simply take advantage of the instabilities necessary to the taste-oriented educational functions of soaps. Also, as a weapon of defense—and hence in some sense also a form of "resistance"—strategic shifting isn't accomplished by "recoding" soap-opera ideological representations. That is, the resistance involved here is not a matter of introducing "discontinuities" or "excesses" or whatever that disrupt some fixed schema of representation. Indeed, it isn't directly keyed to specific representations within the field at all, but to the possibilities permitted by field constitution. Thus to the extent principles of constitution—especially the way in which temporal duration negotiates the intersections of working conditions and conditions of consumption—are ignored, resistance in this form becomes at best invisible, at worst misrecognized as "passive" compliance with coded ideologies, as being trapped within soaps' field of representation and unable to create alternatives.

Once you assume what's at stake in soaps is a matter of what they represent and how they represent it, you've already bypassed the battle for viewing time and what *it* might represent, how in this context "escape" from soaps or challenges to soap representations is not the issue at all. Your taste is located at such a distance from the mediations of working conditions and conditions of consumption that the stakes can appear in terms of ideological representations. From this distanced perspective, it is altogether likely that those viewers for whom the battle for viewing time *is* a primary concern will appear to be in need of "education," of having their eyes opened to both the "reactionary" codes that can appear in soaps, and the "radical" means of disrupting their powers. As viewers, they will appear to be struggling (if struggling at all) with obsolete, outdated equipment and knowledges. (As indeed they may be, since they would probably not recognize themselves in up-to-date visions of Baudrillard's "hyperreal" or Deleuze's "nomads" or Giroux's "genuine opposition" and so on.) The point, however, is not only that the "obsolete" in this sense is what they have available to work with, but that one of the targets of resistance is, precisely, that determination of obsolescence; resistance involves a refusal to grant that the stakes necessarily appear elsewhere. Rather than simply "disrespect" for "intellectual" standards and "high-culture" taste, what's involved is then a certain disrespect for *taste itself.* That is, it's not only a matter of different "standards" of taste, but of resistance to taste's logic of direction toward consumer fields, where it becomes no longer functionally useful in relation to the implacable demands of working conditions. As a result, no matter how taste might be reconstituted to include a valorization of soap operas, it misses the point of what resistances are all about in these terms.

I don't want to imply that viewers caught up in the particular kind of negotiations I've described between working conditions and conditions of consumption never attend at all to ideological representations or are oblivious to the peculiarities of narrative form in soaps. What Bourdieu would call their dispositions toward viewing, however, don't automatically locate such frames of attention as the most immediately crucial. Nevertheless, the instabilities of field constitution that do function immediately are themselves linked to what, borrowing from Modleski's argument, I indicated initially about instabilities of narrative and representation. A "well-made" plot, for example, moving inexorably from beginning through middle to end, may lend itself to a certain kind of absorption, but not the absorption that can go hand in hand with a simultaneous promise of intermittence. Likewise, in soaps, fundamental character changes that from the perspective of ideological coherence can and often do appear astonishing and "unmotivated" function as a condition for keeping both promises alive. More important, while I've discussed working conditions so far as if they were gender-indiscriminate, obviously they aren't. It might be anticipated that viewer negotiations of working conditions and conditions of consumption will not only vary across gender-marked possibilities, but almost inevitably intersect at some point with ideologically coded gender representations in soap programs, especially when, even provisionally, the soap-opera promise of absorption is taken up. In turning more directly to these issues, however, it should be anticipated as well that resistances will continue to be intricated with negotiations of working conditions in ways that elaborate what I have identified as a counter-taste.

III

As the name implies, soap operas have been an explicitly gender-identified field. With the proliferation of very different kinds of soaps and soap-related programming, such as talk shows, however, and the differentially indexed products now typically advertised throughout the wide spectrum of soaps, the field no longer seems unambiguously feminine. This is not only a matter of actual percentages of viewers, but of role permissions and of the segmentation visible in advertising. Likewise, soap viewing no longer seems securely identified with an "uneducated" and "lower-class" audience. College students and college-educated people are a recognizable audience as well. I think it's a dangerous generalization, however, to move immediately toward some implication that soaps thereby appeal to a large "popular taste," that their "appeal" somehow transcends gender and educationally marked social boundaries. Among other things, my discussion of promise and of field constitution is intended to suggest that a so-called popular taste for soaps is by no means uniform. Further, it evidences a great many different *uses* to which soap viewing might be put, and to that extent can function as a counter-logic to taste's mediating powers. Thus while college-educated men as well as working-class women who aren't college educated, for example, may both watch soaps, the viewing will function differently for the latter than for the former.

The very diversity of soaps and the diversity of their viewing audiences, however, while indicating the dangers of assuming some transcendent "popular appeal," also suggest a sense in which, educationally, soaps do mobilize a great deal of the spectrum of mass culture constructions, in something of the same way a core discipline functions within the institutions of formal education. What's at stake educationally in soaps affects any number of other fields as well, again much like developments in core disciplines in the university. Advertising constructions, for example, will depend on market research analysis that tries to collect as much data as possible about segmented soap audiences, in order to predict how best to reach whom and when, how high to set advertising rates, and so on. Within mass culture as also mass education, soaps as a kind of core discipline then afford an obvious place to recognize how taste is educated to perform in terms assigned by indices of lifestyle. In this context, instabilities of narrative form and ideological representation can on the one hand be linked to the double promise of field constitution, through the latter helping to ensure a certain size and diversity of audience. But on the other hand, they must be recognized as modeling particular strategies of performative agency. Within the social organization of class-as-lifestyle, destabilization by no means equates immediately to subversive ideological disruption. The lack of a well-made plot and clearly motivated characters may disturb certain traditional academic expectations, but such things aren't at all incongruent with promised powers of performative agency.

Rather than trying to sketch the detail of representational instabilities in soaps, it's worth beginning instead by what in this context appears as an anomaly, the one character position in soaps that possesses an often remarkable *stability* of representation. And that, of course, is what Modleski identifies in *Loving with a Vengeance* as the position of the "villainess," the targeted "bitch" who continually keeps any number of plot sequences in motion. To be sure, there are male "villains" in soaps, but in contrast to the villainess, it's increasingly rare to find a villain who remains the same throughout. Indeed, as Susan Jeffords has argued, it's no longer a surprise to find in soaps a male character who in earlier episodes had been involved even in the violence of rape, say, to emerge later as a "reformed" sensitive hero, someone to be forgiven and supported in his newly realized sensibility ("Performative," 111–13). Such a dramatic change is altogether unlikely to happen to the villainess.

Further, male characters who fundamentally change positions, like our "reformed" rapist, typically then come to possess a certain freedom of crossing back and forth across traditional gender roles, adopting specific roles at their option. That is, the "reform" itself in this case is likely to come about insofar as our hero learns to "identify with" the victim of rape, and hence learns not only a refusal of the "attitudes" that led to the rape in the first place, but how to continue the freedoms of a mobility of social position no longer constrained by fixed gender roles—without, of course, ever losing the sense of being a man. Men, in other words, can act differently as men. It's true enough that the typical soap villainess will often also possess a remarkable mobility—she's likely to be one of relatively few women in soaps who can move at ease in any number of different social situations—but that mobility remains nevertheless fundamentally different: whatever social spaces she occupies, she never really crosses gender roles. She may in certain instances act or "masquerade" as a man, but she is not permitted the performative agency of male characters, the sympathetic "identification with" that frees their newly emergent mobility.

More and more frequently, however, it's become possible to find "upwardly mobile" women in soaps: women who have, for example, gone to work in traditionally male fields, even at relatively high levels, and so on. But in these cases, there's still a third form of mobility at work, which might be identified as involving a rather curious oscillation: sometimes the character is a woman, but sometimes she is to be perceived as beyond gender markers altogether. That is, where the mobility of male characters will often be realized through a freedom to cross gender roles, and where in contrast the mobility of the villainess preserves gender identification as woman, here mobility across different social spaces seems predicated on at once preserving positional markers as woman and yet evidencing as well the capability on occasion to "rise above" all such "mere" gender identifications. If that capability—whatever exactly it may involve—doesn't appear, the role slides toward the positionality of the villainess, toward simply "being a bitch." It is not only soap operas that emphasize the dangers inherent in such a slide. One cartoon in a recent issue of *Working Woman* (a magazine directed at an upscale audience) illustrates the point dramatically, showing a well-tailored, clearly executive woman who in her secretary's eyes appears with the head of a dog.* In principle, at least, it would then seem that one obvious way to avoid these "dangers" would be to take up the option available even to rapists in soaps: namely, to learn the "identification with" that permits the freedom of crossing fixed gender roles. That such an option never really appears is a good clue to who actu-

---

*I owe the cartoon reference to Michelle Kendrick, who called my attention to it in "Coaxing Little Sister: Contemporary Women's Magazines and Construction of Gender," p. 13.

ally benefits from the mobilities of performance in the organization
of class-as-lifestyle. The destabilization of gender-identified roles
facilitates what nevertheless remains a primarily *masculine* power of
behaving differently. Men, again, can act differently as men; women
can act differently only by somehow appearing "beyond gender."

This process helps explain more clearly just what is involved in
the production of gender as "obsolete," a fundamental condition of
the emergent dominance of class-as-lifestyle organization. For valorized male characters, the obsolescence of gender appears to the extent gender identifications can be marked as optional; such characters
are in a position to choose, taking up whatever gender identifications might best be performed on the occasion. Upwardly mobile
women may of course be valorized in soaps, but here in contrast the
"option" is constrained to a matter of knowing when to function
"as a woman," and when instead it's necessary to move beyond such
merely social categories. That is, women in effect rarely get to function differently *as women* without risking being perceived as bitches.
Thus the obsolescence necessary to class-as-lifestyle is not really
the social category of gender, but specifically feminine-marked gender identifications, for women. These are embodied in soaps in the
position of the villainess, whose mobilities never escape her gender
role. The villainess, quite simply, is the perennially obsolete. Thus
all her contrivances and strategies, and all the powers of mobility
through which she deploys them, can't finally succeed. However, as
Modleski points out, they never completely fail either. As obsolete,
she won't eventually disappear completely into the past; she must
be continually produced in order to sustain the organization of the
present. In soaps, quite literally, it is the villainess who generates the
continual movements of the narrative

There is in principle still another character position available to
women in soaps, that of the "good mother," the woman who is at
once, like the villainess, securely anchored in a gender identification,
but utterly unlike her in that she has virtually no power of mobility.
Outside her "kingdom" in the home, she appears completely at a
loss. In a particularly interesting turn of her argument, Modleski
suggests that this position is relatively rarely represented as such in
the programming (92–93). It is instead reserved primarily for the
viewer, the woman watching the program, who if she could only
move into the complicated interstices of the action might somehow

manage to bring everything right. She can't, of course, and hence must be content with writing "fan letters" and the like, instructing particular characters of the dangers they're about to fall into. To the extent, however, that the good mother and the villainess are obviously linked in their fixed identifications, for Modleski this leads to a particular kind of psychological bind for women viewers:

> Since the spectator despises the villainess as the negative image of her ideal self, as she watches the villainess act out her own hidden wishes, she simultaneously sides with the forces conspiring against fulfillment of those wishes. As a result of this "internal contestation," the spectator comes to enjoy repetition for its own sake and takes her pleasure in the building up and tearing down of the plot. In this way, perhaps, soaps help reconcile her to the meaningless, repetitive nature of much of her life and work within the home. (97)

If, however, the psychological stakes for at least some women viewers (for it's dangerous to generalize too rapidly here) in this "internal contestation" have to do with positive and negative images of self, in social terms they involve the gender codings of powers of mobility. Unlike the good mother, whether as represented in the program or as a position available to the viewer, the villainess does have certain mobilities. The same fixed—albeit in psychological terms contradictorily valued—identification yields two very different powers of mobility. In social terms at least, the "way out" of that bind would then seem to be available in the positionalities of upwardly mobile women, that is, women who like the villainess can "move," but unlike the villainess, in "approved" ways.

But when you look a little more closely at what I called the "oscillation"—sometimes a woman / sometimes as if beyond gender identifications—on which such a way out would depend, it's far from clear exactly how it could ever be *learned*. If you ask in terms of actual performative strategies what it would be like to behave as if "beyond gender," it would seem to be necessary to begin by exploring the details of specifically indexed masculine behavior. It's difficult to know how you would know you were acting "beyond gender" without some learned understanding of masculine behavior as well as feminine behavior. But to "act like a man" is of course to risk appearing a "bitch," like the villainess masquerading as a man for "secretive," "manipulative" ends. Acquiring powers of mobility thus seems to require learning to perform the shifting balance of sometimes a woman / sometimes beyond gender, but educationally the latter remains a mystery. Even if in principle it might have some performative content, there's no way to learn what it involves without risking an identification that would effectively cancel the reason for which to learn it. Psychologically, the bind might be located for some women, as Modleski describes, in the doubleness of positive and negative images of self: around the figures of good mother and villainess. In social terms, however, that bind appears instead in the contradictory promise of mobility appearing in the ostensibly valorized positionalities of upwardly mobile women in soaps; it is their need to learn what remains a mysterious set of practices. Given the directions in which taste points for consumer identifications, the circumstances seem implacably circular. Any way out only turns into a dynamic that projects you back into the situation from which you needed to escape in the first place.

However, to the extent Modleski's argument begins to recover not only a field of consumer identifications but also a sense in which soap viewing might negotiate the demands of often very different working conditions, I think the possibility of certain resistances can be recognized. They would of necessity function less as countertastes than, again, as a counter-taste, an other direction altogether. This is so because, for women whose work might well lie both within the home and elsewhere, working conditions not only permit but enforce a certain kind of mobility, require action in very different social spaces. And while, as Modleski suggests, the work in either case may seem "meaningless" and "repetitive," by means of an identification with the villainess women can resist demands to perform both kinds of work, even challenge these demands, rather than succumbing to a kind of exhausted circularity.

In this context of enforced mobility, what becomes immediately valuable about the villainess is her ability to remain in control of herself across multiple social situations. She may then *represent* a "bad self," but that's less important than how her control of her actions suggests she possesses some "inner reserve" that enables such control. To have this reserve is useful if you must move back and forth between the demands of work at home and work elsewhere. The work tasks may not become any less meaningless and repetitive, but it doesn't follow that in doing them you also become meaningless and repetitive. Like the villainess, whose "real self" so often remains hidden behind a facade of behavior, you have a reserve available. Further, it's a reserve that can be "filled" in very different ways than with the "bad self" represented by the villainess. Precisely to the extent that the tasks performed seem meaningless and repetitive, they obviously aren't performed for your own "manipulative" ends. That is, they can't be felt as emerging from the designs of a "bad self" that resembles the villainess.

To resist in this way is not to escape the ideological coding of the villainess, but to repair the soap image of the villainess for strategic use. What in soap-opera terms is marked as the obsolete—the fixed-gender identification of the villainess whose scheming and manipulations will never really succeed in "today's world"—becomes available nevertheless as a weapon of resistance. To make use of the obsolescence of the villainess thus requires a certain labor of ideological repair. In soap-opera terms, the villainess represents not only a now obsolete "technology" for social mobility, but a "broken" one, one whose manifestations of self are obviously twisted, perverse, malign, and so on; and these manifestations of self never undergo the itinerary of reform available to rapists and other wonderfully reconstituted exemplars of male behavior. Yet broken, obsolete, or whatever, it's not really a position the motive force of soap plots can do without, and in its continually produced obsolescence it becomes continually available for use in resistance. It's always there, to be patched up and *used*, not in the consumer identifications of taste, but for the resisting purposes of a counter-taste.

The villainess is no less obsolete in the postmodern terminology of Baudrillard, for example, for whom any such notions of "reserve" and "control"—let alone "self"—appear as just so many littered fragments of a now vanishing social organization. Thus in a direct sense, the resistances an education of taste as carried out through soaps can never finally prevent, insofar as it remains impossible to get rid of the positionality of the villainess, can at least be rendered nugatory by a postmodern academic education. Whatever versions of Baudrillardian logic are at work simply function to complete the lesson, to take over where mass culture education ends, marking the "taste" at issue as hopelessly out of date. What mass culture can't eliminate, academic education obligingly makes, at best, invisible.

IV

There's little point here in idealizing the forms of resistance I've been describing; they don't eliminate the necessities imposed by the

demands of working conditions, nor the possibility of being perceived by family and co-workers as a "bitch." But they do wedge
a sense of control out of implacably difficult circumstances, and a
functional agency that remains vital to that control, even if by the
standards of performative agency it is hopelessly obsolete. Politically, then, unless resistances can be recognized in these terms and
built on, extended, and multiplied, not much can be expected of
them in terms of any "larger" social changes. Academic education
can begin to consolidate these resistances by not cooperating to preserve invisibility, which paradoxically might involve learning *not* to
take "popular taste" seriously. The pleasures of popular tastes may
seem to challenge the very notion of the serious; but the deeper reason is that taking popular taste seriously in academic terms is almost
inevitably to "update" it, to make this or that conception of popular taste "competitively innovative" in academic circumstances—to
make it, in short, a matter of taste rather than the practices of a
counter-taste. A taste for villainesses is not quite the same as the
repair of the villainess.

As updated to "taste," the obsolete and the uses of the obsolete
then become something like the esthetic of "leftovers" that Andy
Warhol describes in a passage Ross quotes almost at the end of the
section on camp in *No Respect*:

> I always like to work on leftovers, doing the leftover things. Things that
> were discarded and that everybody knew were no good, I always thought
> had a great potential to be funny. It was like recycling work. I always
> thought there was a lot of humor in leftovers. . . . I'm not saying that
> popular taste is bad so that what's left over is probably bad, but if you can
> take it and make it good or at least interesting, then you're not wasting
> as much as you would otherwise. You're recycling work and you're re-
> cycling people, and you're running your business as a byproduct of other
> businesses. Of other *directly competitive* businesses, as a matter of fact. So
> that's a very economical operating procedure. It's also the funniest oper-
> ating procedure because, as I said, leftovers are inherently funny. (Ross,
> 170; Warhol's italics)

Warhol's explanation has in fact not just one, but two very different antagonists, both of which are relevant to academic locations
of taste. There's not only the remote enclaves of the seriousness
of "high culture," but perhaps even more fundamentally the grim-
ness of a so-called puritan left politics that also still thrives in the
university, ready at a moment's notice to stuff all such nonsense as

"embourgeoisement," the near-fatal disease of "good" revolution-
aries, wanting to have the things possessed by the bourgeoisie. And
Warhol's esthetic is "competitively innovative" indeed, neatly es-
caping both. On the one hand, he would demystify the high-culture
banquet, making it possible under the board as well as across the
board. And on the other hand, he would mock the "dangers" of embourgeoisement by *not* wanting to have, showing you instead how
to play with the banquet's leftovers endlessly in a simulation of the
very embourgeoisement marked as so dangerous. In appropriately
modified ways, Warhol's moves then continue to have an obvious
utility to the circumstances of academic criticism trying to make the
obsolescences of popular "tastes" something "directly competitive."
He successfully demonstrates how to thread a way among competing values and organizations of academic practices, how to make
room for taking popular taste seriously as, if perhaps not "inher-
ently funny," at least as competitive as the other businesses at work.
But such moves come at the expense of "recycling people" no less
than work and ideas, of permitting them visibility only when put
through the filter systems of a kind of treatment plant for taste.

"When I win the lottery," the first chorus of the Camper Van
Beethoven song of that title goes, "gonna buy all the girls on my
block, color TV and a bottle of French perfume." There's a sense
in which that chorus might be perceived as parody of a familiar
conservative rhetoric of "welfare patrons," who in ostensibly "des-
perate" circumstances and needing assistance nevertheless "throw
away" money on inessentials. (Warhol, from the other end, might
well have gleefully seized on it as an already recycled leftover with
the humor still intact.) Yet in a rather different context, apart from
either perception, it helps a great deal to explain the mechanisms of
tasteful exploitation, which don't just consist of "creating" in "poor
people" a desire for the things possessed by those who are "better
off." Taste exploits by organizing a social world where the *proliferation*
of necessities is itself a necessity, the precondition for the expansion
of available fields where taste can be exercised. The more necessities, that is, the more opportunity to "go beyond" mere necessities
into finer and finer discriminations of taste. If televisions and perfume were themselves simply luxuries, relatively little taste value
of discrimination could be realized from what kind of television or
perfume you had. But "poor people" aren't after all culturally op-

pressed by the impossibility of keeping up with this always changing fashion. Their positions are exploited by the structures of *necessity* fashion changes leave in their wake, the way in which televisions and perfume are insinuated into every corner of social life, in order to maximize the occasions for the exercise of taste across discriminations of "which television" and "which perfume." The education of taste, after all, must demarcate and enforce continually new zones of necessity in order to valorize new indices of taste, and it is that process that functions as exploitative.

Taste, as I argued, always carries in some sense the residue of the directional transformation it accomplishes from working conditions to conditions of consumption. But what I want to suggest now is that, more important, the process of *educating* taste intensifies the pressures on work, which in effect must be made to do the impossible for many people, to yield the resources to satisfy the demands of the necessary in order to make available "beyond" these necessities the opportunity to perform in fields of taste at all. For all that taste seems located within the labors and pleasures of consumption, as the consumer appropriation of and "reproducing" of consumer products of all kinds, in the social organization of class-as-lifestyle *educating taste is not finally "about" consumption.* That is, while indices of taste lie within consumer fields, the education of taste functions instead to extend, authorize, legitimize, and proliferate the social relations of work as a matter of class-as-lifestyle division.

A so-called consumer society not only depends on a massive organization of the working relations of a service economy, as I argued in chapter 2, but also on filling the spaces of the necessary in consumption, constitutively linking up the details of "everyday behavior" through possession of what must then come to appear as the necessities of that everyday behavior. Consumer society doesn't really make former "luxuries" available to everybody; it transforms luxuries into necessities in order that division can be preserved across the mere possession of these newly necessary resources and the capitalizations of performative agency. More and more people more and more of the time must work more and more in order simply to keep up with this proliferation of the necessary. Educating taste is then less a matter of inducing consumption than of inducing work. The better you're able to recognize the educationally discriminated intricacies of taste's performative powers, the less mere possession

exhausts the possibilities of consumption. You find yourself caught
up not in a hyperfrenzy of always increasing consumption, but of
always intensifying work performance in pursuit of a continually
receding calculus of consumer possibility.

The result is a social world where it must be made to seem increasingly impossible to do without certain things, and where to
some great extent it will then in fact become impossible to do without them in negotiating the organization of that social world. Tressell's Frank Owen in *The Ragged Trousered Philanthropists*, standing
somewhere near the beginnings of this massive proliferation of the
necessary, is then also an early avatar of a long tradition of left politics, as someone who never quite grasped the sense in which his
comrades' repeated expressions of interest in "more jam" rather than
in Owen's abstract lectures about capitalism was the most charac-
teristically *un*bourgeois element about them.* For wanting *to have*
"more jam" after all can't really be an exercise of taste as an expression of "bourgeois" desire for distance and social distinction. That
is, it's neither a recognition of the necessary as "merely" a point
of departure for the logic of taste, nor a simulation of possession,
such as Warhol's esthetic. Like the dream of the lottery player in the
Camper Van song, it's a wish to *have* the necessary.

The forms of resistance I've sketched in this chapter obviously
exist at certain points of labor demands where, far from being "distraction," consumption is inevitably a battle of negotiating the impositions of working conditions. But in those circumstances people
continue as well the hopes of Owen's comrades, developing resistances into multiple forms of a counter-taste. In contrast to educating taste, the education of a counter-taste then expresses precisely
(and perhaps never more clearly than in dreaming the lottery) *taste-
as-consumption*, something it can never really be in the educations of
nostalgia, retro, the estheticizing of "leftovers," the whole vast apparatus of performative agencies in class-as-lifestyle with their intensi-
fications of work. For over and above the uses "mere things" might
afford in the circumstances of work, of the endless daily negotiations
with labor demands and the education of "taste," *having* more and

*For a particularly useful discussion of Tressell in this context, see Pamela Fox,
"Recovering the 'Narrow Plot of Acquisitiveness and Desire': Reproduction, Resistance and British Working Class Writing, 1890–1945."

more things will always be welcome, not just "mere." Last year's ideologies can be had no less than color TVs and French perfume, with next year's lottery promising CDs and postmodern simulations soon to be available too as "things of the past." Fashion's leftover structures of necessity eventually become the junkyard of the obsolete—but these supply the useful tools of resistance And if from soaps you can get the obsolete controlling reserve of the villainess, in the final chorus of the Camper Van song you get "silver-plated sixshooters" to do something with it.

SIX

"What Are You Doing Here?"

I want to begin with a small parable of sorts constructed out of two series of recent events, one that took place in "consumer culture," the other in the immediately recognizable political sphere of presidential decision. I hope that like all good parables it will sustain a lot of commentary, because I want to use it as a guide for a brief look at the history of Reaganism in the United States as a political culture. As I have argued throughout, that political culture seems to me best understood as educational (that education occurring not only—or even primarily—in the school system, but rather across consumer fields). This is a lot of weight for a parable to bear; my justification is that it should function also as a convenient summary of much of the argument of preceding chapters, with the commentary then as conclusion and as a way to locate possibilities for a countereducation as Reaganism itself has begun to evidence signs of fundamental changes.

The Mazda Miata was designed to resemble the very limited-production, hopelessly unreliable, and prohibitively expensive Lotus Elan of the sixties. The introductory advertising campaign, however, chose to deemphasize the design similarity. Typically, it conjured up instead images of a vast, almost *American Graffiti*–like retro glossy, but with a kind of fuzz-glare around each object, to emphasize the construction itself, and heartbeated by the only thing missing to complete the picture, which finally emerges as the Miata. The advertising decisions were documented, albeit after the fact, in *Advertising Age* and elsewhere, but it is important to recognize the reasons for choice as contingent. For the initial Miata sales did far exceed expectations; it's not like the "choice" of advertising strategy was some profoundly thought-out guaranteed plan for consumer manipulation and control of the market. As in any form of educational operation, changes in consumer education more often than not begin in an improvisational play across the familiar and the available, with no one knowing for sure exactly what will happen. You discover the "logic" of the operation in the register of effects rather than in inventories of intention, however fascinating such inventories might be—after the fact. In any case, and in contrast to the more obvious and familiar strategy potentially available because of the design similarity, the effects of the Miata advertising campaign in terms of a positional education were stunning.

An emphasis on similarity would have yielded a "now you can too . . ." advertising promise of ownership and rewards. Such a strategy was likely already anticipated by Ford Motors for marketing their planned Capri convertible, and by GM for marketing the Geo Metro convertible; even after the success of the Miata, both campaigns still bore traces of it, "readjusted," however, in light of what happened with the very different Miata strategy that actually emerged. The immediate trouble with this kind of familiar advertising—it's used, after all, not only for cars but for everything from art reproductions to American Express tours to "third world" countries—is that its very familiarity makes it more susceptible to what advertisers dread as a "consumer backlash," in the form, crudely, of the standard comedy line, "I wouldn't want to belong to any club that would have me." If I can get an updated Elan any jerk can, so what's the point? "Backlash," that is, takes its cue from how, educationally, this strategy can quickly slip into a lesson that first humiliates you, by reminding you of a past in which you could have played no part, and then compounds the humiliation by asking you to be grateful to the auto makers (or whomever, given the circumstances of different products) for cheapening that past enough to make it available to just anyone in the present. The Miata ad strategy, however, offers a past that was *always* yours, if over time dissipated, diffused, obscured, perhaps even taken away by vaguely malignant powers; but now it is in your power to repossess it, this time the way it ought to unfold, under the enabling sign of constructive energies available to you in much the same way they're available to the makers of the ad in their version of the construction as shown in the ad itself.

There is a certain resemblance here to the "baseball, hot dogs, apple pie and Chevrolet" ads earlier in the eighties, but with two fundamental differences. First, the stress in the Chevy ads falls on *Chevrolet* always having been there, with then the faint but unmistakable whining of reproach that "you deserted us, fell for that Japanese crap, but generously we'll invite you back where you've always belonged." Without ever having to say so directly, the Miata ads can imply in contrast a sinister presence at their boundaries, a sense that Something Else got to your past, disinheriting you, rather than your absence being a matter of your active "desertion." Unlike the Chevy ads, which appear so "dated," these ads—even in the miseries of current auto sales, and even though they tout a "Japanese" rather than an "American" car—nevertheless continue to fit far more comfortably and congruently into a world of Hollywood movies and TV shows featuring soon-to-be-forties men affirming it's not too late to reverse things and repossess—and without the need to go on a cattle drive like Billy Crystal in *City Slickers* or to get a bullet in the head like Harrison Ford in *Regarding Henry* or to relearn how to fly like Robin Williams in *Hook*. Just need a car . . .

Second, and equally important for my purposes, the Miata ads simply refused to acknowledge the force of structuration of positionality necessary to both the "now you can too . . ." and the Chevy ad strategies. To emphasize directly the Miata-Elan tie would reinforce a structure of positional exchange equivalents, with its promise of directional "up" because you already know where up is. But then the possibility of "backlash" arises, a perception that would question the very nature of the exchange necessary to direction. The Miata ads articulate position instead across the emergence of altered powers of structuration, where rather than promising a positionality once available only to Elan owners, they make available the energies for constructive repossession of *your* past as yet not settled into positionally related linkages and clear itineraries of up and down. That is, they promise up/down itself as still "up" for grabs by means of an emergent structuration—a "back to the future" opening rewriting the present by producing the past—counter to the already settled territory devolving from a remote and inaccessible Elan world to which you inevitably come belatedly. In this configuration of possibility, cars like the Elan then become obsolete, less because technologically superseded than because they recede into the minatory

blur of a just-visible Something Else, the lurking constraints of implacable temporal order blocking passage, a past claiming itself as
unchangeable.

After its immense immediate success, the Miata itself has begun to
fade; prices that had at one time skyrocketed to ten and even twenty
thousand dollars over MSRP in west-coast markets have returned
to "normal" (although as of this moment at least the Miata remains
immune to the rebates attached to nearly every other car). Contrary
to a lot of speculation in the media, the fade is hardly one more sign
of some "revolt" against the "greed is good" eighties but, as linked
with the phenomenon of its initial success, a useful way to read
the developing logic of what's at stake through the eighties straight
on into the nineties with a recessionary economy. "Lifestyle" reports, in *Time*—and in books such as Amy Saltzman's conveniently
automobile-titled *Downshifting: Reinventing Success on a Slower Track*—
as well as movies such as *City Slickers* and *Regarding Henry*, and the
deepening effects of the recession, all suggest that "materialism" is
over. Actual interviews, however, don't register the change in quite
such dramatic terms, as Saltzman herself admits: "Most of us have
no interest in forsaking everything we have worked for to live out
a romantic ideal in the woods. What we do long for is a middle
ground: a place where the modern conveniences and intellectual and
professional challenges of big-city life do not take us over but merely
give our lives depth; where the cost of living does not force us to
give up our own happiness to meet a monthly mortgage payment;
and where success has a more personal meaning than continually
moving ahead in a job" (176).

You'd look a long time, however, to find a better description of
the "world" of Miata ads. The point is how the Miata itself became
a victim of this success of the educational lessons available in and
heightened through the advertising campaign. So successful was the
lesson that in the rush to "put it into practice" by means of a Miata,
prices quickly escalated to the extent that the car itself could no
longer "qualify" as central to the lesson. The logic of the ads can
now find far better expression in what local Seattle news writers
refer to, in the "rural" town of Port Townsend (on the edge of the
wilderness Olympic National Park, and about an hour's drive and
ferry ride from Seattle), as "one-downsmanship," a "practice of 'ag-
gressive humility,' whereby anyone, no matter how well off, always

makes sure to make do with less: an older pickup truck, a more
frayed flannel shirt, something bartered, or better, recycled" (*Seattle
Post-Intelligencer*, section C, 8). In the kind of emergent structuration
imaged in the Miata ads, again, up/down must be up for grabs. So-
called materialism was never really the stake in any case, but simply
a turbo boost that upped the "up" to the point where newly emergent structurations could become plausible, featuring older pickups
and such, and likewise newly emergent ways of capitalizing on the
shifting indices of up/down.

The political relevance of what I've been outlining as relations of
position and structuration in Miata advertising is twofold. On the
one hand, it's a version of how lifestyle identities are constructed
across the capitalization of change that I described in chapter 2, and
is then linked to what I called the educating of taste in chapter 5. That
is, substituting "older pickups" for Miatas occurs within the development of the same configurations of taste set up by the Mazda ads,
across the performative capitalization of being able to change objects from Miatas to older pickups. On the other hand, however, and
what concerns me here particularly, is the way the advertising contributes to a redefinition of ideologies of rising social expectations.
This has nothing to do with "slower tracks" or "middle grounds"
as desirable aims, but with a certain substitution of "freedom from"
for "rights to" as a crucially constitutive element of expectations.

In this context, think again, for contrast, of the "now you can
too . . ." strategy that might have been deployed for the Miata. Both
its promise, and its potential for "disastrous" backlash, are at some
level located in its assumed constellation of expectations with rights.
Ownership of an Elan came with and reconfirmed certain rights of
position; expectations for "moving up" by purchase of an updated
Elan-now-Miata would likewise imply rights to what a "higher"
position affords. Rather than rights, however, the actual strategy in
contrast links expectations to a promise of "freedom from" by means
of shifting structurations into new territory. You have no necessary
or guaranteed rights in that territory—up/down is up for grabs—
but the promise is that constraints have been suspended. The past is
not irrevocable but available, to be produced by a power of choice
in the present. "Most of us," Saltzman suggests, "have no interest
in forsaking everything we have worked for." What the Miata ads
offered was the opportunity to intervene in a continual redefinition

of "everything we have worked for." The political logic projected by such exercises in consumer education is then very different indeed from the previous ones. It would require a *social* organization whose principles for structuring positional relations must be capable of expansively producing new territories of structuration in order to effect a guarantee of "freedom from," but at the same time eliminating guarantees of "rights to" as themselves potential constraints on that freedom, insofar as such rights are made to seem limiting, infringing on the possibilities of continual redefinition.

Juxtaposing advertising strategies and the processes of political decision making shouldn't any longer seem particularly farfetched, but I want to insist on rather more intricate connections than simply the recognition that advertising now plays a significant role in politics. While Bush's nomination of Clarence Thomas for Supreme Court justice (my chosen example here), like the Miata, was the subject of a considerable advertising campaign, the similarities don't end there. Legal affirmative action "quotas" also ineluctably link rights and expectations: if this specific situation exists; if you are positioned exactly here in the situation; you can not only expect a particular outcome, you have a right to the realization of that outcome. Quotas, that is, would have provided an obvious strategy for the Thomas nomination, were it not for the fact that both Bush and Thomas were adamantly opposed to quotas. Yet even without the retrospective documentation now beginning to appear, nobody in their right mind could have imagined Thomas was nominated with no consideration whatsoever of his race, any more than someone who knows cars could have missed the resemblance between the Miata and the Elan. Administration attempts to portray the decision as based on "pure merit" must have sounded silly even as they were being considered, and the "advertising" didn't try to push the point very far. Miata ads, however, do suggest a different set of terms altogether to understand the strategy at stake.

It was the *nomination* and not Thomas himself that was made to occupy a space—like the Miata in the ads—that emerges within an altered structuration of positionality, where in contrast to what is implied by quotas, expectations instead appear in terms of freedom from constraints. Constraints, in other words, are lifted from the act of nominating Thomas, with the result that the discriminatory positional powers of the *white* race became the Elan-past of this political narrative. And rather than "others" now being promised positions (and rights to position) in the present that had formerly belonged only to white men, the new structuration of territory in the nomination was a "back to the future" indeed, rewriting a present wherein constraints have been removed in order to produce a past *for whites* that "runs" on into the future, unlike the Elan. As bell hooks has remarked, "Ultimately the Thomas hearings were not only a public political spectacle orchestrated by whites but . . . whites were, indeed, the intended audience. The rest of us were merely voyeurs" ("Feminist Challenge," 22).

Thomas himself was joined to the space of the Miata-nomination as available-to-be-"upped" to the Supreme Court, no quotas and no "rights to" in evidence (with the "minor caveat" for many conservatives, of course, that Thomas nevertheless still seemed "curiously" to adhere to a now hopelessly obsolete and useless doctrine of "natural rights," as if trying to argue for the merit of a Capri convertible after just having been handed a Miata). Like the "miracle" of capital emerging out of nothing in the eyes of good bourgeois economists, symbolic capitalization of positional identities in this "new" politics "happens" once constraints have been removed. There's the nomination, full-blown on screen like that fuzz-glared Miata. While Thomas hadn't been "turned white," any more than the Miata is an Elan, the relations of position and structuration had been politically reshaped every bit as surely as in Miata advertising. Anita Hill's charge of sexual harassment posed a threat, because it intervened to disrupt this new structuration, refocusing attention on Thomas himself and on "outdated" issues of gender and race that had been made to seem invisible.

Thus the lines of congruence I'm marking between my two examples don't quite form some "Jacobean imaginary" (Ernesto Laclau and Chantal Mouffe's term) of already totalized social structure; there was Hill's intervention and the long process of the hearings that followed. But they do involve linked productivities of structuration, which even if not quite a "symmetry" should certainly be fearful enough for any would-be oppositional political education, especially given what happened with Hill's intervention. That is, it's hardly "wrong" to argue, in good poststructuralist fashion, as Laclau and Mouffe do in *Hegemony and Socialist Strategy*, that "the incomplete character of every totality necessarily leads us to abandon, as a terrain of analysis, the premise of '*society*' as a sutured and self-defined totality. 'Society' is not a valid object of discourse. There is no single underlying principle fixing—and hence constituting—the whole field of differences" (111). But the necessary corollary is that "society" and "the social" are everywhere at stake in discursive production.

The issue here isn't a matter of some structural identity between Mazda's economic interest in marketing Miatas and Bush's political interest in the nomination of Thomas. It's a matter of education for political citizenship, in that however oddly the intersections occur across these "interests," there are intersections and not simply endless parallel lines through the "field of differences." This education links the lessons of consumer culture and the lessons of political decision making across the social vision of freedom from constraints, of the endless mobilities of consumer choices. The nomination after all reflects not Thomas's productive "merit," but the "free" exercise of Bush's consumer approval.

In response to a question about hegemony, Stuart Hall arrived at what he calls a "rough example" to characterize the hegemonic powers of "the Thatcherite project," which depends, he argues,

> on seeing the mother, who is trying to represent and understand the inability of her child to get on in a competitive education at school, as the same mother who is concerned about women who go out to work and neglect their responsibility to the family, the same as the woman who says to the miners, "You can't possibly go on strike tomorrow because your wives and children don't have enough to live on." These are all different positions, but the point where people begin to recognize themselves in all of them is what I call the "point of articulation." By the notion of hegemony I want to invoke precisely the capacity of a political formation to intervene on all these different sites. ("Toad," 61)

Relations of hegemony, Gramsci reminds us, are always also pedagogical relations, where what Hall calls the "point of articulation" occurs, in the examples I've connected of education for political citizenship, in the discursive restructuring of expectations as a matter of freedom from constraints. "Different positions" indeed can "recognize themselves" *in this process of structuration*, which again doesn't imply " '*society*' as a sutured and self-defined totality" of fixed positions, but does focus attention on the discursive productivities of social structuration across very different positional interests.

Reaganism, as I will suggest, has been permeated by a certain horrified fascination with "what went wrong" in the sixties, with the borderlands likewise just visible at the boundaries of the Miata ads. Reaganism has developed, however, toward the possibility of "reconstruction" implied by the Thomas nomination, which would produce the obsolescence of race and gender across "innovative" new possibilities of social organization. I have relatively little interest here in issues of what was actually "wrong" or "right" about the sixties, but a great deal of interest in how Reaganism has embedded reconstruction in a politics of education for citizenship, linking economics with mass culture and with "reform" proposals for institutional education.* The image of the child-becoming-citizen, that is, conveniently locates the subject of educational policy. What I will sketch as a quick history of Reaganism then foregrounds a development from the multilevel attacks on the "spoiled children" of the sixties that marked Reagan's terms in office, to both Bush's and Clinton's campaign visions of an entrepreneurial state charged with the responsibility for educating its "forgotten-child" citizens and Perot's recent campaign that promised the ultimate politically educative technology available to everyone.

Challenges to Reaganism have little to gain by following a lead like Clarence Thomas's attempt to ground political rights in natural qualities. Yet in the context of an educational agenda for change, there seems to me much to gain from making strategic use of "obsolete" ideologies such as notions of rights, and "obsolete" institutions such as public education understood as an authority instrumental in changing configurations of social position. My chapter title is a familiar enough soap-opera line, occurring on any number of differ-

---

*Lawrence Grossberg, in *It's a Sin*, distinguishes Thatcherism from an American New Right insofar as a New Right "agenda operates in the conjunction of economics and popular culture rather than that of economics and the State" (32), as Thatcherism does. And while on the whole my argument supports Grossberg's contention about the importance of that particular conjunction between economics and popular culture as Grossberg understands the term, it is also important to recognize that a New Right is by no means the only constituency of Reaganism. Indeed, the interests largely in the ascendancy during the Bush administration have been from the beginning considerably more attentive to the powers of state apparatuses, with one effect being that New Right thinking itself has increasingly focused on the state as well. Thus in what follows, I will emphasize, as in my initial "parable," how the reconstruction of the state has played a larger and larger role within the development of Reaganism.

ent occasions, but more often than not as an expression of outrage at the appearance of the villainess, as a sign of trouble to come. I've tried to suggest in chapter 5 how it's possible to repair the obsolescence of that soap-opera image for use in other situations, and I think a politics of oppositional education can learn a great deal from a process of resistance understood in these terms of repair. In both her obsolescence and her ubiquity, the threat posed by the villainess is not only in what she knows, but where she is when she knows it: "What are you doing *here*," the refrain that greeted Anita Hill from the Senate's "soap-opera" hearings. For left politics, the "here" in which we have no business is the social spaces—including both Senate hearings and Miata ads—now largely occupied by the forces of Reaganism.

I

Political analysts in the United States frequently have claimed that Reagan's election marked the emergence of the first significant new coalition in U.S. politics since F.D.R. and the New Deal. In Britain, theorists such as Stuart Hall and Andrew Gamble have gone much further, arguing that Thatcherism must be understood as nothing less than the formation of a kind of Gramscian *"blocco storico"* of the right. Critical debate about such assertions for the most part has focused on the importance they assign to ideology and ideological constructions; on whether either Thatcherism or Reaganism really possesses the ideological coherence implied, and indeed if ideological terms in any case afford the best means of understanding the political power at stake; and on the so-called New Times agenda in Britain that emerged out of this reading of Thatcherism. But however these "larger" issues might ultimately be decided, it seems to me clear that Reaganism in the United States has produced some rather astonishing ideological effects. Consider, for example, from relatively early in the history of Reaganism, William Rusher's "new class" analysis that would become an important theme in Reagan's first election victory:

> A new economic division pits the producers—businessmen, manufacturers, hard-hats, blue-collar workers, and farmers—against the new and powerful class of nonproducers comprised of a liberal verbalist elite (the dominant media, the major foundations and research institutions,

the educational establishment, the federal and state bureaucracies) and a semipermanent welfare constituency, all coexisting happily in a state of mutually sustaining symbiosis. (quoted in Edgar, 68)*

Even from the obligingly convenient distance of retrospection, it would be a mistake to dismiss such statements as merely a "negative politics" without some attention to the curious logic at work here, which seems relatively impervious to the reasonableness of pointing out the obvious, such as the fact that the owners of "dominant media" are after all "businessmen." Rusher was not only trying to link potentially very diverse interests against a "common enemy" but also articulating a way to mobilize existing resources toward new positional powers—crudely, toward something he assumes *none* of these "producer" groups would feel they possessed, and all would feel they should possess. That is, the key element of Rusher's logic is a specific perception of disproportion and imbalance that positions his own strategic assertion in the role of *oppositional* challenge. It's a picture that admittedly seems even more absurd when you turn to some of the more recent manifestations of this kind of oppositional rhetoric. It's not at all easy to grasp any sense in which a predominantly white, middle- and often upper-middle-class group of "abortion clinic" protesters in Wichita, Kansas, can imagine themselves the vanguard of a political opposition movement whose principal victims after all will be relatively powerless working-class and "minority" women. But like Rusher, the protesters nevertheless deploy a logic of self-definition that positions them in opposition to dominant power.

What I want to suggest initially, then, by these relatively "early" and "late" examples from the political culture of Reaganism, is that the first great ideological success of Reaganism involved a process of redefining social dominance. Without as yet trying to assess the ultimate effectiveness of such redefinition in terms of political coalitions or in its multiple intersections with economic policies and the "social issues" agenda of the New Right, in some form nevertheless it seems to me a pervasive feature throughout Reaganism. Thus

---

*I want to stress my use of David Edgar's essay "The Free or the Good" because it seems to me one of the best comparisons between Thatcherism and Reaganism. Yet Edgar, too, is rather too quick to assume the immediate congruence of social authoritarianism and economic "freedom" in Reaganism at least.

regardless of how effectively redefinition is carried out, it locates a primary pedagogical direction of Reaganism; that is, the process of redefining social dominance functions as both an ideological lesson Reaganism teaches, and a means whereby crucially positioned agents of Reaganism themselves learned a strategic politics of power. The connections I've emphasized between the new structurations of territory in Miata advertising and the constructed space of the Thomas nomination, for example, benefit a great deal from this pedagogical history of Reaganism whose development I will sketch here.

In "The Poverty of Redistribution," one of his many articles for the *Wall Street Journal* in the seventies, collected in *Two Cheers for Capitalism*, Irving Kristol stated a theme that like Rusher's "new class" analysis was repeated over and over in the subsequent mobilization of the right that led to Reagan's first presidential victory: "Poverty as a human condition, as distinct from a statistical condition, is defined to a substantial degree by the ways in which one copes with poverty. . . . And what is true for the way one copes with poverty is also true for the way one goes about abolishing poverty" (241). The statistical feats of prestidigitation in that essay (by Kristol's calculations, poverty had already been abolished in New York City) are remarkable, but as Kristol was intent on pointing out, the statistics are in any case only a sideshow here. For what Democratic spokespeople—defending the disintegrating vision of the Great Society's "war on poverty" and castigating conservatives such as Kristol for reducing poverty to a "state of mind"—failed to recognize was why remarks like the following of Kristol's, from the same essay, would have an immediate resonance for certain audiences:

> Being a "breadwinner" is the major source of self-respect for a man or woman working at a tedious, low-paying job that offers few prospects for advancement. It is also the major source of such respect as he (or she) receives from family, friends, and neighbors. When welfare provides more generously for a family than a breadwinner can, he becomes a superfluous human being. (242)

More and more people were already finding themselves in the situation Kristol describes, "working at a tedious, low-paying job that offers few prospects for advancement." More important, they had a sense of being denied the realization of even whatever necessarily attenuated expectations such work might promise. Kristol's image of a lack of respect, becoming a "superfluous human being,"

was an image in which any number of people could see themselves—
what Hall might well identify as a "point of articulation"—far more
easily than in the elaborate statistical composites of median family
income and redrawn "poverty lines." This does not at all imply that
people simultaneously accepted Kristol's or any similar reasoning for
the cause of the problem, nor in fact that there was any uniformity
whatsoever in why people found the image a recognizable reflection.
And certainly there were available far more comprehensive, complicated, and accurate explanations for why so many people were in
fact working these "tedious, low-paying" jobs than Kristol's statistical shuffle and blaming of the welfare system. The point is simply
that the image became an expressive reality for a great many people
who were necessarily thinking first in terms of relative disjunctions
between expectations and realization, work and reward, in the immediate circumstances of their own lives rather than in terms of relative indices of poverty across a wide social spectrum. *No* explanation
was likely to be convincing that couldn't register immediately and
effectively that expressive reality. That is, it doesn't require imagin-
ing that huge numbers of eventual Reagan voters were completely
convinced—manipulated, or whatever—by Kristol-like conservative reasoning into identifying welfare programs as the culprit to
see why people might nevertheless vote for Reagan. The explanations seemed at least attached to an image of reality, and hence worth
a shot.

Postpone then for a minute questions of whether such a description should imply scorn for the "masses" willing to accept "image"
over political substance, or if it identifies some substance of needs
and interests really if confusingly expressed by that image, or if
it testifies to a postmodern demolition of the "very distinction"
between image and substance, or supports Althusserian interpella-
tions of political subjects, and so on. Given subsequent events, the
itinerary of the image is worth pursuing in terms of what Reaganism's politics made of it. Kristol's essay again affords a good initial
clue: "Meanwhile, there are many poor people (including of course
blacks) in the country who are too proud to go on welfare, who
prefer to work hard at low-paying jobs, earning less than if they had
gone on welfare" (242). In this form, the argument is just smugly
patronizing in both racial and class terms, but of course Reaganism had no mystical intuition into what great numbers of "ordinary

people" wanted, retrospective mythologies to the contrary. Reaganism did, however, recognize and respond to changing circumstances,
as Kristol would evidence in reporting to *Newsweek* in 1976 that "if
there is one thing that Neo-Conservatives are unanimous about, it
is their dislike of the 'counter-culture' which has played so remarkable a role in American life in the last 15 years" (quoted in Edgar,
67). That the statement had so quickly a self-fulfilling corroboration in any number of similar statements by Nathan Glazer, Robert
Nisbet, Norman Podhoretz, George Will, and others suggests both
the depth of the antipathy toward "the sixties" and a tactical means
of shifting ground from the patronizing implied by Kristol's earlier
comment. Linked with the attack on welfare programs, this antipathy made "the sixties" an available emblem of disproportion, and
hence a means for the disposition of critique that could be used in
multiple ways.

The connection, quite simply, was the claim that the "spoiled
children" of the sixties, like the "welfare patrons" of the seventies,
thought they had a right to get something for nothing. That is,
rather than patting people on the head for being "too proud to go
on welfare," with all the implications of immense social distance
and condescension, this form of critique supplied tools by means
of which people could justify for themselves, in their own terms,
that they weren't just schmucks for not getting a "free" welfare ride
or not "letting it all hang out" or not clamoring for everything in-
stantly. What Reaganism learned, in other words, was the strategic
importance of an educational process that seemed to proceed not
by trying to explain for anybody and everybody why a compelling
image was compelling, but instead by constructing corroborative
elaborations of the image that opened a space where people could
continue to fashion and refashion explanations on their own, out of
their own specific circumstances.

And it was out of the education in that educational process that
the Reagan "hit men" such as William Safire and Patrick Buchanan,
following Spiro Agnew's earlier lead, could subsequently launch
their concerted attack on "pointy-headed intellectuals," could image
an entire spectrum of left politics as so much intellectual analysis
trying to tell everybody what to do and why. For this was not at
all merely an appeal to some supposedly long-standing tradition of
"anti-intellectualism" in "American life" (Kristol, for example, had

been quite emphatic that it was capitalism which, wrongly, encouraged a belief that ideas don't count for anything), but almost the
opposite: everybody has a capacity to be an intellectual; don't let
anybody take it away who thinks they know more than you do;
you're quite capable of working it out on your own. Assuming, of
course, that you're not yourself a spoiled child, that you've measured
what it means to be an adult and accepted the responsibility.

In *Breaking Ranks*—appearing at the end of the decade, on the eve
of the first Reagan election victory—Norman Podhoretz supplied in
apocalyptic terms a certain cultural correlative of Rusher's economic
argument, thundering that "there can be no abdication of responsibility more fundamental than the refusal of a man to become, and to
be, a father, or the refusal of a woman to become, and be, a mother"
(363)—that is, for Podhoretz, biologically and culturally a producer-
adult. Kristol had stated a similar position earlier, in quieter if no
less melodramatic terms:

> Indeed, it is my impression that, under the strain of modern life, whole
> classes of our population—and the educated classes most of all—are enter-
> ing what can only be called, in the strictly clinical sense, a phase of
> infantile regression. With every passing year, public discourse becomes
> sillier and more petulant, while human emotions become, apparently,
> more ungovernable. (268)

I've focused immediately on domestic issues, but similar themes
can be found in the range of international policy directions as well.
The United Nations, for example, was attacked for "pandering" to
"third world" and Communist interests who weren't paying their
way like adults and hence deserved no real voice in UN affairs. Likewise, although the build-up of the military was typically justified
for "defense purposes," it seemed nevertheless to involve continual
and direct intervention in the internal politics of other countries—
presumably when those countries entered "a phase of infantile regression." Internationally, most of the rest of the world, like the
home-grown "spoiled children" of the sixties, seemed in the light of
Reaganism's foreign policy to have gained a threatening and dispro-
portionate power by, precisely, acting "spoiled." This meant, then,
that it was time to introduce a little adult discipline into world affairs
as well.

Economically, however, "supply-side" theories in the United

States drew as heavily on the work of Milton Friedman and of F. A. Hayek and the "Austrian school" as the monetarism preferred by Thatcherism in Britain. These theories targeted inflation rather than unemployment as the structural constraint on the "market order" (Hayek's term), and directed themselves everywhere toward "correcting" the imbalances by which government regulation, union power, and the "welfare establishment" had undermined the potential productivity of American business. What Gamble, Hall, and others have pointed out about monetarism then holds for supply-side (with its infamous "Laffer curve") as well: that the rationales for the necessary "freedom" of economic agents weren't particularly congruent with the social issues agenda I've described emphasizing authority and responsibility. *Commentary* and even the *Wall Street Journal* in the United States, like the *Salisbury Review* and other forums in Britain, in fact featured seemingly interminable debates across the differences. Where Gamble sees the success of Thatcherism as having nevertheless forged a synthesis from these divergent ideological directions (Gamble, 121), in the United States at least it seems to me less obvious that the Reagan election victories were dependent on direct linkages of this kind between "economic" and "cultural" priorities.

What I've tried to imply instead is how widely shareable images of disjunction, disproportion, and imbalance could coexist with often radically different conceptions of what exactly constituted, in contrast, coherence, proportion, and balance. This is not at all the same as saying that Reaganism emerged as a "negative" politics, uniting otherwise very diverse interests only in opposition to specifically targeted groups such as those in Rusher's list of "nonproducers." What's new initially about Reaganism is the transformation of a historically familiar, "traditional" conservative defense of established principles and order against "disruptive" threats from the borderlands, into what is instead a vision of dominance itself gone haywire, like the sinister Something Else that surrounds the Miata ads generating all kinds of confused and confusing effects from who knew what mysterious center.

Hence "regression," for example, in statements like Podhoretz's or Kristol's, became not just a biological or psychological metaphor but also an image of social defeatism, a giving in to the chaotic, disruptive, discordant forces dominating the present whose visible

emblem was the "spoiled children" of the sixties. To take another
kind of example, Hayek's account of socialism suggested that so far
from being an economic system toward which we are heading, it
is in fact where we came from and have as yet far from completely
extricated ourselves; indeed, we may find that specifically modern
conditions make it even more difficult to escape. Likewise, Rusher's
"economic division" targets, precisely, "nonproducers": as he saw it,
those who contribute nothing toward the realization of a future but
merely scam what they can from the work of others in the present.
Conservatism in its Reagan version, that is, learned to image itself
across all these different sectors as offering people a chance to organize for and to build a society in which they could get what they
felt they deserved, rather than simply a way to preserve an existent
social structure in order to hold onto what they had.

   The difference is important, for it explains a great deal about
the general failure of liberal Democrats and the more radical left to
convincingly portray Reaganism as a hate politics that set nondominant groups against each other and thus prevented their uniting in
opposition to real, socially entrenched positions of dominant power.
Hate propaganda certainly existed throughout the fundamentalism
of the "moral majority" and the Robert Vigurie version of the New
Right. It functioned for Reaganism, however, as less a kind of extreme shock troops that would pave the way for a more prudent and
sensible return to older virtues than as the necessary if nevertheless
distorted reminder *that dominant power was somewhere else*. This so-
called fringe right was necessary because it foregrounded the crucial
move in the transformation that took place: the dissociation of dominance from what would seem to be obvious locations within the
social formation. But it was also then distorted, because it immediately and mistakenly leaped to the conclusion that homosexuals,
feminists, rioting blacks, welfare cheats, and so on and on actually themselves embodied and/or occupied positions of dominance,
rather than simply being the beneficiaries of a mysteriously skewed
dominant power. In Reaganism's redefinition of dominance, and
like the mystery at the fringes of the Miata ads, dominance must
always appear "somewhere else," visible only in its effects, which
then impinge on and constrain the possible futures of corporate executives every bit as much as corporate janitors, and which appear
throughout the social formation as imbalances and disproportions.

Thus, for Reaganism, what came to identify left-wing politics was a failure to understand what dominance was all about. The left was perceived as clinging to things such as indices of income inequalities, discriminatory practices by race and gender or because of sexual "preferences"—in general, an analysis of dominance based in some now hopelessly obsolete calculus of social hierarchization inherited from nineteenth-century reformers. At worst, the left was imaged as just the antics of "infantile regression," of spoiled children traversed by and enacting the effects of destructive powers beyond their control, or, in Robert Vigurie's updated simile from a speech I heard reported, spitting into the wind without knowing or caring they'd be hit first and hardest the harder they spit.

As this characterization of the left suggests, there is a sense in which the past remained vitally important within Reaganism. The intent was not to go back to it, however, but to realize its best tendencies in the future. Debates between supply-siders and what in the heyday of supply-side Burton Pines could derisively refer to as "the social issues crowd" (329), for example, such as those between Milton Friedman and Kristol, were charged with the enormous energy and import of imaging a future. It was everywhere the left that was perceived as mired in the politics and policies of the past, endlessly rehashing old themes. The point for Reaganism was how to understand the nascent promise of a living past still awaiting what nobody yet knew would emerge as the future.

Reaganism then had its obvious attractions for more old-line conservatives such as Kristol and George Will, not only in its respect for the "best elements" of the past but also in the value it accorded ideas and intellectuals. Reagan himself was so often seen as basically stupid—"living in some B movie" as the Camper Van Beethoven song "Sweethearts" had it—that it was easy to dismiss the intellectual energy and commitment that helped shape Reaganism into a political force. On the other hand, however, Reaganism also caught up the very different politics of radical exclusion that drove the religious fundamentalism of the "moral majority" and the Vigurie-inspired "grass roots" organizations, who found in the shifting redefinitions of social dominance an opportunity to focus their virulent attacks on specifically targeted groups. The result seems to me less an ideological synthesis—to the extent that that implies some recognizable core of shared values, beliefs, and practices—than the

multiple, often quite disparate effects of a fundamental transformation made possible through the conceptualization of dominance as
radically dispersed and menacing everywhere the promise of a future
yet to be built. Reaganism's first great ideological success, again,
was its self-definition as an oppositional vanguard, out to challenge a
dominant power that had robbed the vast majority of the population
of their hopes for a better future.

II

I think, however, that the most immediate and effectively deployed social weapon of Reaganism was economic, which accounts
for my own emphasis in preceding chapters on corporate restructuring, the emergence of a service economy, the developments of
what I've called consumer education, the intensification of work,
and so on. That is, what I've tried to describe has not been some
assumed primacy of economic forces (a technoideological coding of
obsolescence/innovation, especially as deployed within Reaganism,
is no more economic than ideological) but rather the effectiveness,
and the effects, of the economic as a weapon within the political
force of Reaganism. The reason, quite simply, seems to me that
while in electoral terms the constituencies of Reaganism proved to
be remarkably diverse, as in ideological terms its attractions were as
far-reachingly centrifugal as centripetal, its productive power base
was located in the interlocking spheres of corporate, government,
and academic economic practices.

This doesn't at all mean that Reaganism was driven by "economic
interests"; what it means, again, is that the broadly economic was
available first to *implement* whatever multiply imaged possibilities
of social change arose, even if at times in ways that weren't at all
congruent with the interests of specific economic agents within that
power base. (In the event, what "the country" did, for example, was
not exactly "good for GM.") Ideologically, supply-side theorists,
Friedman "Chicago-school" theorists, and so on, had to contend not
only with certain kinds of opposition within Congress but also with
"the social issues crowd" within Reaganism itself. The process of
corporate restructuring, in contrast, for all that those involved may
have felt themselves "harassed" and "constrained" by government
"intervention" and regulatory agency "intransigence," nevertheless

could proceed as rapidly as possible in forcing the issues. Consumer education could also develop with sometimes bewildering rapidity, and, as I argued in chapter 4, often to the horror of both identifiable constituencies and ideological positions within Reaganism. Reaganism indeed comprehends a diversity of interests in "the past," from a more old-line conservatism such as Kristol's to the mysticism of "nation," "race," and "religion" of multiple New Right elements, but the past that mattered most and first for the purposes of policy implementation was located in the already massively developed sectors of the economy.

For reasons I'll suggest, I think it unlikely that the long-term strategies of Reaganism can continue to be understood in and through direct economic implementation of specific policies; Bush's term in office has already supplied evidence of a number of shifts in focus, which are likely to be extended during Clinton's presidency if his campaign is any indication. Yet the effects of the recession, the resurgence of business interests in the Democratic party with Clinton's candidacy, the growing divisions within the Republican party itself under Bush's leadership, all have indicated that the myths of "free" economic growth will continue to exercise a magnetic attraction within the political field of Reaganism. To the extent its policies were forged in the attempt to direct the development of economic changes toward political ends, Reaganism made it necessary to once more think directly in terms of "political economy"—if not quite the same political economy that Marx saw in the nineteenth century. That imperative continues to mind its force in the midst of whatever changes take place in Reaganism itself, as even Bush was forced to acknowledge, if not persuasively enough to salvage a losing campaign.

In my parable of Miata advertising, I stressed the reliance on a notion of "freedom from constraints" as a constitutive force in the definitions of expectations and promises. Such freedoms have a particular resonance in relation to the mix of economic theories within Reaganism. Whether in Friedman's version or Hayek's, and likewise whether in the monetarism of Thatcherism or the supply-side of Reaganism, there was a certain common ground to be found across these economic theories in the principle of removing constraints that had impeded economic growth and interfered with the "free market." Thatcherism arguably faced greater difficulties in these terms, since—to borrow Walter Korpi's useful distinction—Britain was much closer to an "institutional" welfare state. The United States had remained at most a "marginal" welfare state, with correspondingly a still very strong ideological commitment to the idea that "private enterprise" could accomplish most tasks better and more efficiently than they could be handled through the public domain. But for Reaganism as well, there were nevertheless considerable political problems in the state implementation of anything like the economic policies implied by supply-side and its relatives. As I've suggested, there were theoretical objections from within Reaganism itself, from both older conservative positions such as Kristol's, and from the ideologues of the New Right, who were far more interested in "social issues." Further, the consumers of welfare-state services in the United States, particularly of so-called entitlement programs such as Social Security, were considerably more numerous than the "welfare constituencies" vilified by the New Right. What the New Right did was to identify their targeted groups with very specific programs in the United States, with the result that the federal funding cuts that did come were highly selective, isolating specific population groups.

Equally important, however (and what still troubles the construction of Miata ads, which must everywhere disguise the sense in which the Miata is the product of an elaborate corporate design and marketing system), is how in the United States the freedoms of individual agency central to the economic theories from which supply-side was derived had never been linked very strongly with *corporate* organization and its imperatives. Already by the mid-seventies that linkage had become even more tenuous, as Kristol himself had warned in an essay tellingly entitled "The Corporation and the Dinosaur":

> It is fairly clear that the American corporation today really doesn't understand what has happened to it in these past decades. It doesn't understand that, whereas the American democratic environment used to perceive it as being a merely economic institution, it now sees it as being to an equal degree a sociological and political institution, and demands that it behave as such. (74–75)

Much as supply-side theorizing might try to emphasize an economically based "automatic" sequence of connections in the removal of government constraints on corporate business, the resulting increase in productivity, and the general increase to follow in benefits for everybody, ideologically (as Kristol pointed out) there seemed no inherent logic in that sequence at all. Meanwhile, corporate organization in the United States had only begun to face the "dramatic challenges" posed by multinationalism and the revolutionizing of technologies of production, where the "oil crisis" of the early seventies served to highlight corporate failure in these economic terms no less than in the "sociological" and "political" spheres Kristol had emphasized.

The strategic success of Reaganism in this unpromising context was to have transformed its two negatives into a plus. In the early eighties Reaganism was faced on the one hand with the perceived distance between the valorization of individual economic freedoms and widespread suspicion of corporations allowed the freedom to pursue business as usual, and on the other hand with the relative backwardness of corporate organization itself and the reluctance to engage in technological modernization in the face of international competition. The politics of Reaganism transformed these negatives into a series of positive imperatives to advance the cause of "individual entrepreneurship" as the wave of the future. The necessity for corporate restructuring, insofar as that involved both decentralization and the diversification of increasingly specialized sectors— so-called flexible specialization that emphasizes sales of "positional goods" to niche markets could thus be made to seem identical with the reassertion of the freedoms of individual economic agents to reap the rewards of their effort and innovations. Economically, the best was still to come, and would arrive to the extent—as supply-siders wanted, if for rather different reasons—government regulation could be gotten out of the way of new business initiatives acting politically as well as economically in everyone's best interest. While to a certain range of New Right constituencies this seemed still an economic emphasis that ignored the more pressing problems of social issues, arguably it worked to the immense advantage of a New Right agenda, if—as in the case of supply-side theorists and economics—not exactly in the way they would have wanted.

For the "social issues crowd," the sanctity of the family, and of stable patriarchal relations within the family, was first and necessarily a moral and not an economic concern, and called for a reassertion of some mythical past before feminism, before the "influx" of other and racially different cultures, and so on. Economically, the impact of Reaganism was a double one, which indirectly did contribute to establishing conditions where that moral concern could begin to seem an anticipation of the future rather than a futile attempt to turn back the clock. As I argued in chapter 2, corporate restructuring required a larger and larger work force of part-time, temporary, swing-shift, nonunionized, and mobile workers. Women weren't forced out of the labor market—supposedly to return to being morally desirable good housewives—but they were increasingly forced out of good jobs and into anything that was available to pay the bills, while at the same time being subjected to increasing social pressures to stay home, keep the house, and raise children. Just as often, they were forced to themselves work in or to use the services of "private" child-care facilities. Equally important, those on the low end of these circumstances faced the inevitable dislocations of all kinds of family relations, the "feminization of poverty," the drying up of welfare aid, the intensification of work across all the activities of one's life, the deterioration of neighborhoods, an enormous increase of crime. But as the population faced with such conditions continued to grow, its very visibility created a situation where what had initially been resisted even within Reaganism as an "inappropriate" government intervention in "private" life, an imposition of morality, and so on, could instead begin to appear as—after military defense—the most vital *responsibility* of the state. And as in the case of calling in troops to quell the Los Angeles "riots" after the Rodney King verdict, the Bush administration gave every indication of continuing to expand this rhetoric of responsibility in all its interventions.

More generally, that is, Reaganism was again able ideologically to turn its two negatives into a plus, in a way that began to link economic and cultural imperatives directly as Bush followed Reagan into office. The disastrous effects of economic policies and the resistance to imposed moralities as a constraint on individual freedoms were transformed into what might be called by analogy a positive *cultural* entrepreneurship of the state. Thus rather than being an authoritarian presence to discipline the "spoiled children" of the sixties, the necessity of the state—its responsibility *as* a state—emerged full-blown in the Bush administration (in ways echoed throughout the Clinton campaign) as keyed to the image of "the child" in a different sense altogether, "the child" that must be cared for: latch-key; forgotten; abused (or "aborted" before being born), barely able to read or write, if literate at all; bereft of moral guidance even as assaulted on all sides by the temptations of easy drugs and easy sex; threatened by a whole array of sinister "new" diseases; no family role models in sight; and not incidentally sentimentalized almost beyond imagination by media images of careerist yuppies suddenly discovering at relatively advanced ages that child and family are what it's all about. While "ideally" to be the product of committed heterosexual union, as Spielberg's revised version of *Peter Pan* (nastily retitled as *Hook*) clearly realizes, this is a child whose ultimate care and protection requires a relentlessly remasculinized new world order, a new order that Bush has tried hard to identify as the special accomplishment of his presidency.

"The child" in this multiply imaged sense can then be divorced from the ideological imperatives and economic effects of Reaganism's immediate history, which produced the actual conditions in which so many children have to live, and can be made the image of necessity for state intervention and care. This occurs not by means of an "imposed morality" with its legal sanctions but by entrepreneurial government cultural initiatives designed to empower the family as a small-business operator, headed by Podhoretz's "producer-adult" and dedicated to producing a new and capable generation of children. "The child," in other words, became the perfect summary vehicle and image of Reaganism's developed form, the point of congruence between economics and morality, individual freedoms and state intervention, as the bearer of the future yet to come. As now the victim of always menacing "dominant" forces, "the child" is in need of rescue and care by those committed to a new and better future through the entrepreneurial state's cultural initiatives.

I take quite seriously in this sense Bush's announced determination to become "the education president," as clearly Clinton did as well, by echoing the commitment. The entrepreneurial state must be concerned with education in a much wider sense than institutional education (although that has been and will likely become even more directly a focus in the future, as I'll suggest). Gulf War propaganda makes the point neatly. The "lesson" here has to do with what "American character" is all about.* Not only was the pyrotechnical brilliance of the weaponry supposed to be at the service of minimizing to every extent possible the loss of American life, but the conduct of the war from top to bottom by those involved could function as an example of what passage to an educated, responsible adulthood might actually look like and might expect to receive as its reward of public approval on the return home. Comparisons to the Falklands War in which Britain had engaged earlier are then appropriate enough to some extent, but only within limits. That war played largely within Thatcherism's identifications of "nation" and "British" with a certain kind of strong, interventionist state. Here, in contrast, the war also plays with and to the image of possible futures for "the child," of what might emerge from the realization of "American character." As a transformation of early Reaganism's lashing out at the "spoiled children" who helped undermine the Vietnam War effort, the Gulf War thus foregrounded the movement into the developed Reaganism of the Bush administration's entrepreneurial state as a good manager, conscientiously responsible for educating its children for citizenship, a state now under the new stewardship of a determinedly centrist Democratic party committed to "even better" management.

III

Hall's Gramscian reading of Thatcherism in *The Hard Road to Renewal* (see especially chapters 8, 9, and 10) focuses first on the formation of a new hegemonic bloc, on the welding together of diverse constituencies into a political force capable of implementing specific policy directions. Like Hall, I have also relied on Gramsci in my quick sketch of a history of Reaganism, but it is the connection Gramsci emphasizes between hegemony and education that has supplied my primary focus. In my reading the Vietnam War and the Gulf

---

*I owe the reference to "American character" and what it implies to Susan Jeffords's forthcoming essay "The Patriot System, or Managerial Heroism," which brilliantly explores the connections between war technologies and the "character" of its managerial heroes, and how both are keyed to the role of Great Protector for those "children"-victims of the world unable to protect themselves.

War not only suggest conveniently bracketing events for this history but also, as I've implied, mark the emergence and development of Reaganite politics as educational; they are lessons for the growth and training of future citizens of the state. In turning now more directly to Reaganism's policy initiatives and reform directions for public institutional education, it is then important to recognize that they occur in the context of an already pedagogically organized political culture. Reaganism thus confirms in one sense at least a truism of radical left critique, that liberal educational reform alone cannot initiate real social change; for the changes brought about by Reaganism did not begin in the schools or in policies of school reform. Yet at the same time, the success of Reaganism indicates something of the limitations of that critique, in at least two ways.

While it did not begin in the schools, Reaganism nevertheless owes much of its success to a process of economic, political, and cultural education. Because that education did not take place in the schools doesn't make it any the less an education. Second, and despite how the reform of institutional education has been relatively slow to develop within the political culture of Reaganism, institutional education was perceived almost from the beginning as a primary target of Reaganism's self-definition as politically oppositional. Schools, and universities particularly, were identified as the home territory of war protesters, civil rights advocates, feminism, "pointy-headed" intellectuals—most of the familiar gallery of Reaganism's social villains. This is hardly "real history" in any sense, but it is deeply expressive of the importance attached to political education by Reaganism. It is in effect a reverse image of what Reaganism itself set out to achieve educationally; that is, perhaps the easiest way to grasp an emergent political self-definition of Reaganism is by attending to where it locates the primary effects of the politics it would challenge.

If paradoxically then, institutional education as now an increasingly and specifically targeted sector for new policy initiatives and reform directions becomes also a potential lever for social change in opposition to Reaganism. To the extent Reaganism reads its own teleology as culminating in the necessary reconstruction of the schools, institutional education identifies a space for effective challenge to Reaganism. The "idealism" of earlier liberal hopes for social reform through education begins to assume a certain material reality because of, and not despite, the remarkable itineraries of change initiated by Reaganism. Such material realities, however, impose their own conditions of possibility. There's no inherent logic at work in the "system" that guarantees this strategic importance to institutional education, nor is there any reason to think Reaganism utterly incapable of altering its own self-definitional directions. But there is reason at the moment to take advantage of what the immediate situation does offer, which requires, I think, some way of understanding Reaganism's direction of school reform other than as a return to a "traditional" curriculum.

As I have implied, Miata ads, as part of a complex consumer culture, can help in the understanding of what's wrong with a characterization of Reaganism as simply a defense of the established order and positional privileges of the past. Despite their retro look and obvious plays of nostalgia, there's nothing about the ads that suggests any desire to return to the past of Elans and their owners, or even to make available in the present some direct re-creation of the world of those past Elan owners. The ads are about expectations for the future, which only look to history within a "personalized" image of one's own past of youthful hopes and ambitions for the future. Films such as *City Slickers*, *Regarding Henry*, and *Hook* are, again, powerfully represented intensities of what this "personalization" is all about.

Its political significance can then appear across the terms of my juxtaposition of the Miata ads with Bush's nomination of Thomas, which in its denial of quotas and rights is also and everywhere a denial, like the Miata ads and the films, of any personal involvement in or benefit from the past as a *social* history. That is, expectations in this cultural imaginary have to do strictly with an assumption of the perennial "starting over" of individual itineraries made possible through the removal of constraints, against which the insistences of quotas, rights, and the like can be made to seem only the sad, sick, guilt-driven obsessiveness of defeatism, unwilling and unable to move with the times. Bush's nomination of Thomas will in contrast be made to appear an act of exemplary citizenship, which so far from being constrained by some false ideal of redressing the past, or desperately clinging to past privileges, can be dedicated to the spirit of a voluntary, generous—even selfless—and open engagement with the present as the construction site of a better future for everyone. The space opened by the nomination is an arena for this image of responsible, masculine, adult action, educationally charged with the responsibility not only of role model, but of recognizing the adulthood of others at the appropriately indicated time, across whatever barriers of race—or gender—might present themselves (hence Bush's insistent attempt to separate himself and his nomination of Thomas from the process of the hearings as a congressional operation). Most important, it functions then not for preserving positions of privilege from the past, but for creating the privileges of positional dominance in the future, for it is Bush, not Thomas, who is freed to act within the space of the nomination, even to command his subordinates to say nothing "negative" about Anita Hill, to remain politically "above the fray."

That educationally, social history has become of little interest to Reaganism may seem an odd assertion in the face of the efforts made by William Bennett, for example, as the Reagan administration's most visible and abrasive spokesperson for an educational vision located in the past and in "tradition." But here again, Miata ads are useful, given the title of Bennett's most famous statement: *To Reclaim a Legacy*. Miatas aren't Elans, and the story Bennett has to tell bears no more relation to a return to a "classically humanist" curriculum than Miata advertising to a return to the past of Elans and Elan owners. The "legacy" Bennett had in mind lies in the familiar territory of individual expectations and freedoms from constraint. Like the Miata ads, the retro imagery of his report appears early, in the fuzz-glare evocation of central texts in the humanities, describing them as those that "tell us how men and women of our own and other civilizations have grappled with life's enduring, fundamental questions: What is justice? What should be loved? What deserves to be defended? What is courage? What is noble? What is base?" (3). What is invoked here is not social history, but personally accented memory to serve as representatively exemplary: Remember when you were children and "dared" to ask such immense questions of the world? The point, as Bennett himself argued, "is not a return to an earlier [Elan] time when the classical curriculum was the only curriculum and college was available to only a privileged few" (2), nor is it a "now you can too . . ." promise of cheapened versions now, available to everybody. It's the expectations of a personal history, a personal past, to which you are invited to "return"; you are told to measure against it all the obscurely menacing dispossessions of the present that have constrained the freedoms of realization that should be yours.

The space available for action is then the present, if not only for yourself, as in the Miata ads, but for those children who are in danger of being subjected through "dominant" educational trends to a far worse dispossession, to the possibility of never really having that childhood to begin with. That is a theme Roger Kimball made central in *Tenured Radicals*, his "report from the front" about what is happening to the humanities: "Because many professors have been the beneficiaries of the kind of traditional education they have rejected and are denying their students, it is the students themselves who are the real losers in this fiasco" (xvii). Having inherited Elans for themselves, such professors are now busy pointing out all the car's many faults to a whole generation of students, who should be able to expect instead the contemporary promise of an educational Miata if they behave like adults.

The issue then is hardly some deep congruence between the economic interests of car advertising and the political interests of Reaganism, but the way in which consumer culture has learned from political events, and in turn how political programs have taken advantage of and shaped the lessons of consumer culture. While Reaganism has produced any number of sharp critiques, from writers such as Kristol and George Will, it has also addressed and aggressively reshaped the legitimacy of consumer culture as a field of citizen expectations and freedoms. It has found ways of making the logics of consumer culture a part of its own political and educational territory. This means that, more than ever, it's a mistake to identify Reaganism with the specific ideologies of those such as Kristol, instrumental in its early development, who offer a more familiar intellectual contempt for "mass culture" that can easily be dismissed as elitism. Kimball, like Allan Bloom, himself seems a recent reviver of Kristol-like arguments—in his savaging of Ann Kaplan and her work on MTV, for example. But Kimball has benefited from a considerable political history since Kristol; his crucial point, after all, is the following: "Not that her [Kaplan's] book is intended to be a popular account of this popular entertainment medium" (43). In other words, she has no idea why MTV is *popular*, and hence what its real potentials and dangers are, nor is she really interested. In fact, she has no business here at all, but should go back to what she was trained for.

While Kimball's argument, like Bloom's and Bennett's, targets recent developments in the humanities and thus has an immediate relevance to those of us who teach in these disciplines, it belongs nevertheless within a much broader range of educational initiatives within the development of Reaganism. His attack can be linked on the one hand to the "concerns" expressed often, in *Fortune* magazine for example, about corporate difficulty in finding the highly skilled work force they need, and on the other to "public choice"–inspired analysis of an educational "establishment" and its "vested interests." In this context the effect of Kimball's long, long "summaries" of papers and conference proceedings is a demonstration of incompetence. That is, beyond all the Marshall-amp noise about abandoning Western values and ideals, et cetera, is a claim that radical scholars simply don't know what they are talking about; how can they be expected to educate others? Likewise, if for *Fortune* as well as for any number of other and similar promulgators of "concern" from the "business community," the educational system is not training students in the skills required for "today's" work force, the clear implication is that educators themselves lack the necessary skills and knowledges.

What "public choice" analysis contributes is an explanation for these deficiencies in terms of the special interests of educators themselves, who will be motivated less by the "public good" in any sense—whether of Western values or of business productivity—than by maximizing their own authority and control over the workplace. Such motivations can't ever be eliminated entirely, but educational institutions can be "restructured" so that the motivations of educators can be more closely aligned with the needs of the clientele—parents, students, the business community—they supposedly serve. (If, for example, teachers could be held directly accountable to parents, then the avenues open to maximize their own individual authority and control as teachers would at the same time help realize parents' desires for a particular kind of education for their children.) It is within this larger context that Kimball's arguments suggest the particular relevance of the humanities for such potential restructuring. His critique, even more obviously than Bennett's, is aimed at the "spoiled children" of the sixties so often targeted by Reaganism, who have now themselves moved into positions of power, primarily in the humanities, as an institutional base for their special interests, where they can then coerce cooperation from the educational establishment and subvert the role of the state in properly educating its future citizens for adulthood.

Actual policy initiatives for institutional reform of education, however, were slow to develop while Reagan was himself president. Certainly a great deal of talk centered on education during his first term of office, but what happened was for the most part a long, slow slide of federal funding (as a percentage of aggregate outlays, funding for education, training, and employment fell from 5.3 in 1980 to 3.4 in 1984), with no real policy direction and nearly everybody furious, if for different reasons. It was also in 1984 that Bennett, as chair of the National Endowment for the Humanities, published *To Reclaim a Legacy*, and his elevation to education secretary was clearly an attempt to establish direction. The slide had been disastrous for the very process of corporate restructuring the administration had tried to encourage, as well as having devastating effects on many of the working-class and lower-middle-class constituencies the Reagan election campaign had encouraged so assiduously with visions of "entrepreneurial" success.

Bennett, however, while certainly definite, visible, and "abrasive," wasn't particularly effective. He never quite seemed to have grasped the sense in which corporate incentive for supporting state investment in an educational system had its payoff at the top, in the resources higher education supplied for technological development, and in providing highly skilled and specialized personnel. In his own way Bennett was (if paradoxically) "democratic" in his understanding of educational organization, because convinced that reform had to proceed across the board from the very lowest level of educational institutions, with the immediate task of higher education being to initiate the process. The benefits would then eventually be felt at the top, in a "new and improved" student population that had gone through a more rigorous selection process that had imparted considerably more real training and knowledge. "Social issues" folks of course liked his stress on fundamental values—religious training included—and his emphasis on standards and accountability played well enough through all the ideological positions of Reaganism. But the comprehensive sweep of his reform proposals seemed to have displaced more immediate and necessary priorities.

If perhaps inadvertently, however, Bennett did help create conditions for the emergence of a primary focus of reform on so-called student culture or, more often, "school culture." Rather than Bennett's comprehensive goal of addressing from the beginning questions of curricular reform, faculty responsibility, educational funding, and institutional change all at once, a "school culture" focus begins instead by asking what seems a much more limited question: What do students actually do in educational institutions, or more typically, following a relatively peripheral direction in Bennett's scheme, what *don't* they do? As Bennett's successor at the Endowment, Lynne Cheney wrote the 1988 report *Humanities in America*, strongly emphasizing how little had changed since the publication of *To Reclaim a Legacy*:

> In 1988–89, it is possible to earn a bachelor's degree from:
> —37 percent of the nation's colleges and universities without taking any course in history;
> —45 percent without taking a course in American or English literature;
> —62 percent without taking a course in philosophy;
> —77 percent without studying a foreign language. (Cheney, 5)

The subsequent discussion generated by the report and by such studies as Robert Zamsky's *Structure and Coherence. Measuring the Undergraduate Curriculum*, published the following year, was by no means confined to what students might not have to do, but extended to what "in fact" they didn't do.

Strategically, there's a certain initial leverage from this apparent "bottom-line" emphasis on school culture (which Bennett had pointed to, even if he failed to fully exploit it). Whatever educators may say about reform and innovation, about "meeting new challenges" and so on, school culture indices of measurement suggest there has been little visible effect on students. A "bottom line" of school culture thus affords Reaganism—as has happened in so many other instances as well—a way to turn liability to advantage. The slow drift of Reagan's first six years in office reappears in a "larger context" as an image of the ineffectuality of entrenched educational policies of the sixties that at best left school culture in the hands of students, who had no idea what to do, and at worst of course in the hands of the "spoiled children" of the sixties now become "tenured radicals."

Further, for all it seems initially a limited focus, school culture reform permits a remarkable new space of explanation for restoring attention to standards and assessment, in elementary and secondary schools as well as in colleges. Standardized tests, for example, rather than being a questionable imposition of standards, emerge in this logic as first of all a source of "information," a way of finding out what students actually do in schools and what they know. Tests are removed from the context of debate over "imposed" values versus diversity, censorship versus academic freedom, and so on, and made to function instead as the means of generating data on which to base subsequent policy decisions. (If *this* is what they know, then . . .) Hence Bush defended the *America 2000* recommendation for regular, standardized skill testing as simply an instrument rather than a policy, a way to discover what's going on in the schools, unobscured by the motivations of special-interest groups and the conflicting ideological values brought to bear on proposals for curricular reform. A focus on school culture in these terms thus makes possible some accommodation between the more economically oriented ideologies of Reaganism and the "social issues crowd," by locating a common field of "problems" that can be addressed by a variety of flexible reform proposals. At the same time, it softens the overt antagonism to the "special interests" of an educational "bureaucracy" that had been so pervasive earlier in the development of Reaganism, and which had almost required administrators to speak out in defense of their faculty as well as themselves. Rather, school culture reform can appear open to the initiatives of administrators who are willing to work toward the goal of improving "coordination" and efficiency.

Most important, however, the very notion of school culture creates a sense in which student knowledges, practices, values, expectations, and beliefs are to be understood, precisely, as *school* culture: as the effects of educational organization, curriculum, and instruction, as if the school were a hermetically sealed unit within which students existed as children and where the relevant measure of the appropriateness and efficiency of schools could then be read off from the student "product" generated, much as one might evaluate the success of corporate organization in terms of the "bottom line" of product quality and sales. Thus it blocks any attention whatsoever to how students have been affected by the economics of Reaganism, by its political culture, and by the lessons of consumer education they experience in the marketplace. This school culture image of the student-child to be shaped by educational practices is especially absurd at the college level, given simply the changing demograph ics of the college population. Already, by the mid-eighties, 40 percent of those enrolled in college were over the age of 25, and 40 percent of the total college population were enrolled part-time and working. The number of women enrolled in college had risen from roughly one-third of the student population in the fifties to over one-half by the eighties, and many of these women were over 25 and part-time students. Further, while the rate of African-American and Hispanic high-school completion increased by 62 percent from the mid-seventies to the mid-eighties, college enrollment for these groups declined from 35.8 percent to 26.9 percent (Eaton, 132–33).

To address even the changes registered by such statistical profiles, let alone the entire complex of economic-cultural changes over the last two decades, as a matter of school culture and its "deteriorating" product represents a massive ideological intervention whose effects will be ours to deal with as educators for some time to come. While in one sense a school culture focus reinstalls education as a national priority—already advertised everywhere in the proliferation of "public service" announcements and special programs dedicated to convincing students to "stay in school, get an education"—in another sense it fundamentally alters an understanding of what that priority involves.

I V

Historically, the emergence of a goal of universal public education in the United States in the second half of the nineteenth century and the early decades of the twentieth century was shaped in detail through the insertion of educational institutions within more and more social territories, if in very different ways for different institutions. Education, that is, could be recognized as potentially universal, and hence the necessary focus of national policy initiatives, insofar as educational institutions became directly functional operators within more and more sectors of the social field. In his inaugural address as president of Harvard, Charles William Eliot had argued that "we do not apply to mental activities the principle of division of labor; and we have but a halting faith in special training for high professional employments. The vulgar conceit that a Yankee can turn his hand to anything we insensibly carry into high places, where it is preposterous and criminal" (11). This often-quoted statement, however, anticipated not only what the future process of training and assessing Harvard students would be like but also a different form of authority and a different institutional presence for Harvard in the midst of "high professional employments." Harvard would be "there" because expectations of exactly how "high professional employments" should best be carried out required its presence.

Likewise, if in an obviously different register of social fields, Alexander Inglis's proposals in 1918 for the development of "vocational education" in the public schools spoke to both curricular and assessment changes, and called for an effective educational presence in the workplaces of industrial production. For Inglis, education, in some form at least, belonged in such workplaces every bit as much as in the places of "high professional employments" that had concerned Eliot earlier. These examples could be multiplied many times over, for the point again is that education became a national priority as educational institutions were built into an arterial system of transport across the multiple territories of a social formation, with stations everywhere and the promise of rail lines linking them. Whether you were certified as competent to work as a consultant engineer doing metal stress analysis for building contractors, or alternatively as a specialist in corporate law, or as a sheet metal finisher, your education was assumed capable of getting you "there," wherever in the instance "there" might be. This was so because institutional education was a designated system of transport to its own existing station already "there," within whatever given field. Thus, as I argued in chapter 2, education became the perceived vehicle for ideologies of rising social expectations. Education promised a ticket to ride, and a visible map of social territory organized around the proliferation of institutional stations of education.

A school culture focus marks a fundamental break with this history of education. It defines education as a national priority by openly *disconnecting* and removing schools from other social territories. Schools instead market a student-product, package students with their purely internal "culture." Students then may or may not emerge from school culture as responsible adults, morally desirable persons, politically informed citizens, capably trained workers, or whatever. But they *will* be available to and taken up by employers, political parties, cultural groups, and so on, if the quality of the product is approved, much as Thomas's nomination to the Supreme Court reflects first of all Bush's consumer approval rather than Thomas's productive merit. Schools, that is, function as specific social marketing to maximize opportunities and remove constraints on movement, but they increasingly can't "move" anybody anywhere, because their institutional stations throughout the social formation are being progressively abandoned and boarded up, tracks left rusting, like some vast derelict railway system left over as an obsolete relic from the past. Institutional education no longer supplies a useful map of the social field. Educational reform thus becomes a matter of the reform of education in order to make its products more desirable, rather than being a lever with which to transform the rest of society, as both Eliot and Inglis had imagined. Likewise, student expectations are to be redefined in terms of "freedom from" constraints on opportunities, rather than "rights to" transport on the basis of educational achievement.

Marxist models of educational reproduction have offered a powerful critique of the educational system in the United States, by assuming from the beginning that schools only rarely "moved" any body anywhere in any case. Education for these critiques recreates in different and ideological form the more fundamental and already existent determinations of social position. Schools are the ideological "factory" producing students whose training and positionalities then reproduce the larger configurations of social organization. Such critique thus identifies an educational system as the primary means by which a dominant social formation transforms each new generation of students, like the heterogeneous "raw material" of factory production, into a necessarily limited range of "socially accepted" roles suitable for the slots already available.

School culture reform, however, is not open to critique in quite the same way, because it is not organized around ideological (re)production in this sense, but rather through indices of marketability that recognize an always proliferating expansion of consumer "needs" and "demands." In other words, the model here is the service sector rather than the factory; the organizing principle is located in market research analysis of consumer needs rather than in control of (re)production; and student itineraries through an educational system must conform to the flow patterns of shifting consumer demands rather than to a production schedule identifying the steps from raw material to finished product.

While "product" remains a term that is applied to services generally as well as to the commodities of industrial manufacture, there is a crucial difference in the meaning of the term. As product, services name what is being marketed ("our product is service"), with no necessary reference either to a process through which raw material is transformed or to a location such as a factory where the transformation is accomplished. Students in this sense are then the "product-services" marketed by the schools, not the raw material that the schools transform into a commodity-product to fit the appropriate slot. As educators, our product too is service, in the form of the students we make available to meet the shifting demand curves of the marketplace. Our work thus becomes a matter of market research analysis on the one hand and product distribution possibilities on the other. And the schools where we work will no longer seem to be massive factories linked by the interstices of a transportation system to every sector of the social field, but simply supply and distribution centers, services available on demand, adjacent to but not impinging on other sectors.

The immediate effects of school culture reform internally will then involve redefinitions not only of teacher responsibilities but also of teacher expertise. If it is responsible for student marketability, teacher expertise must look first to the specificities of consumer "needs." Disciplinary field training within an academic structure becomes subordinate to the ability to read field demand outside the schools, in response to pressures from both parents and students to ensure a marketable education. Educational administrators will then have a greater role in defining expertise as well. Unlike in the early development of Reaganism, to the extent that administrators are encouraged and rewarded for initiatives to improve efficiency, coordinate programs more effectively, and introduce increasingly detailed assessment procedures and standards for merit raises, they will also be positioned to identify and oversee the permissible boundaries of expertise. At the university level, that will mean stricter and more regularized tenure and promotion review procedures that inevitably penalize scholarly work whose "payoff" is not immediately obvious, and programs such as women's studies and ethnic studies whose faculties cross disciplinary territories. At the secondary and elementary level, as Sara Freedman had recognized about merit pay proposals (24 28), the already elaborate practices of labor intensification (such as the use of pre-testing, designed as much as anything to check whether teachers have adequately prepared students for exams) will increasingly focus on teacher as well as student skills, which, given the primary labor force of elementary and secondary schools, will then also target women specifically and directly.

Externally, the effects of school culture reform will function to protect other social sectors from educational interference. To the extent school culture is understood to "reproduce" anything, what it reproduces is not the determinations of "the social formation" generally, but school culture itself. Students then become available to potential consumers of educational services located elsewhere in the social formation *at the option of those consumers*. Service labor of whatever kind, as I argued in chapter 2, is expected to advertise in the very process of the work, and teaching as service in this sense is no exception. In the emerging terms of school culture reform, a book such as Kimball's *Tenured Radicals* is only a first step, a way of "exposing" radical criticism to view. The isolation of schools as an internal formation in school culture reform can then imply that the labor process exposed is only bad advertising. Despite Kimball's own apocalyptic warnings about the decline of Western culture, et cetera, the more "crudely appropriate" response available is simply the continual reiteration that it doesn't sell. If radical education really offered a valuable service to potential consumers, people would be snapping it up; they aren't, so it isn't. A school culture reproduces a school culture, and as a result it has no necessary or intrinsic connection to any other social sector whatsoever. Nor do would-be radical scholars have any expertise or authority to speak relevantly to other sectors. A culturally entrepreneurial state expects entrepreneurial education, where, in that famous Thatcherite phrase, you could get "value for money," not some radical teacher's idea of what the social world should be like.

School culture reform identifies education as a national priority,

and has begun to generate policies that would implement the restructuring of educational institutions. Schools in this vision will be very
different from what earlier educators such as Eliot and Inglis imagined as the locationally functional network of institutions spread
throughout the social formation, or from that familiar Marxist critique of such ideals as in fact involving an ideological (re)production
factory. Schools will instead be responsible, like any other specific
sector, for the processes and practices that maximize their product
quality and attractiveness. Likewise, as I argued in chapter 2, their
"failures" will be identified in terms of obsolescence, of clinging to
the no longer viable assumptions and values of an educational past
that like factories, railroads, and the whole panoply of an industrial
sector seems merely a relic of another economy. Would-be radical
scholars within that economy will then increasingly be made to appear "frozen in amber," less the menacing threat of Kimball's "tenured radicals" than an aging brat pack unable and unwilling to see
an emergent future for what it is, for all their claims to newness and
innovation.

Despite the often considerable volume of a rhetoric of return (to
a traditional curriculum, general standards, mandated assessment
levels, and so on), school culture reform is not finally about a return
to anything. It is driven by a vision of education as a service mar-
keter and distributor, making available a student "product"—in the
service meaning and not the industrial meaning of the term—where
and when it is needed. It is postindustrial education for a postindustrial, service economy. And like service employees everywhere, the
work force of educational institutions will be expected not only to
offer a service, but, as I argued in chapter 2, to advertise the service
in the practices of the job. Teacher work will be continually on view
in and through the visible advertising supplied by student product
quality. School culture reform after all begins in the assessment procedures of that student quality as a direct index of teacher work.
Teachers' product, too, is service.

One of the many ironies here is the success of this Reaganite
vision in soliciting the help and support of a great many ostensibly
"conservative" scholars in the humanities, who don't exactly see
themselves as the service reps they're in effect destined to be. While
there's perhaps a certain amusement value in registering the eventual
fate of "conservative" scholarship in these terms of school culture

reform, oppositional education must think first of students. And there's nothing amusing in the recognition that the school culture—reformed educational institutions of the future would also be expected to supply, in ever increasing numbers, the terminal throwaways on which the political order of Reaganism depends.

V

The notion that left politics can learn something from Reaganism is not easy to accept, as Hall discovered in trying to argue the point in reference to Thatcherism in Britain. Without trying to be as comprehensive as were Hall's suggestions, it seems to me worth taking up part of his argument and applying it to Reaganism. Hall is concerned not only with exposing the ideological grounds of Thatcherism, but with learning how Thatcherism implemented its policy directions. That point has become especially important, for at least a couple of reasons. First, as Hall himself has acknowledged, if "Thatcherism" (or "Reaganism" in the context of the United States) is understood as naming a specific set of policies initiated while Margaret Thatcher was prime minister, then the conditions under which Thatcher herself came to power and within which she set certain policies in motion are not themselves the product of nor synonymous with "Thatcherism." As a result, analysis of Thatcherism is a matter of asking how and in what ways the Thatcher government exploited those conditions to political advantage, while at the same time asking what alternative directions might be possible. Thatcherite policies, in other words, are not an inevitable "tendency" of the present, nor can the political present be understood simply as "Thatcherism."

Second and correlatively, however, there remains a necessity to recognize that Thatcherism, and Reaganism, must also identify much more than a specific set of policies and policy directions. They have become what Gramsci might well understand as a kind of political "common sense," the largely unacknowledged assumptions that "make sense" of current conditions and hence set parameters within which certain policies seem plausible and realistic, while others in contrast seem hopelessly naive, utopian, out-of-date, or incoherent. "The Welfare State," for example, is likely to appear in current political debates as neither the great enemy to economic productivity it seemed to supply-siders nor the best hope of liberal technocrats but rather, across the political spectrum, just a kind of residual combination of dreamy idealism and bureaucratic inertia no longer remotely adequate to the needs of the present. That perception seems just common sense, but it's a perception nevertheless that depends on the political culture of Thatcherism in Britain and Reaganism in the United States, even when that political culture reaches a specific policy voice, as it were, in Bill Clinton that differs from the policies of Ronald Reagan or George Bush. Common sense, as Gramsci explained, is hardly a unified political philosophy or a consistent interpretation of existing conditions. Pointing out contradictions in common sense, however, is not the same as changing the configuration of boundary conditions by which, contradictory or not, common sense permits the implementation of specific policy directions.

Learning from Reaganism is a matter of understanding the formation of a political agency capable of transforming that passive voice "common sense permits" into an active intervention that initiates political change. Reaganism itself, that is, offers a certain model of escape from a very narrowly based internal movement politics—caught in the dilemma of trying to balance ideological purity against pragmatic compromise—into a movement able to implement wide-ranging policies across a vast number of social sectors. And while I can't imagine any good reason to want to build a political movement that looks like Reaganism, and even less reason to think such a movement might have its "base" in university humanities departments, it does seem to me necessary at every specific location of potential political challenge to Reaganism, including university humanities departments, to find ways of escape from that purity/compromise dead end. This is necessary even if it does mean learning from the very politics of Reaganite hegemony that must be challenged.

The increasingly visible conservative image of the humanities as a threateningly radical political enclave, and the no less widespread—if less dramatic—image of narrow and sectarian incompetence, seem to me to make that process of learning an important one. Perhaps the first and simplest lesson, however, involves recognizing where the humanities are perceived as threat. It is, I think, a question first of *where* the threat lies, rather than of what is threatening, as even Kimball's argument implies: "Thus what began as an intoxicating intellectual spree at a few elite institutions—places such as Yale, Johns Hopkins, Brown, and certain campuses of the University of California—has quickly spread to many other institutions. This metastasis is indeed one of the most troubling developments in the story of the crisis of the humanities" (xiii). As history this may be silly, but it does explain something about the strategic politics of Reaganism's interventions, which will be positioned as "tolerant" of virtually any such "intellectual spree" so long as it remains an appropriately isolated operation. It is perceived as a threat when it's perceived to go where it doesn't belong, and where it might then seriously affect the quality of the educational product. The "silly" history is crucial to this strategic positioning, for it helps establish an imagery of viral disease spreading from isolated sectors throughout the body politic, a disease which must be contained, by school culture reform most obviously. Learning from Reaganism is not a matter of granting the plausibility of such "explanations," but of understanding how Reaganism could be positioned as capable of delivering explanations in the first place.

At least part of the answer to that "how" involves what seems to me the rather frightening range of knowledge in a book such as Kimball's *Tenured Radicals*. This is a different matter than the accuracy of his knowledge —whether he has a clue what's really at stake in Derrida's discussions of feminism, et cetera—and far different from questions of whether he's misunderstood arguments or taken them out of context. In some simple, direct sense, he knows enough to do what he wants to do, which is to place himself as a reporter "inside the radical walls" with the expertise to deliver reliable information to be judged and acted upon by others located elsewhere. While there's a lot of relatively easy-to-dismiss apocalyptic nonsense in Kimball, there's also a remarkably detailed itinerary of titles, names, dates, places, terminologies, and academic practices; and Kimball isn't so intent on delivering his message of the underlying ideologies of "tenured radicals" that he ignores this surface.

It is the detail of the surface that supplies the crucial leverage of the argument, that the humanities are not just a large, complex, mysterious field of benignly remote academic practices, but are shaped by specific political constructions toward particular ends. Even those who wouldn't necessarily accept his vision of what the humanities ought to be can recognize a sense in which support of or even indifference to whatever exactly they are need not be automatic or obvious. The perception of the humanities as politically interested has been very much a part of critiques of the humanities by the scholars Kimball attacks (if in rather different terms). What Kimball does is redirect the force of critique such that it is his book that appears to be the means to open the humanities from the outside for inspection, discussion, and challenge. By seeming to position himself on an inside, his strategic power then lies precisely *in having constituted the terms of "outside" and "inside."* It is that constitutive division that puts "radical scholars" in the unenviable position of appearing to fear, resist, and impose constraints on the freedoms of everybody to "inspection, discussion, and challenge." The immediate effectiveness of *Tenured Radicals* is then to have created a space for explanation, an explanation that Kimball is quite happy to deliver.

What Kimball doesn't try to do is deliver an explanation before there's space available. Yet more often than not, a certain rush to explain has been the preferred strategy of left politics—not entirely without reason, for in one sense it is blindingly obvious that, for example, Hayek, Friedman, Gilder, such think tanks as the Institute of Economic Affairs or the Heritage Foundation, and so on, are not particularly good sources for understanding what "multinational capitalism" is "really" all about. Likewise, it's true that Glazer, Lemann, Moynihan, Scruton, and the others aren't likely to deliver any understanding of racism. As a result it's impossible to explain the policies of Reaganism by turning to such sources. Nevertheless, to the extent that one political goal involves doing what's possible to disengage the level of public support that has permitted the *implementation* of Reaganism's policies, it's necessary to recognize that no explanation, no matter how impeccable its sources or its logic, will have even a remote chance of success without first carving a space for explanation out of the territories now occupied by all these Reaganite names and policy constructions. They are important to know, not in order to "explain" Reaganism, but to determine how to act on that knowledge, to do something about Reaganism. This is not at all to deny the importance of what can be known about multinational capitalism and racism and how knowledge must necessarily be drawn from other sources altogether, but it is to stress the politically effective importance of *where* you know it. Kimball's strategic success, again, lies in appearing to speak *for* the outside, but *from* the inside, and it is the power of that intervention that must be contested.

Kimball's targets are so often what he sees as the fraudulent "ideological" politics of race, gender, and class issues that it's easy to overlook the territories on which his own attacks tend to focus, which is more often than not that of critical analysis of "mass culture" constructions. It's not only specific political directions of critique that exercise him. What he isolates over and over are discussions such as those of Ann Kaplan on MTV, Mary Ann Doane on films, Houston Baker on blues and rap, Stanley Cavell on Springsteen and *Star Trek*, and so on. The rationale for his concern is expressed in terms of an "idea of literary quality that transcends the contingencies of race, gender, and the like or that transcends the ephemeral attractions of popular entertainment" (xv). The danger of such a rationale lies not only in the implications of "literary quality" but also (as I argued in chapter 5) in how it protects the "attractions of popular entertainment" as, precisely, "ephemeral." To some very great extent, Reaganism has become a politics of "everyday life" that can be expected to support all such initiatives as Kimball's that promise the refocusing of critical attention on "literary quality" (or whatever) that might "transcend" the ephemera of everyday life and its entertainments. The ephemera thereby are left as territories to be occupied exclusively by the political culture of Reaganism itself.

School culture reform, however, would radically extend this enforcement of territory, far beyond anything Kimball's book might accomplish. While in its broad outlines a concept of school culture speaks to and by means of policy decisions that affect the organization of institutional education, in its molecular detail the goal of isolating the process of education that takes place in the schools will increasingly have to do with specific matters of curriculum as well, such as the study of "mass culture." Once again, the difficulty for oppositional politics involves a question of where as well as what you know, of where knowledges can be put to effective use.

I've had occasion often enough to suggest how Reaganism managed to turn liabilities to its own advantage, and I think the emergent educational reform process involved in the concept of school culture imposes a need to learn the trick very quickly indeed. School culture will not only limit ideological mobilities, creating pressures that make it much more difficult, for example, for educators in the humanities to engage with other disciplinary territories, let alone "market forces" or the "ephemera" of consumer culture. It will also limit institutional mobilities, the effective presence of educational institutions in other sectors of the social formation. It would leave us as teachers stuck in the midst of an isolated institutional apparatus increasingly imaged as obsolete, and often then coerced into defending practices that in the past have themselves been for good reason targets of left political attack. This is an all-too-familiar position with respect to any number of characteristic forms of the so-called welfare state as it came under fire from Reaganism. The liabilities, then, are considerable, but there do seem to be ways in which they can be turned to advantage.

While school culture reform is in some sense *about* students and very obviously directed *at* students in multiple ways, it is not at all *for* students, and certainly not for all students. As I argued in chapter 2, what in economic terms a service economy requires from an educational system is the *present* production of obsolescence, of more and more "children" whose expectations and whose skills and whose lives are throwaways, terminal junk. Likewise, in cultural terms, the kind of "legacy" imaged by Bennett, Kimball, and others, whose appeal is based in their versions of "personal memory," can have little resonance for many students, any more than the attenuated yuppiedom of back-to-farm-and-family would charm migrant farm workers. Consumer education's far more diverse lifestyle identities and choices are often for good reason immensely attractive, but for all that Reaganism has appropriated these logics of choice into its own politics, they don't have to remain there. As Stuart Hall has argued often and persuasively, "choice" is hardly a concept invented by the right for its exclusive use. School culture can legitimize a remarkable range of reform proposals directed toward educational restructuring, but the grounds of legitimation must necessarily avoid what *students* know very well: that their choices, knowledges, and expectations are by no means derived solely from the internal "culture" of an educational system. To the extent opposition to school culture can escape the confines of ideological "purity," that student awareness can become available as a crucial lever of opposition within the schools targeted by reform. It is useful in this context to learn something of how Reaganism itself emerged from an impasse of ideological "purity."

Conceptually, Reaganism drew on a number of sources for its opposition to the welfare state, from the market philosophies of Friedman and Hayek to the religious fundamentalism of the "moral majority." But much to the dismay of its own ideological purists, Reaganism did not rely on the assumed value of these conceptual resources to become a politically effective bloc. To some great extent Reaganism overcame its own deficiencies and liabilities by learning to create images of opposition through attending to the expressions of fears, hostilities, frustrations, perceptions of disproportion, and dismay at an imminent future across an enormous range of social territories and potential constituencies. The creation of that oppositional imagery likewise opened a wider and wider space for the subsequent "explanations" and policy directions of Reaganism's political culture. The lesson is clear enough, and usefully applicable to our own immediate context of educational institutions.

Given the visibility of Reaganism's political culture, and its intricated connections with the instabilities of consumer education, it won't always be possible to find students who express dissatisfaction with educational institutions in "politically correct" ways, and who thus seem available as a "natural" constituency for left politics. (It will be more difficult at the university level, given what "reforms" have already accomplished with selective admissions policies and financial aid.) This doesn't imply, however, some necessity to abandon any notion of political correctness, but to recognize at the same time that dissatisfactions exist even when the languages of pc don't—deeply, fundamentally, and throughout a remarkable range of the student population. Students do know well enough that they are not solely the "product" of school culture. The more left politics hears *only* its own conceptual assumptions, however, the less likely it is to register student knowledges and hear student dissatisfactions for what they are. Rather than a "pragmatic" requirement to then negotiate some treacherous path between "purities" and "compromises," the alternative is to abandon any assumption of immediately available "natural" constituencies. It is to think instead of how to develop capacities to go somewhere else where the languages are different and perceptions of the issues occur in other forms; to create spaces of explanation and learn new directions accordingly; to develop and change assumptions and values that can work effectively in those spaces; and most obviously, to do so in ways that

always remember that left political commitments to education, unlike Reaganism, must be not only to and about but for all students.

As I've suggested frequently enough throughout, political work
in these terms will then often find itself engaged with "obsolete"
ideologies, in the patchwork repair of yesterday's ideologies no less
than the yesterday's technologies with which deteriorating school
"physical plants" are crammed. Historically, it's easy to demonstrate
how the educational linkages of rising social expectations and rights
to social position were grounded in a bourgeois politics of individual, democratic citizens (and in the much earlier challenges of
"natural rights" to aristocratic social hierarchies). But that historical
context is perhaps not the best one in which to hear current student
dissatisfactions that are nevertheless very often expressed in the languages of rights. Those dissatisfactions must be heard instead as the
use of what resources seem immediately available to be mobilized
against all the ways in which consumer education and the political
culture of Reaganism have functioned to redefine expectations as
"freedom from" constraints rather than "rights to" position. However obsolete, that is, languages of rights at least seem available to
students, to use in resisting all the pressures toward "marketability"
that will only increase with the policies of school culture reform,
and even more immediately as recession "inexplicably" continues.

Marketability in these terms involves something different from
the commodification of skill training and of students themselves.
Within a logic of class-as-lifestyle and of freedom from constraints
in the realization of performative agency, the demand to become
marketable induces less some fatally self-alienating anxiety of commodification than the sense of losing command of location. As I have
argued, the logic belongs to the rapid movements of a postindustrial service economy rather than to a factory model of transforming
student "raw material" into a commodity. As a result, marketability
can never really be tested where you are, with what you have, but
requires movement somewhere else, entry into a seemingly interminable series of checkpoints linked by no discernible rationale of
"progress" beyond the imperative to move again as quickly as possible. Reaganism has learned to exploit to the fullest the ways in
which such freedoms of movement may feel wonderful at the controls of a remote TV monitor, in the midst of the endless "choices"
of consumer culture. But it feels rather less so in the bounce from

McDonalds counter work to an Office Assistant II position to part-time day-care-center help, across the accumulating hours of night classes, advising appointments, transcript evaluations, financial-aid deadlines, check float, apartment shifts, and bus schedules, and so on and on. When in perpetual motion through all this, and wherever ideas of "rights" came from, its languages promise what seem some possibilities of enabling control with which to contest the forces that keep you in motion.

Neither consumer education nor the political culture of Reaganism have been blind to such possibilities, and thus in any number of contexts have made rights an object of nostalgic affection, which can be trotted out when useful, as in the identification of so-called reverse discrimination and in claims that "politically correct" university faculty are suppressing the "right" to free speech on the part of conservatives. But the use of nostalgia here, as so often, signals a recognition of dangers which nostalgia must function to contain, and which often explode in unexpected ways, as recently in the David Duke election campaign in Louisiana with its slogan of equal rights for whites.

It was a mistake, I think, to dismiss immediately the disavowals of Duke on the part of Republicans, from the Bush administration on down. The danger for Reaganism was not that the Duke campaign might give the game away, reveal the "real" racism otherwise more effectively disguised. It's that Duke didn't know how to play the racism that has "worked" for Reaganism, the racism that has constituted itself as political representative of and facilitator for those "innovative blacks" who have modernized themselves—moved with the times—and helped make "race issues" a "thing of the past"; the racism that will retain notions of "rights" only as nostalgia productions; the racism that promises to take care of all its "children." Bush's racism, for example, like the Miata advertising and his nomination of Thomas, continued to play freedom from constraints, depending everywhere on producing the obsolescence of race as a primary category of social relations. It would rewrite the promise of new social positions from a matter of rights to a matter of freedom from constraints, where for whites again race becomes, precisely, just a now obsolete constraint of the past.

New trends in corporate human resources management also contribute to a perception of race as obsolete. In his significantly titled *Beyond Race and Gender* (published in 1990, and introduced with a foreword by Avon CEO James Preston), business consultant R. Roosevelt Thomas joins a great many other authors to recognize so-called managing diversity strategies as the key to corporate competitiveness in the current business climate. A conception of diversity must be expanded—"beyond race and gender," as Thomas's title implies—to include difference "with respect to age, functional and educational backgrounds, lifestyle preferences, tenure within the organization, personality traits, and ways of thinking" (170). White men are then also constituted as "different," and included with everyone else rather than segregated, as often happens in diversity workshops.

In these arguments, freedom from constraints appears as in effect the "right" of corporations to determine hiring practices without the guidance of merely "reactive" (Thomas's term) policies such as affirmative action. Once managers recognize that a diverse work force offers competitive advantages and reorganize "corporate culture" accordingly, there will be a "natural creation of a diverse work force" and a "natural upward mobility for minorities and women" (28) within the corporation. "Natural" in this context doesn't mean conformity to some universalized norms of human nature, but conformity to the new "nature" of the corporation, free from the constraints of external guidelines such as affirmative action. "True, all groups will benefit" from managing diversity strategies, Thomas argues, "whether they are different in terms of age, lifestyle, gender or race." Lest it be forgotten, however, what the point of managing diversity is, Thomas then adds: "But their benefit is not the driving motivation. Managing diversity presumes that the driving force is the manager's, and the company's, self-interest" (168). Or as Ann Morrison argues a similar reminder in *The New Leaders*: "The explicit goal is to strengthen the organization by leveraging a host of significant differences" (7).* Like Miata advertising, managing diversity strategies promise a present power of choice for whites that runs on into the future.

In contrast to these new corporate directions and to Bush ad-

---

*For an extended discussion of managing diversity strategies, see Evan Watkins and Lisa Schubert, "The Entrepreneurship of the New: Corporate Direction and Educational Issues in the 90s."

ministration policies, and despite his facelifts and media "manipulations," Duke was an educational dropout from the political culture of Reaganism. Hence his classroom disruptions would be imaged as disparagingly by more "mainstream" Republicans as the "infantile disorders" of the left, if for very different reasons.

Like Duke, however, and even more insidiously, Pat Buchanan's racism also reinvents, out of the very matrix of consumer education, rights as a crucial category (and a racially marked category), borrowing Duke's infamous slogan of "equal rights for whites." The danger for any would-be oppositional politics is that genuinely alternative possibilities are foreclosed across this political field, as from one side corporate strategies deploy the resources of a consumer culture toward a politics of freedom from constraints, and from the other Buchanan's "backlash" appropriates rights itself as an exclusive category of white choice. This means that for left politics Buchanan and the corporate world are not two versions of what is at bottom the same thing, but two very different things that require very different political strategies to contest. Corporate policies for managing diversity are simply not open to the same kinds of challenge as are Buchanan's appeals to the rights of whites.

I'm not then suggesting some left metaphysical investment in the languages or concepts of rights. Wherever they appear, from expressions of student dissatisfactions to the Duke campaign itself, the languages of rights shape a region that requires an ability for strategic shifting. Rights can be a usefully repaired technology of social empowerment to be deployed against the demands for marketability imposed by school culture reform, and at the same time something that, as in the Duke campaign, appears a threatening engine of repression that must be dismantled. "The differential mode of oppositional consciousness," Chela Sandoval argues in "U.S. Third World Feminism," "depends upon an ability to read the current situation of power and of self-consciously choosing and adopting the ideological form best suited to push against its configurations, a survival skill well-known to oppressed peoples" (15). And the development of an effective oppositional consciousness, as I've argued throughout, can never afford the luxury of dispensing with the socially designated obsolete, the out-of-date, and the outmoded. Oppositional consciousness must instead learn the skills of repair, and where these skills can be most usefully deployed.

The repair of the obsolete can be strategically inventive, even if the invention will never count as "innovative" in the dominant coding of obsolescence/innovation. Within educational institutions, if what can be heard in student dissatisfactions involves a perceived loss of rights and limitations on choice, then that's the territory of repair and invention that must be worked in educationally, even if it involves working on throwaway ideologies and conceptual relics "from the past." One crucial lesson to be learned from Reaganism itself, after all, is that no alternative educative process can work without first creating a space for its operation in existing territory.

Far more directly than either George Bush or Pat Buchanan, however, it was Ross Perot's campaign that attempted to repeat the first great ideological success of Reaganism: its self-definition as an oppositional vanguard, engaged in challenging a menacing and mysterious dominant power whose effects show up anywhere, everywhere. Yet repetition—as Marx recognized long before it became a truism of poststructuralist thought—is always repetition with a difference. Perot abandoned his campaign and then returned to it again. The immediately crucial difference, however, is less in how Perot in any case never really collected the personal prestige Reagan enjoyed than in the rapidity with which his *campaign*—even before officially announced as a campaign—collected corroborating replies. If in 1979 Reagan and his proposals still looked, even to some Reagan voters, "too simple" for an increasingly complex world, Perot in contrast was figured by means of the staggering feat of *successfully* appearing to have no real proposals at all, not even "too simple" ones. As campaign strategists on this new team, Ed Rollins and Hamilton Jordan would have been required to convert the "outsider" rhetoric that Jordan had tentatively crafted for Jimmy Carter, and that Rollins had helped perfect for Reagan, into an image of Perot as a "no-sider," the ultimately competent new political technology to unlock constraints once and for all, to realize everyone's dreams. It was an image more or less successfully grafted onto the Clinton campaign and subsequently onto his creation of a "transition team" drawn from diverse interests.

Looking backward, Marx could claim that history the second time around is farce rather than tragedy. Looking backward on the history of Reaganism is a luxury we don't yet possess. For all the signs of significant shifts and new policy directions emerging during and after the recent presidential campaign, Reaganism as I have argued remains the political common sense of the present. And in the midst of this particular repetition of early Reaganism's redefinition of dominance, it seems to me likely Marx's formula might have to be reversed. Reaganism made a farce of the promise of "new times" and new possibilities, seized the occasion to exploit the rapidity of shifting formations and to institute policies that produced altogether new intensities of division and of hopelessness for countless numbers of people. Farce, as even so pristine an intelligence as T. S. Eliot's could recognize, is vicious in its brutality.

Even had he remained a candidate from the beginning of the campaign, it's not very likely that Perot would have won election in 1992. His candidacy all too clearly was beginning to function for all too many people as a visible, insistent way of recognizing that Reaganism, as it involved specific policies, policy directions, and political consequences, was by no means identical with the oppositional imagery of promised new times that it rode to power. Perot himself became a figure of that imagery; the promise of the campaign, like the promises of early Reaganism, thus involved far more than victory in any given election for a specific candidate. It was a campaign out to make "politics as usual" obsolete, which in practice was not exactly what Reaganism was organized to do. Yet in the circumstances of the historical repetition marked by the Perot campaign, farce can easily become the grimmest of tragedies. For Perot's fundamental premise (and that of Clinton himself or whoever might succeed Perot as a figure of repetition) to the contrary, it's not possible for everyone to play in the game of producing obsolescence, any more than it's possible for everyone to become rich. Marx understood as well as anyone nineteenth-century capitalism's "rules" for producing the division of rich and poor. In our time, Perot seemed to his supporters to be someone who had mastered Reaganism's political culture, with its technoideologically coded divisions of innovation/obsolescence, like no one else. But Reaganism's farce of new times will become a tragedy of new times without Marx's further awareness that the point of understanding isn't to play the rules better, but to change them altogether. It will never be the case that everyone can play in the production of obsolescence.

In some crude and direct sense, the goal of school culture reform is to ensure that relatively few will ever have the opportunity to try. Thus any alternative politics of education that would work with a student audience, that would repair now precariously poised political languages of rights and empowered positionalities, must nevertheless address itself to more than a student audience. The policies of school culture educational reform will continue to disconnect educational institutions from other social territories, to limit institutional mobilities. A willingness to work with and for expectations as linked to rights to position that fails simultaneously to challenge those limitations can then only be another series of false promises. Commitments to the social importance and *connectedness* of educational institutions, that is, involve still further repair of still another kind of obsolescence, where invention will then seem obviously risky business, given the historically constituted ideological effects of the educational system in the United States and given all the naively liberal salvational politics of education as the best lever for social change. Like a notion of rights, the structure, functions, and locations of institutional education often seem a part of the ideological past perhaps best left obsolete. But of course they can't be, for school culture *will* make education a "national priority." Again. If we aren't "there," it will do so in ways that continue to speak to and about students, at all levels of education, while at the same time creating a social world *for* students where more and more of them will be condemned to the terminal obsolescence of throwaways.

In the event, however, the "there" is already "here." "What are you doing here?"

Works Cited

Works Cited

Aaker, David A., ed. "The 1909 J. Walter Thompson *Blue Book on Advertising*," in *Advertising Management*. Englewood Cliffs, N.J., 1975.

Adorno, Theodor. "On Popular Music," in *Studies in Philosophy and Social Sciences* 9 (1941).

Altman, Rick. "Television/Sound," in Tania Modleski, ed., *Studies in Entertainment: Critical Approaches to Mass Culture*. Bloomington, Ind., 1986.

Ang, Ien. *Watching Dallas*. New York, 1985.

Ascher, Carol. "Selling to Ms. Consumer," in Donald Lazere, ed., *American Media and Mass Culture*. Berkeley, Calif., 1987.

Babbage, Charles. *On the Economy of Machinery and Manufacture*. Philadelphia, Pa., 1832.

Barrett, Michèle. *Women's Oppression Today: Problems in Marxist Feminist Analysis*. London, 1980.

Baudrillard, Jean. "The Ecstasy of Communication." Trans. John Johnston, in Hal Foster, ed., *The Anti-Aesthetic: Essays on Postmodern Culture*. Port Townsend, Wash., 1983.

Bennett, William. *To Reclaim a Legacy: A Report on the Humanities in Higher Education*. Washington, D.C., 1984.

Bourdieu, Pierre. *Distinction: A Social Critique of the Judgment of Taste*. Trans. Richard Nice. Cambridge, Mass., 1984.

"Brake and Muffler Shops," *Consumer Reports* 54 (Aug. 1989).

Braverman, Harry. *Labor and Monopoly Capital*. New York, 1974.

Cheney, Lynne. *Humanities in America: A Report to the President, the Congress, and the American People*. Washington, D.C., 1988.

Cohen, Stephen, and John Zysman. *Manufacturing Matters*. New York, 1986.

Conant, James. *Education in a Divided World*. Cambridge, Mass., 1948.

———. *The Revolutionary Transformation of the American High School*. Cambridge, Mass., 1959.

Eaton, Judith. *The Unfinished Agenda: Higher Education and the 1980s.* New York, 1991.

Edgar, David. "The Free or the Good," in Ruth Levitas, ed., *The Ideology of the New Right.* Cambridge, 1986.

Eliot, Charles William. "Inaugural Lecture as President of Harvard College," in Eliot, *Educational Reform: Essays and Addresses.* New York, 1905.

Fernández Kelly, María Patricia, and Anna M. García. "Economic Restructuring in the United States: Hispanic Women in the Garment and Electronics Industries." In Barbara Gutek, Ann Stromberg, and Laurie Larwood, eds., *Women and Work,* vol. 3. Beverly Hills, Calif., 1988.

"Five Compact Sedans," *Consumer Reports* 55 (March 1990).

Foster, Hal, ed. *The Anti-Aesthetic: Essays on Postmodern Culture.* Port Townsend, Wash., 1983.

Fox, Pamela. "Recovering the 'Narrow Plot of Acquisitiveness and Desire': Reproduction, Resistance and British Working Class Writing, 1890–1945." Ph.D. diss., University of Washington, 1990.

Freedman, Sara. "Master Teacher/Merit Pay—Weeding Out Women from 'Women's True Profession': A Critique of the Commissions on Education," *Radical Teacher* 25 (Nov. 1983).

Gamble, Andrew. "Thatcherism and Conservative Politics," in Stuart Hall and Martin Jacques, eds., *The Politics of Thatcherism.* London, 1983.

Gendron, Bernard. "Theodor Adorno Meets the Cadillacs," in Tania Modleski, ed., *Studies in Entertainment.*

Glenn, Evelyn Nakano, and Charles M. Tolbert II. "Technology and Emerging Patterns of Stratification for Women of Color: Race and Gender Segregation in Computer Occupations." In Barbara Drygulski Wright, et al., eds., *Women, Work and Technology.* Ann Arbor, Mich., 1987.

Gramsci, Antonio. *Quaderni del carcere,* ed. Valentino Gerratana, 4 vols. Turin, 1975.

———. *Selections from the Prison Notebooks,* ed. Quintin Hoare and Geoffrey Nowell Smith. New York, 1971.

Grossberg, Lawrence. *It's a Sin: Essays on Postmodernism, Politics and Culture.* Sydney, 1988.

Hall, Stuart. *The Hard Road to Renewal: Thatcherism and the Crisis of the Left.* London, 1988.

———. "The Toad in the Garden: Thatcherism Among the Tories," in Cary Nelson and Lawrence Grossberg, eds., *Marxism and the Interpretation of Culture.* Chicago, 1988.

Hall, Stuart, and Martin Jacques, eds. *New Times: The Changing Face of Politics in the 1990s.* London, 1990.

Haraway, Donna. "A Manifesto for Cyborgs: Science, Technology, and Socialist Feminism in the Last Quarter." In Karen V. Hansen and Ilene J.

Philipson, eds., *Women, Class, and the Feminist Imagination*. Philadelphia, Pa., 1990. Originally published in *Socialist Review* 80 (March–April 1985).

Harrison, Bennett, and Barry Bluestone. *The Great U-Turn: Corporate Restructuring and the Polarizing of America*. New York, 1988.

Heath, Stephen, and Gillian Skirrow. "An Interview with Raymond Williams," in Tania Modleski, ed., *Studies in Entertainment*.

hooks, bell. "A Feminist Challenge: Must We Call All Women Sister?" *Z Magazine* 1 (Feb. 1992).

———. "Overcoming White Supremacy." *Zeta* 1 (1988).

Inglis, Alexander. *Principles of Secondary Education*. Cambridge, Mass., 1918.

Jameson, Fredric. "Postmodernism and Consumer Society," in Hal Foster, ed., *The Anti-Aesthetic*.

———. "Reification and Utopia in Mass Culture," *Social Text* 1 (1979).

Jeffords, Susan. "The Patriot System, or Managerial Heroism," forthcoming in Donald Pease and Amy Kaplan, eds., *Cultures of Imperialism*. Durham, N.C.

———. "Performative Masculinities, or, 'After a Few Times You Won't Be Afraid of Rape at All.'" *Discourse* 13:2, 1991.

Kendrick, Michelle. "Coaxing Little Sister: Contemporary Women's Magazines and Construction of Gender." M.A. Thesis, University of Washington, 1990.

Kimball, Roger. *Tenured Radicals: How Politics Has Corrupted Our Higher Education*. New York, 1990.

Kristol, Irving. *Two Cheers for Capitalism*. New York, 1978.

Laclau, Ernesto, and Chantal Mouffe. *Hegemony and Socialist Strategy*. London, 1985.

Lemann, Nicholas. "The Origins of the Underclass," pts. 1–2. *Atlantic* 258 (June–July 1986).

Marx, Karl, and Friedrich Engels. *Manifesto of the Communist Party*. In *K. Marx, F. Engels, V. Lenin: On Historical Materialism*. New York, 1974.

McCabe, Colin, ed. *High Theory/Low Culture*. New York, 1986.

Meehan, Eileen. "Why We Don't Count: The Commodity Audience," in Patricia Mellencamp, ed., *Logics of Television: Essays in Cultural Criticism*. Bloomington, Ind., 1990.

Mellencamp, Patricia. "Video and the Counterculture," in Cynthia Schneider and Brian Wallis, eds., *Global Television*. Cambridge, Mass., 1988.

———, ed. *Logics of Television: Essays in Cultural Criticism*. Bloomington, Ind., 1990.

Modleski, Tania. "Femininity as Mas(s)querade: A Feminist Approach to Mass Culture," in Colin McCabe, ed., *High Theory/Low Culture*. New York, 1986.

222   *Works Cited*

———. *Loving with a Vengeance: Mass Produced Fantasies for Women.* Hamden, Conn., 1982.

———, ed. *Studies in Entertainment: Critical Approaches to Mass Culture.* Bloomington, Ind., 1986.

Morley, David, and Roger Silverstone. "Domestic Communication—Technologies and Meaning." *Media, Culture and Society* 12 (1990).

Morris, Meaghan. "Banality in Cultural Studies," in Patricia Mellencamp, ed., *Logics of Television.*

Morrison, Ann. *The New Leaders: Guidelines on Leadership Diversity in America.* San Francisco, 1992.

Mort, Frank. "The Politics of Consumption," in Stuart Hall and Martin Jacques, eds., *New Times: The Changing Face of Politics in the 1990s.* London, 1990.

Murray, Robin. "Fordism and Post-Fordism," in Stuart Hall and Martin Jacques, eds., *New Times.*

Newfield, Christopher, and Ron Strickland, eds. *After PC: Nineties Prospects for the Human Sciences,* forthcoming.

Pines, Burton. *Back to Basics.* New York, 1982.

Pinkerton, James. "Post-Modern Politics: The Search for a New Paradigm." Speech, Sept. 18, 1991.

Podhoretz, Norman. *Breaking Ranks.* New York, 1979.

Polan, Dana. "Brief Encounters: Mass Culture and the Evacuation of Sense," in Tania Modleski, ed., *Studies in Entertainment.*

Ross, Andrew. *No Respect: Intellectuals and Popular Culture.* New York, 1989.

Saltzman, Amy. *Downshifting: Reinventing Success on a Slower Track.* New York, 1992.

Sandoval, Chela. "U. S. Third World Feminism: The Theory and Method of Oppositional Consciousness in the Postmodern World." *Genders* 10 (Spring 1991).

"Service Loses Its Smile," *U.S. News & World Report* 108:25, June 25, 1990.

Skirrow, Gillian. "Hellivision: An Analysis of Video Games," in Colin McCabe, ed., *High Theory/Low Culture.*

Tartar, Helen. "Abject, Technician, Metonym: The Acquiring Editor and the Scholarly Community." Unpublished ms.

Thomas, R. Roosevelt, Jr. *Beyond Race and Gender: Unleashing the Power of Your Total Workforce.* New York, 1991.

"Urban Refugees," *Seattle Post-Intelligencer,* July 22, 1991.

Walker, Richard. "Is There a Service Economy? The Changing Capitalist Division of Labor." *Science & Society* (Spring 1985).

Watkins, Evan. *Work Time: English Departments and the Circulation of Cultural Value.* Stanford, Calif., 1989.

Watkins, Evan, and Lisa Schubert. "The Entrepreneurship of the New:

Corporate Direction and Educational Issues in the 90s," in Christopher Newfield and Ron Strickland, eds., *After PC.*
Watney, Simon. "The Spectacle of AIDS," in Douglas Crimp, ed., *AIDS: Cultural Analysis, Cultural Activism.* Cambridge, Mass., 1988.
Williams, Raymond. *The Country and the City.* New York, 1973.
————. *Television: Technology and Cultural Form.* New York, 1974.
Willis, Susan. *A Primer for Daily Life.* London, 1991.
Wilson, William J. *The Declining Significance of Race.* 2d edition. Chicago, 1978.
Wollstonecraft, Mary. *A Vindication of the Rights of Woman,* ed. Carol H. Poston. 2d edition. New York, 1988.

Index

In this index an "f" after a number indicates a separate reference on the next page, and an "ff" indicates separate references on the next two pages. A continuous discussion over two or more pages is indicated by a span of page numbers, e.g., "pp. 57–58." *Passim* is used for a cluster of references in close but not consecutive sequence.

Absorbed and intermittent viewing, 147–51
Abstract labor, 67–69
Adorno, Theodor, 97–98, 142–43
Advertising, 50, 53–55, 61, 70–71, 114–27 *passim*, 152–53, 201f, 211; and automobiles, 99–101, 109n, 164–71, 173, 175, 183, 191f. *See also* Market research
Advertising Age, 164
Affirmative action, 169, 212
Agnew, Spiro, 177
Altman, Rick, 108–10, 113, 120n, 121
American Graffiti, 89f, 164
Ang, Ien, 108n
Arachnophobia, 124
Ascher, Carol, 115, 116n
Automobile maintenance literature, 88–105 *passim*. *See also* Brake repair
Avant-garde, 18, 26, 39–40, 135. *See also* Postmodernism

Babbage, Charles, 15–16, 17f, 22
Baker, Houston, 207
Barbie, 136
Barrett, Michele, 112f
Baudrillard, Jean, 6, 29, 36–37, 68–69, 78, 84, 87, 92, 95, 97–98, 151, 158
Beethoven, Ludwig Von, 97f, 136–44 *passim*
Bel Geddes, Barbara, 107, 110, 122, 124
Bennett, William, 191–95 *passim*, 208
Blaming the victim, 58–59, 60
Bloch, Ernst, 37, 98
Bloom, Allan, 192f
Bluestone, Barry, 42
Bourdieu, Pierre, 70, 135–43 *passim*, 149, 151
Brake repair, 62–63, 65
Braverman, Harry, 41–42, 44, 76
Breaker-point ignition, 89–90
Buchanan, Patrick, 177, 213–14

Bush, George, 3, 5, 9–14 *passim*, 59–60, 77, 97, 103, 120n, 169–72, 183–91 *passim*, 196, 199, 211–14 *passim*

Caddyshack, 139
Camper Van Beethoven, 136, 139, 144, 160, 163, 181
Capitalization of change, 4, 32–38, 67, 70–71, 168, 170
Carter, Jimmy, 214
Cavell, Stanley, 207
Census categories, 41–42, 44, 96n, 116
Cheney, Lynne, 195
Chevrolet, 100, 166–67
Child, image of, in Reaganism, 172, 177–78, 186–88, 191–92, 208, 211
Chilton manuals, 91–94
Chinatown, 89
City Slickers, 166f, 190
Class, 7, 14, 23–24, 36, 39, 47–60 *passim*, 87–88, 90, 94–95, 98, 104–5, 125–26, 152, 175–76, 194
Class-as-lifestyle, 9, 49–82 *passim*, 94, 96, 105, 114, 125–33 *passim*, 139, 141, 150, 153, 155, 161f, 210
Class division, 13–14, 49–51, 66–72, 80–82, 125–26, 129–33, 161–62
Clay, Andrew Dice, 59f
Clinton, Bill, 5, 9, 172, 183, 187, 204, 214f
Cohen, Stephen, 42
Cold medicine, 137ff, 147
Colonialism, 33, 102
Commentary, 179
Commodity, 3–4, 42, 68, 109, 200, 210–11
Common sense, 5, 203–4
Conant, James, 73, 102–3

Concrete labor, 67–69
Consumer Reports, 61–65, 70, 78, 100
Consumption, 6, 12–14, 43–82 *passim*, 92, 97–98, 101, 103, 112, 114–24, 132, 137–63 *passim*
Corporate restructuring, 6, 39, 42, 182–86 *passim*, 194, 211–13
Counter-taste, 141–42, 152, 157–61 *passim*
Cultural exploitation, 125–28, 130f

Dangerfield, Rodney, 138f
Darman, Richard, 83n, 139
Debord, Guy, 68
Deleuze, Gilles, 151
Derrida, Jacques, 205
Destabilization, 31–32, 44–48 *passim*, 55, 69, 76, 153, 155
Dire Straits, 77
Distraction, 140
Doane, Mary Ann, 207
Doogie Howser, 139
Duke, David, 211–13

Edgar, David, 173–74
Edwards, Alba, 116n
Electronic ignition, 28, 89–90
Electronics industry, 29–31, 34–38
Eliot, Charles William, 198–202 *passim*
Eliot, T. S., 213
Embourgeoisement, 160
Engels, Friedrich, 17, 22
Entitlement programs, 184
Entrepreneurship, 185–88
Exchange value, 67–68

Family, 112–17 *passim*, 125–29 *passim*, 132, 185–87
Fashion, 135, 161, 163

Fernández Kelly, María Patricia,
30–35 *passim*
Fields of taste, 135–63 *passim*
Finch, Anne, 17, 21
Finnegans Wake, 138
Fiske, John, 108n
Flexible specialization, 185
Ford Motors, 165
Fortune, 193
Foucault, Michel, 22–23
Fox, Pamela, 162n
Fredericks, Christine, 116n
Freedman, Sara, 201
Friedman, Milton, 179, 181ff, 209
Fuchs, Victor, 41
Fundamentalism, 136, 180f, 209

Gamble, Andrew, 173, 179
García, Anna M., 30–35 *passim*
Garment industry, 29–33, 37–38
Gender, 7, 13, 45–49, 55–60, 69,
72, 81, 87–101 *passim*, 112, 115,
131, 151–58, 170, 172
Gendron, Bernard, 97
General Motors, 21, 44, 61f, 100–
101, 165, 182
Gentile, Giovanni, 13–14
Giroux, Henry, 151
Glazer, Nathan, 177
Glenn, Evelyn Nakano, 30n–31n
Gramsci, Antonio, 1, 2n–3n, 5,
12–14, 52, 101, 171, 173, 188,
203–4
Grossberg, Lawrence, 172n
Gulf War, 85, 187–89
Guns N' Roses, 77, 80, 132

Habermas, Jurgen, 2n
Hall, Stuart, 5, 6n, 10, 140, 171–79
passim, 188, 203, 208
Hammer, M. C., 136
Happy Days, 107f, 111, 122

Haraway, Donna, 2, 3n, 19–26,
29, 38–39
Harrison, Bennett, 42
Hatch, Orrin, 58
Hayek, F. A., 179f, 183, 209
Henry, Jules, 2n
Heritage Foundation, 206
High-culture taste, 135f, 140f,
147–49, 159–60
Hill, Anita, 170, 173, 191
Homewood Suites, 54
Hook, 166f, 190
hooks, bell, 48, 170
Household, 109–31 *passim*
Housewife, 115–18 *passim*, 122–28
passim
Human resources management,
211–12

Iacocca, Lee, 35n
Industrial economy, 15–22 *passim*,
26, 97; and service economy,
29–33, 42–44, 46f, 53, 72–76,
198–200, 202
Inglis, Alexander, 198f, 202
Institute of Economic Affairs, 206
Intellectuals, 136–39, 142–51 *passim*
Intelligence testing, 74–75
Intermittent and absorbed view-
ing, 147–51

Jameson, Fredric, 84–87, 92,
98–102 *passim*
Jeffords, Susan, 153, 188n
Jordan, Hamilton, 214

Kaplan, Ann, 192f, 207
Kendrick, Michelle, 154n
Kimball, Roger, 9n, 134–35, 136,
142, 192–94, 201f, 204–8
King, Rodney, 3, 59, 186
Korpi, Walter, 184

Kristol, Irving, 175–85 *passim*, 192

Laclau, Ernesto, 170–71
Laffer curve, 179
Lemann, Nicholas, 24–25, 56–57
Lifestyle, 7, 35, 37, 49, 94, 96, 105, 134, 167f, 208. *See also* Class-as-lifestyle
Lotus Elan, 164–70 *passim*, 190ff
Luxemburg, Rosa, 102
Lyotard, Jean François, 34

Mahler, Gustav, 139
Market research, 46, 49, 61. *See also* Advertising
Marx, Karl, 1, 3–4, 17, 21f, 50, 67–68, 69ff, 183, 214–15
Mazda Miata, 164–75 *passim*, 179f, 183f, 190–92, 211
McDonald's, 53, 143–44
Meehan, Eileen, 109n
Meineke Brake Shops, 62
Mellencamp, Patricia, 87–88
Midas Brake Shops, 62f
Modleski, Tania, 46, 97–98, 99, 132, 147, 151–57 *passim*
Montagu, Lady Wortley, 17
Moral Majority, 181
Mork and Mindy, 107f, 111, 121
Morley, David, 108n, 119n–20n
Morris, Meaghan, 140
Morrison, Ann, 212
Morrison, Toni, 130n
Mort, Frank, 6n, 49
Mouffe, Chantal, 170–71
MTV, 24, 27, 131–32, 192
Murray, Robin, 30n

Natural coding, 2, 20–25, 27, 33–36, 46f, 57f, 74–75, 76, 112, 117. *See also* Haraway, Donna

Necessity and taste, 135, 137, 142, 146, 160–63
New class analysis, 173–74
Newness, 10–14. *See also* Avant-garde; Reaganism; Technological innovation
New Right, 125–33, 172n, 174, 180, 183ff. *See also* Reaganism
Newsweek, 177
New Times agenda, 6n, 173
Nicholson, Jack, 84
Nisbet, Robert, 177
Nostalgia, 26, 39, 85–88, 90–92, 129–32, 162–63, 190, 211

Obsolescence, 46–51 *passim*, 56–57, 58ff, 72, 79, 80ff, 113f, 125, 131, 142, 150–51, 155–63 *passim*; and technological innovation, 2–3, 7–40 *passim*, 84–93 *passim*, 98–104 *passim*; and Reaganism, 166–73 *passim*, 181f, 199, 202, 208–16 *passim*
Opposition and dominance in Reaganism, 174–82, 189, 209, 215

Pastiche, 84–86, 89, 92, 99
Performance, 48–51 *passim*, 61, 64–71, 80, 82, 93, 96, 103, 127, 132, 139, 141, 150, 153–58, 162. *See also* Class-as-lifestyle
Perot, Ross, 172, 214–15
Piers Plowman B, 77
Pines, Burton, 181
Pinkerton, James, 11–14
Pirsig, Robert, 92
PMLA, 147
Podhoretz, Norman, 177f, 187
Polan, Dana, 107–11 *passim*, 121
Political correctness, 11–12, 14, 209–10

Post-Fordism, 30n
Postmodernism, 77, 83–84, 92, 95,
    98, 107, 111f, 123, 141–42, 146,
    158, 163; and technoideological
    coding, 11–12, 14, 20, 34–40
    passim
Preston, James, 212
Progress, 15–18, 20, 28, 33
Proust, Marcel, 139, 147ff
Public choice analysis, 193–94
Public education, 4–6, 8–9, 50–
    51, 71–82, 99–106 *passim*, 113–16
    passim, 130–33, 159–60, 172,
    189–216
Public Enemy, 139
Puig, Manuel, 132

Race, 7, 18, 23–25, 46–49 *passim*,
    55–59 *passim*, 72, 81, 104–5, 126,
    131, 169–70, 172, 211–13
Radio, 119–20
Rating services, 109
Reagan, Ronald, 3, 173, 181
Reaganism, 5–14, 77, 81, 105, 126f,
    132, 164–216 *passim. See also*
    Child, New Right; Opposition
    and dominance
Reed, Donna, 107, 110, 122, 124
Regarding Henry, 166f, 190
Repair, 10–11, 14, 88–96 *passim*,
    142, 158–59, 173, 210–16
Resistance, 8, 51, 141–42, 150–52,
    157–63, 173
Right to social position, 168–73,
    199, 210–14
Rocky Horror Picture Show, 137
Rollins, Ed, 214
Rose, Axl, 78, 80, 132
Ross, Andrew, 137, 138–39, 159
Rousseau, Jean Jacques, 17, 21
Rusher, William, 173–80 *passim*

Safire, William, 172
Salisbury Review, 179
Saltzman, Amy, 107
Sandoval, Chela, 3n, 4, 213
Saturday Night Live, 123
School culture, 77, 81, 195–216
    passim
Schubert, Lisa, 26n, 212n
Sclar, Donna, 91
Scott-Heron, Gil, 15, 40
Self-help literature, 48, 61–71
    passim, 80, 88–96, 101, 150
Service economy, 5, 6–8, 41–82
    passim, 125, 130f, 161–62, 182,
    200–203, 208, 210
Service labor, 44–45, 47, 52–55,
    62–66, 93–96, 143–45
Sherman, Cindy, 137
Silverstone, Roger, 108n, 119n–
    20n
Simulation, 77, 84f, 89, 92, 99,
    132, 160, 162f
Sixties, the, 172, 177f, 180, 186,
    193–94, 196
Skirrow, Gillian, 85–86
Slumming, 136, 145
Soap operas, 145, 146–58, 159, 163,
    170
Soap Opera Weekly, 146
Social Darwinism, 1–2, 3, 18–19
Sociology of work, 143–45
Spin-offs, television, 107, 111,
    121–22
Stigler, George, 41
Supply-side economics, 178–85
    passim

Tartar, Helen, 56
Taste, 8, 134–63, 168
Technoideological coding, 2–8,
    10, 21, 24, 25–27, 31–36, 38–40,

46–52 passim, 56–60, 89, 125,
134, 182, 215
Technological innovation, 15–
17, 22, 25f, 27–29, 89–90, 95,
118–20
Technology, 2, 15–40 passim,
83–96 passim, 100–105 passim
Television, 27, 40, 107–24 pas-
sim, 129, 131–32. See also MTV;
Soap operas
Television flow, 108–10, 113, 120–
24, 129
Temporal duration and taste, 140,
144–47, 149–51
Terkel, Studs, 143
Test marketing, 123–24
Thatcherism, 5, 6n, 9f, 173, 179,
183–84, 188, 203–4
Thomas, Clarence, 11, 58, 169–73,
175, 190–91, 199, 211
Thomas, R. Roosevelt, Jr., 211–12
Thompson, J. Walter, 118–19
Time, 167
Tolbert, Charles, 30n–31n
Tollet, Elizabeth, 17
Tressell, Robert, 162
Tune-up, automobile, 89–90

United Nations, 178
Use value, 26n, 67, 142, 149–50,
151f, 157–63 passim

U.S. News & World Report, 54

Vacuum cleaners, 145–46
VCRs, 108n, 122
Veblen, Thorstein, 68
Video games, 85f
Vietnam War, 188–89
Vigurie, Robert, 180f
Villainess, in soap operas, 153–58,
159, 163, 173

Walker, Richard, 42–43, 44
Wall Street Journal, 175, 179
Warhol, Andy, 159–60, 162
Watney, Simon, 3n
Welfare policies, 176f, 183–84,
208f
Will, George, 177, 181, 192
Williams, Raymond, 11, 16n, 84,
107–9, 113, 140
Willis, Susan, 26n, 47, 53, 138n
Wilson, William J., 23
Wollstonecraft, Mary, 16–17, 21,
23
Wordsworth, William, 16–17, 20
Working Woman, 154

Young, Neil, 85

Zamsky, Robert, 195
Zyman, John, 42

Library of Congress Cataloging-in-Publication Data

Watkins, Evan, 1946–
Throwaways : work culture and consumer education /
Evan Watkins.
    p. cm.
Includes bibliographical references.
ISBN 0-8047-2249-8 (cl.)   ISBN 0-8047-2250-1 (pbk.)
1. Social change.   2. Social status.   3. Consumption
(Economics)   4. Culture.   I. Title.
HM101.W278   1993
303.4—dc20
93-19270

⊗ This book is printed on acid-free paper.
It has been typeset in 10/12 Bembo by
Tseng Information Systems.